Russia on Reels

RUSSIA ON REELS
The Russian Idea in Post-Soviet Cinema

Edited by

BIRGIT BEUMERS

I.B.Tauris *Publishers*
LONDON • NEW YORK

First published in 1999 by I.B.Tauris & Co Ltd,
Victoria House, Bloomsbury Square, London WC1B 4DZ
175 Fifth Avenue, New York NY 10010
website: http://www.ibtauris.com

In the United States of America and in Canada distributed by
St Martin's Press, 175 Fifth Avenue, New York NY 10010

A full CIP record for this book is available from the British Library
A full CIP record for this book is available from the Library of Congress

ISBN 1 86064 389 2 (hardback)
ISBN 1 86064 390 6 (paperback)

Library of Congress catalog card number: available

Set in Monotype Calisto by Ewan Smith, London
Printed and bound in Great Britain by CPD Wales

Contents

KINO: The Russian Cinema Series
General Editor's Preface

Cinema has been the predominant popular art form of the first half of the twentieth century, at least in Europe and North America. Nowhere was this more apparent than in the former Soviet Union, where Lenin's remark that 'of all the arts for us cinema is the most important' became a cliché and where cinema attendances were until recently still among the highest in the world. In the age of mass politics Soviet cinema developed from a fragile but effective tool to gain support among the overwhelmingly illiterate peasant masses in the civil war that followed the October 1917 Revolution, through a welter of experimentation, into a mass weapon of propaganda through entertainment that shaped the public image of the Soviet Union – both at home and abroad and for both élite and mass audiences – and latterly into an instrument to expose the weaknesses of the past and present in the twin processes of *glasnost* and *perestroika*. Now the national cinemas of the successor republics to the old USSR are encountering the same bewildering array of problems, from the trivial to the terminal, as are all the other ex-Soviet institutions.

Cinema's central position in Russian and Soviet cultural history and its unique combination of mass medium, art form and entertainment industry, have made it a continuing battlefield for conflicts of broader ideological and artistic significance, not only for Russia and the Soviet Union but also for the world outside. The debates that raged in the 1920s about the relative revolutionary merits of documentary as opposed to fiction film, of cinema as opposed to theatre or painting, or of the proper role of cinema in the forging of post-Revolutionary Soviet culture and the shaping of the new Soviet man, have their echoes in current discussions about the role of cinema *vis-à-vis* other art forms in effecting the cultural and psychological revolution in human consciousness necessitated by the processes of economic and political transformation of the former Soviet Union into modern democratic and industrial societies and states governed by the rule of law. Cinema's central position has also made it a vital instrument for scrutinising the blank pages of Russian and Soviet history and enabling the present generation to come to terms with its own past.

Russia on Reels

This series of books intends to examine Russian and Soviet films in the context of Russian and Soviet cinema, and Russian and Soviet cinema in the context of the political and cultural history of Russia, the Soviet Union and the world at large. Within that framework the series, drawing its authors from both East and West, aims to cover a wide variety of topics and to employ a broad range of methodological approaches and presentational formats. Inevitably this will involve ploughing once again over old ground in order to re-examine received opinions but it principally means increasing the breadth and depth of our knowledge, finding new answers to old questions and, above all, raising new questions for further inquiry and new areas for further research.

The continuing aim of the series is to situate Russian and Soviet cinema in their proper historical and aesthetic context, both as a major cultural force in Russian history and Soviet politics and as a crucible for experimentation that is of central significance to the development of world cinema culture. Books in the series strive to combine the best of scholarship, past, present and future, with a style of writing that is accessible to a broad readership, whether that readership's primary interest lies in cinema or in Russian and Soviet political history.

Richard Taylor
Swansea

Acknowledgements

The present volume is based on papers presented at the conference on 'Russian Cinema in the 1990s' held at the Watershed Media Centre in Bristol in October 1997 and generously supported by the British Academy, the Foreign and Commonwealth Office, Bristol University Alumni Foundation, the British Universities Film and Video Council (BUFVC), and the Dean of Arts at the University of Bristol, Michael Liversidge. Special thanks to all of them, and to Mark Cosgrove at the Watershed. I should also like to thank the Embassy of the Russian Federation, especially Mr Boris Malakhov who helped plan the film week and took part in the conference.

I would like to thank all the participants for their contributions to the conference and/or the current volume, and the Bristol University Arts Faculty Research Fund for generous support in the preparation of this volume. My special thanks go to Sergei Selianov, Oleg Kovalov, Mark Rudinstein and the staff at 'Kinotavr', Sergei Livnev, Daniil Dondurei, Nina Tsyrkun, Miroslava Segida, Svetlana Khokhriakova, Ksenia Yasnova, Svetlana Kriukova, Natasha Synessiou, Ilona Chakliya, Helen Tilly and Julian Graffy.

I am deeply indebted to Gordon McVay for his patience and thoroughness in checking draft versions of texts and translations at various stages of the preparation of the manuscript; and to 'the most important of all', Richard Taylor for seeing this volume through with such competence, and such a great sense of humour!

Birgit Beumers
August 1998

Note on Transliteration

Transliteration from the Cyrillic to the Latin alphabet is a perennial problem for writers on Russian subjects. I have opted for a dual system: in the text I have used the Library of Congress system (without diacritics), but I have broken from this system (a) when a Russian name has a clear English version (e.g. Maria instead of Mariia, Alexander instead of Aleksandr); (b) when a Russian name has an accepted English spelling, or when Russian names are of Germanic origin (e.g. Yeltsin instead of Eltsin; Eisenstein instead of Eizenshtein); (c) when a Russian surname ends in -ii or -yi this is replaced by a single -y (e.g. Dostoevsky instead of Dostoevskii), and all Christian names end in a single -i; (d) when 'ia' or 'iu' are voiced (at the beginning of a word and when preceded by a vowel) they are rendered as 'ya' or 'yu' (e.g. Daneli*ya*, *Yu*ri) – with the sole exception of the name Asya to avoid confusion with the continent, Asia. In the scholarly apparatus I have adhered to the Library of Congress system (with diacritics) for the specialist.

Notes on Contributors

Birgit Beumers is Lecturer in Russian at the University of Bristol.

Nancy Condee is director of the Graduate Program in Cultural Studies at the University of Pittsburgh.

Daniil Dondurei is the editor-in-chief of *Film Art* (*Iskusstvo kino*).

David Gillespie is Senior Lecturer in Russian at the University of Bath.

Julian Graffy is Senior Lecturer in Russian at the School of Slavonic and East European Studies, University of London.

Mikhail Iampolski is a Senior Research Fellow of the Institute of Film Studies, Moscow and, since 1991, has taught at New York City University.

Oleg Kovalov is a film historian and film-maker. He lives in St Petersburg.

Nikita Mikhalkov is a film-maker, actor, and chairman of the Filmmakers' Union.

Tatiana Moskvina is a film critic, who writes for *Film Art* (*Iskusstvo kino*) and *Seans*. She lives in St Petersburg.

Graham Roberts is Lecturer in Russian at the University of Surrey.

Sergei Selianov is a film-maker and producer. He is the director of the St Petersburg film studio STW (CTB).

Richard Taylor is Professor of Politics at the University of Wales, Swansea.

Nina Tsyrkun is a film critic, who serves on the editorial board of *Film Art* (*Iskusstvo kino*). She is also Research Fellow of the Institute of Film Studies, Moscow.

Emma Widdis is Assistant Lecturer in Russian at the University of Cambridge, and Fellow of Trinity College.

Natasha Zhuravkina is a Language Instructor at the University of Bath.

Illustrations

Illustrations 3, 4, 7, 13, 14, 16 have kindly been made available by Miroslava Segida; illustrations 2 and 5 are courtesy of STW; illustration 8 courtesy of the Gorky Film Studios; illustration 6 (a) courtesy of Pathé, illustration 6 (b) courtesy of TriTe; illustration 9 courtesy of Artificial Eye; illustration 10 courtesy of Ingeborga Dapkunaite; illustrations 12 (a) and (b) courtesy of Blue Light, illustration 15 courtesy of Nikola Film.

1. Introduction

Birgit Beumers

Film and reality

Soviet cinema, this 'most important of all arts', had primarily been seen as a means for propaganda. Film-makers of the 1920s discovered its potential to construct a different reality, to build through montage the perfect Utopia, and thus made it open to abuse for the purpose of constructing a myth instead of an identity. It existed to raise the spirit of the people, to set moral standards, to show 'reality' in positive and bright colours, or to depict the path to the 'bright future'. In the 1930s the creation of such a perfect reality on screen was linked to the concept of entertainment, so that cinema would attract the masses.

After the collapse of communist ideology, film-makers rejected demands to construct the future, but also abandoned the concept of the (formerly under-ground, dissident) film-maker who defended spiritual values. Instead, they began to portray the reality that surrounded them without the ideological constraints hitherto imposed. What they saw was a bleak picture: beggars on the streets, impoverished pensioners, economic chaos, street crime, Mafia shootings, porno-graphic magazines and videos, decaying houses and ramshackle communal apartments, and the emergence of a new class, the New Russians, who adapted quickly and learnt how to make money in a society under reconstruction. Literature and film, visual art and music which are set in this bleak reality are commonly referred to as *chernukha* (literally: that which is made black).

The mainstream of Russian cinema largely indulges in this bleakness, or blackness, and offers neither alternative nor perspective. Film-makers have rejected their 'mission' to act as prophets (as they had done in the Soviet period), or to guide morally and aesthetically. The audience, in turn, rejects films which offer no positive outlook or spiritual guidance amid the chaos, and have turned instead to Latin American soap operas screened daily on Russian television.

In the eyes of the state, though, cinema remains to the present day a most powerful means of expressing moral values and of providing guidance. At the same time, there are movements in Russian cinema to liberate cinema from these fetters, and to return to either the narrative style characteristic of the Hollywood movie industry, or to develop poetic, 'auteur' cinema.

The central question for contemporary Russian film-makers is a crucial one: what is the function of cinema in the new Russia? Can cinema offer what reality cannot provide: an aim, a goal for people to live up to at a time when politics and ideology fail to provide directions? Can cinema help in defining the identity of the new Russia?

Film and industry

The Soviet film industry had always relied on the state to finance and distribute its films. The film studios, such as Mosfilm, Lenfilm and the Gorky Studio, would produce the film, employ directors, actors and technical personnel, provide all the facilities for shooting and editing, and take charge of distribution to state-owned movie theatres. Audience considerations were not crucial for the funding of a film; although several films attracted over 50 million spectators, 'auteur' or art-house films could be made without market pressures.

This system collapsed with the demise of the Soviet state. What remained were large, unmanageable film studios which were gradually split up into small, independent production companies and privatised. At the same time, Goskino, the State Department for Cinematography, continued to subsidise film production.

The ensuing crisis of the film industry has become fully evident only since 1995. The full funding of films came to a halt when Goskino's funds were cut considerably. Film production plummeted even faster than it had rocketed (from an average 150 in post-war Soviet times to its peak of 300 in 1990 when it had been a convenient method of money-laundering and therefore attracted large investments).[1] After 1990 the number of films released rapidly declined.

The sharp drop in film production also reflects a crisis in the role and the function of cinema in a changing society. The Soviet state had built large movie theatres for the masses; these needed to be refurbished, converted into multiplexes and fitted with Dolby systems. The huge, cold theatres were unable to compete with the expanding television and video market, allowing more and more people to watch films comfortably, at home (about half of all households in Moscow are equipped with a video recorder); most cinemas were therefore rented to retail outlets. Only a few were refitted, and less than half a dozen cinemas in Moscow operate on a profit basis at present, such as the American House of Cinema in the Radisson Hotel, the Kodak Kinomir, the Pushkin Hall (formerly Rossiya), the Cine-Centre (Kinotsentr), the House of Cinema (Dom kino), and the Arts Cinema (Khudozhestvenny). Moreover, television has turned audiences away from both cinema and theatre: most films are shown on television soon after their release. Finally, the growing video market has made any film, foreign or Russian, available for the price of a cinema ticket, or less:

Introduction

Table 1.1: Films released, 1990–98[2]

Year	Number of films released
1990	300
1991	213
1992	172
1993	152
1994	68
1995	46
1996	28
1997	52
1998	ca.80

ticket prices for the cinema are around $10, while a video film costs between $5 and $8. Video piracy became an immense problem, since most films were copied illegally, and thus there was no financial return for the film industry. The fight against video piracy has now reduced the sale and circulation of illegal video tapes by about half.

Goskino (under Minister Armen Medvedev) supports the national film industry and was instrumental in formulating the new law on cinema in 1996.[3] With its annual budget it finances around a dozen films fully, and some others partly. The average cost of production is just under $1 million, while low-budget films cost less than half. The average return of a film is $80,000 from theatrical release (i.e. in cinemas), $200,000 from video release, and $30,000– 50,000 from television rights. Under such conditions, no film would normally recoup its production cost.

As long as the state has no law in place offering tax incentives to investors, cinema will rely on the state for funding. And while cinema relies on the state for funding, it remains self-centred and seeks no contact with the audience, does not aim to cater for the masses, nor to entertain and serve a commercial goal. Yet as long as cinema remains exclusively self-centred, investors will not be interested, especially when there is not even the slightest chance of a return. The divide between 'auteur' cinema and commercially driven film production could not be greater. Festivals, national and international, are the main target for contemporary Russian film-makers.

In 1997/8 the situation took a dramatic turn: the Gorky Studio launched its project for low-budget cinema to boost film production; audience-oriented films, promulgating positive values, are being made for release on video. Several films (*The Thief, The Prisoner of the Mountains, Mother and Son*) have achieved international success, winning Oscar nominations or international festival awards. The construction of several multiplexes is well under way. Video piracy has almost ceased – the licensing is controlled, at least partly, enough to ensure a return to the producer; tax laws are in place and reinforced by raids on the street markets. Finally, the election of Nikita Mikhalkov to the chairmanship of the Film-makers' Union promises more enforcement of the return of sales and profit to the producer.

The 'Russian Idea' and Russian cinema

The articles in this volume derive mainly from papers given at a conference held at the Watershed Media Centre in Bristol in October 1997. The focus chosen for the conference and for this volume is the theme of the 'Russian Idea': after the collapse of an all-powerful ideology which defined nationhood and identity, which created myths of a bright future and rewrote the past, and which invented moral standards at the expense of religion, Russia now seeks to redefine its identity, its values and its history. These attempts are reflected in all the artistic activities of the post-Soviet era, but they are especially relevant to the art of cinema, seen under the Soviet system as 'the most important of all arts' (Lenin) both to promulgate ideology and to set moral standards.

The 'Russian Idea' is a concept that has kept appearing on the agenda of Russian thinkers throughout the nineteenth and twentieth centuries. The question of Russia's place in the world, and in world history, is pertinent to past and ongoing debates on the theme of Russia's identity. Both the nineteenth-century philosopher Vladimir Soloviev and his pupil Nikolai Berdiaev devoted much of their writings to the issue of Russia's history and destiny: Russia is deemed to have a special mission, to function as a bridge between East and West. The Russian character thus combines and unites within itself binary oppositions. These oppositions and contradictions, the suspended state between two poles without ever touching ground, is a theme which constantly recurs in the speeches and the work of contemporary Russian film-makers.

The perception of cinema as a medium that provides guidance on the issue of national identity at a time of political disparity has emerged ever more distinctly in 1997–98. Russian cinema underwent a radical change reflected both in an increase in production and in the election of Nikita Mikhalkov to the chairmanship of the Russian Federation's Film-makers' Union in December 1997; he chose to hold his first congress in May 1998, a full twelve years after the historic 1986 Congress when Mikhalkov's warnings about an all too radical rejection of past traditions and values were rebutted.[4] Mikhalkov envisages that the Union should subsidise film production and distribution through an extra-budgetary fund which will collect levies (instead of taxes) from video licences and sales. The Union would thus partly assume the functions of Goskino, which, despite the new Law on Cinema (1996), cannot implement tax collection in these areas until the necessary amendments have been made to the tax code.

This volume thus covers a period which saw the deconstruction and reconstruction of the country's history, the collapse of one ideology and the creation of a new value system, and the transition from a state-controlled and state-manipulated film factory to a genuine film industry and a proper film market.

In 1995, commemorating the centenary of cinema, the British Film Institute commissioned a film on the history of Russian cinema. Film historian and critic Oleg Kovalov wrote the script for a film directed by Sergei Selianov, entitled *The Russian Idea*. This film is an attempt to retrace the main stages in the depiction and interpretation of this historical and cultural phenomenon in the Soviet cinema of the 1920s and 1930s. By the 'Russian Idea' Kovalov chiefly means the search for some 'ideal' existence for the nation in a radiant future, transcending history. Such an idea would normally be ruinous to most individuals, states or to the world as a whole, but it somehow proved to be a fertile one for Russian culture. According to Kovalov, Eisenstein resolves the contradiction between any 'old, national' mythology and a 'new, social' one because he makes the latter either a particular example or an aesthetic element of the former.

The Russian Idea also traces in the films of Vsevolod Pudovkin the evolution of the relationship between the director and the official propaganda of the Soviet regime. Kovalov concludes that there was a growing contradiction between Pudovkin's ideas and his depiction of them on the screen. In the cinema of the 1920s and 1930s, the 'Russian Idea' often became a formal device for expressing some 'eternal' concepts, as well as the source of a new cinematic language.

Kovalov's synopsis for *The Russian Idea* disputes the view that cinema in the Soviet Union was not pertinent for defining a Russian national identity because it was abused to further the socialist cause (the creation of a Soviet identity). He traces in the films of Eisenstein and Pudovkin a concern with the 'Russian Idea' by analysing their subtle subversion of the social plot through religious imagery, and by delineating reality and the dream world of a communist Utopia in their films. He proves that Soviet cinema in effect continued to draw on pre-Revolutionary images.[5]

It is thus only with the decline of the generation of film-makers of the 1920s that the concern with 'Russianness' vanishes from the screen. Soviet ideals take over in the identification of the Soviet state as the Fatherland in the Second World War. The collapse of the Soviet ideal, of communism, with its potential to realise the bright future and create paradise on earth brought the 1990s into a bleak reality, without any perspective of a bright future. The essential contradiction between reality and dream, present and future, this world and the world beyond, had sustained the 'Russian Idea' until the late 1940s, while in the 1990s the belief in the socialist Utopia had shattered the notion of Russia's special mission – to bridge the gap between Europe and Asia, between past and future, between hell and heaven, and to attain the serene state of the communist paradise. It is against a background of this eternal contradiction that the films of the 1990s will be seen.

The four parts of the volume provide different angles on the theme of the 'Russian Idea'. First, by placing the concept of the 'Russian Idea' in a historical and cinematographic perspective; second, by offering a view of contemporary films through the socio-geographical-political lens and investigating the process of fragmenting, remapping and mythologising the present; third, by looking at the ways in which the past, historical and cultural, is seen through the lens of the present, with attempts to find in it a definition of Russianness; and finally, by offering close studies of the work of individual film-makers, Alexander Sokurov, Kira Muratova and Dmitri Astrakhan, who represent not only different generations, but also the entire spectrum of attitudes of film-makers in their varying degrees of concern with the Russian theme.

Part I opens with an article by Nancy Condee in which she looks at the historical and philosophical dimensions of the 'Russian Idea', and follows it through Russian cultural history. She identifies two opposed representations of the figure of Christ: a pantocratic Christ, who judges, and a kenotic Christ who redeems. Analysing the concept of Hesychasm, a monastic movement relying on inner quietude, mysticism and abstract representation, she perceives it as the source of the search for mystical alternatives to any institutional power, including the Soviet state, a search which the Russian people would be drawn to continuously throughout their history. Condee also links with this mysticism the notion of the film-maker as a prophet. The binary opposition between two world views creates two paradigms: the model of inversion (the world beyond as different from this world), and that of analogy (this world as a mirror of the world beyond), which is reflected in cinema in the tension between the real and the imaginary.

Richard Taylor then examines whether 'Soviet cinema' existed as a distinctive construct. He distinguishes its four constituent elements: the 'ideological'; the 'industrial/structural'; the 'economic/financial'; and the 'cultural'. This involves a discussion of the historical, political and cinematic contexts in which Soviet films were produced. The chapter examines the legacy of this distinctive construct for post-Soviet Russian cinema by using the same constituent elements as a framework in which to pose fundamental questions about the nature of Russian cinema in the 1990s.

The three speeches gathered under the heading 'Russian Cinema – National Cinema?' were given between October 1997 and May 1998. They elucidate cinema's concern with national identity and establish the position of Russian cinema at the watershed between ideological instruction and mass entertainment.

In October 1997 Sergei Selianov, director and co-author of *The Russian Idea*, delivered a speech at the Bristol conference in which he juxtaposed two opposed theories of the relationship between cinema and reality: film is a reflection of life, while it has no resemblance to life whatsoever. In the Soviet period film used to be more than life, while at present life is more interesting than art. At the same time, the myth of another world, another reality outside the geographical borders of the former Soviet Union has collapsed; in a world where everything is permissible and possible, the film-maker has lost his status. The loss of limitations which are a necessary obstacle to be overcome by the artist in the process of creation has left the film-maker deprived of the special status of a seer or prophet. Selianov's view here clearly relates to the 'spiritual cohorts' Nancy Condee refers to in her chronological analysis of the 'Russian Idea'. Although Selianov is aware of cinema's potential to create a national idea, he hopes, while remaining nostalgic about the special function cinema had in the past, that it will take a middle path, and that film will be just that: film.

Daniil Dondurei's speech (delivered at the III Congress of the Russian Film-makers' Union in the House of Cinema in Moscow in December 1997 before the election of Mikhalkov to the chairmanship) was remarkable: Dondurei, editor-in-chief of *Iskusstvo kino* (Film Art) and senior adviser on a number of governmental committees, spoke in optimistic terms of the state of the film industry, while he underlined the lack of positive values and the absence of a belief in the future in the national repertoire. He implied that the value system of the nation is being undermined by communists and oligarchs who wish to gain popular support for a different sort of system by painting everything black and depriving the people of ideals. Dondurei is in agreement with Selianov in recognising the artist as a prophet, a function which contemporary film-makers have lost.[6]

Finally, Mikhalkov's speech to the IV Congress in the Kremlin Palace of Congresses in May 1998 makes perfectly clear what the task of a national Russian cinema should be. In a clip with extracts from a number of contemporary films (mainly low-budget films from the Gorky Studios, such as *Snake Spring* [Zmeinyi istochnik, 1997] and *The Body will be Committed to the Earth and the Senior Warrant Officer will Sing* [Telo budet predano zemle, a starshii michman budet pet', 1998], he pointed out the preponderance of scenes of cruelty, violence and murder in contemporary Russian films which contradicted reality; he claimed that the representation of violence in film was not in proportion to reality. He argued strongly for the need to instil hope in the cinema audience, and dwelt on the need to create the myth of a Russian national hero in order to regain a spirit of patriotism that bonded the Soviet Union in the past, and that bonds America now. He proposed practical solutions for the reorganisation of the film industry to guarantee financial returns.

These three positions reflect on the one hand the concern of film-makers and critics alike with the formation of national identity, and the acknowledgement that cinema can play an important role in its creation. Moreover, they also make clear that the construction of a national identity does not put artistic or aesthetic aspects at stake. However, once cinema is no longer state subsidised but relies on returns from cinemas, television and video sales, it will be fully

Russia on Reels

dependent on the spectator; at this point market structures will replace the lever of ideological control held, in the past, by the state. Selianov's position is that of an artist in the first instance, and not that of a manager of culture. He acknowledges that the state realises the power of cinema to formulate a national identity, but defends – although he is a producer – the complete independence of the artist.

In Part II the authors investigate the loss of a sense of unity, location and direction that follows from the collapse of a system, and the loss of an idea that, through its belief in the bright future, united, bonded and contextualised.

Nina Tsyrkun explores different areas of myth-making. Myths in post-modernist culture are constructed with the help of old myths; thus she begins by looking at how myths of the past are being rewritten. In the 1990s, image-making has become a way of mythologising identity: it is a creative process. Contemporary films also subvert the myth of paradise on earth into hell in the underground (the Moscow metro); or they dismantle the myth of the Fatherland and of father-figures; and finally, they turn the film into a fairytale, a dream-land, a world 'beyond'. Tsyrkun concludes that myths draw away from reality and create instead a virtual reality. The escape from reality through myth forms a central part of the inability to come to terms with the present.

The process of re-creating the map of the new Russia is a prominent and important theme in everyday life with the renaming of streets and cities. Emma Widdis investigates the process of remapping through Selianov's film *The Time for Sadness Has Not Yet Come* [Vremia pechali eshche ne prishlo, 1995] where the attempt to define Russia (the protagonist is a land surveyor) is linked to the attempt to reassess the values of the inhabitants of a small settlement in the vast open countryside. Widdis touches on such themes as 'Russian' and 'Soviet', on the ironic treatment of the reappropriation of the past, on the lost identity of 'Soviet' nations. The film debunks the myths of abroad and of the centre as illusions. Nevertheless, the surveyor Methodius reconciles the characters who live for the future with their present, everyday existence, so that eventually they take their lives into their own hands. Widdis links her discussion to the cinematic representation of space. Selianov's film is identified as one offering reconciliation with the present.

The loss of direction and the deconstruction of national values is the central theme in the chapter entitled 'To Moscow! To Moscow?', the quest of Chekhov's *Three Sisters* in search of the lost past (and the lost future) at the turn of the last century, which reverberates in Danila Bagrov's statement at the end of Balabanov's *Brother* [Brat, 1997], when he leaves St Petersburg for Moscow, the centre, the capital of crime. Post-Soviet films develop three types of heroes: the escapist hero (who follows false ideals) and the war hero (who has no Fatherland to fight for) both follow ideals that are hollow, so that the Soviet hero turned Russian becomes a 'criminal knight', or the killer-hero. Balabanov belongs to a new generation of Russian film-makers who refrain

Introduction

from moral judgement, but who challenge by juxtaposing the aesthetic and the ethical.

The contributors to Part III assess the way in which contemporary film-makers view the past, whether historical or fictional. A number of films in the 1980s had dealt with a reassessment of the past: the 1930s and the figure of Stalin became a theme that fascinated film-makers, as did the theme of the Fatherland, the father-figure, and the figure of the leader. The most prominent person here is Nikita Mikhalkov, actor, director, president of the Foundation for Culture, chairman of the Film-makers' Union, presidential adviser, Oscar-winner.

Tatiana Moskvina's article vividly reflects the ambiguity with which Russian critics view the figure of Nikita Mikhalkov. She considers Mikhalkov's public and artistic profile, both in terms of his creative work and his evaluation of the past in his films, but also as a public image, frequently attracting criticism because of his nationalist views. She compares his life with the rewritten and reversed myth of Hamlet. Moskvina assesses his films in the light of the theme of power, fatherhood and love. She discusses his ideas of nation and state, democracy and despotism, war and peace as represented in his life and his films. She asserts that Mikhalkov lives and creates in another reality that ignores everyday life. As such, she links Mikhalkov to that branch of the 'Russian Idea' that is preoccupied with the past and future rather than the present. Mikhalkov's views on issues of Russian identity are considered.

Natasha Zhuravkina investigates the father-figure in connection with the theme of freedom and tyranny in a number of films from the late 1980s to the present. She traces the reasons for the preoccupation with the past: revisioning and rewriting the past frees the individual from responsibility, while at the same time the values of the Fatherland are smashed to pieces.

David Gillespie looks at contemporary screen adaptations of nineteenth-century classics (Tolstoi, Leskov, Gogol and Sologub). Adaptations reveal the way in which the cultural heritage of the past is relevant for the present, how it is adapted for a society which needs to define its identity. In *Katia Izmailova* [Podmoskovnye vechera, 1994] the theme of fiction and reality is intermingled with the main narrative; in *The Prisoner of the Mountains* [Kavkazskii plennik, 1996] meekness and aggression in the two main characters are identified as two halves of the Russian character.

Finally, the work of three individual film-makers forms the subject for the last three chapters, covering the spectrum of 'auteur' cinema and commercial entertainment: Alexander Sokurov, Kira Muratova and Dmitri Astrakhan represent not only different generations, but also the entire spectrum of attitudes of film-makers – the spiritual, the absurd and the commercial. Thus they show varying degrees of concern with the Russian theme.

Sokurov is one of the most poetic film-makers in Russia, often compared to Andrei Tarkovsky, while his work is comparatively less known in the West.

Russia on Reels

Mikhail Iampolski scrutinises Sokurov's latest films, including *Mother and Son* [Mat' i syn, 1997], which is a slow-moving account of death, filmed in the painterly tradition of European Romanticism. Iampolski therefore uses a film about the painter Hubert Robert as a key to Sokurov's representation of decay and death. He explains Sokurov's treatment of the camera image and demonstrates how he manages to aestheticise what is not normally considered aesthetic, and how he instils in the spectator a serenity that helps the spectator overcome the bleak reality of contemporary life, and the all-pervading images of death. In that sense, Iampolski places Sokurov above the film-makers bound by reality, and fixes him both among the 'prophets' of Russian cinema, and within a universal tradition of film language.

Kira Muratova is one of the most highly regarded film-makers in Russia today. Her latest films move away from her earlier realism towards stylisation, and thematically show a concern with the meaninglessness of everyday life, as Graham Roberts demonstrates in his article. The uncertainty of existence, the lack of hope in transcendence, the absence of direction, the themes of fate and chance, the breakdown of language, the superficial distractions in life which cannot deflect from death are features which reflect the loss of direction, but also, on a more universal level, the loss of meaning. Roberts shows how the plots become more and more fragmented, which echoes the process of fragmentation in the country and in society.

Dmitri Astrakhan is one of the most popular film-makers in Russia today, offering a rare happy ending in his film hit *Everything will be OK* [Vse budet khorosho, 1995]. Julian Graffy looks at the reasons for Astrakhan's popularity, and the response of Russian critics who, while complaining about the lack of positive heroes and of a bright future in their national cinema, subject Astrakhan's films to severe criticism again and again. Graffy identifies the central values of Astrakhan's films as 'community, family, home', which are threatened by upheavals so that characters have to make choices. He also examines the way in which Astrakhan rejects the myth of abroad, the 'American dream': real happiness can be found only in Russia.

On the one hand, this volume is concerned with the problems arising from the collapse of one value system, one ideology, one concept of nationhood, and the need to define, construct, create another, new, national identity. On the other hand, the issue of the function of cinema, the role of the film-maker, in this new society is addressed: is he to be a prophet, an artist, or a mass entertainer?

Russian film-makers and critics may have addressed the issue of industry and the function of cinema, but they have not clearly and sufficiently examined the role of the artist as an artist, as a creative person without a spiritual or social mission.

Since the conference in October 1997 the changes in the Russian film world have taken shape: after the 'thinnest' ever Sochi Film Festival (the 1997 competition programme, normally including between fifteen and twenty selected titles, consisted simply of all the twenty films produced in the previous year), the 1998 competition not only represented a distinct selection, but several films had to be excluded because they had already been in festival competitions abroad, such as *The Thief* [Vor, 1997] and *The Land of the Deaf* [Strana glukhikh, 1997], released at the Venice and Berlin festivals respectively. There is reason to believe in the 'radiant' future of Russian cinema.

2. The Russian Idea: Synopsis for a Screenplay

Oleg Kovalov

Nikolai Berdiaev wrote that diametrically opposed characteristics reside organically in the Russian people:

> despotism, the hypertrophy of the State, and on the other hand anarchism and licence; cruelty, a disposition to violence, and yet also kindliness, humanity and gentleness; a belief in rites and ceremonies but also a quest for truth; individualism, a heightened consciousness of personality together with an impersonal collectivism; nationalism, self-glorification, alongside universalism and the ideal of the universal man; an eschatological messianic spirit of religion, and an external religiosity; a search for God and a militant godlessness; humility and arrogance; slavery and revolt.

Throughout Russian history it has proved impossible to reconcile and unite in a harmonious whole the mutually exclusive components which form the face of the nation – here, now, at the present instant. That is when the mind of the philosopher, the politician, the poet turned towards the world of the past or, more often, to the promised future; there, it seemed, a radiant paradise had already been created for souls torn from the prison of a dirty, agonisingly imperfect reality. 'The true kingdom is the City of Kitezh,[1] which is to be found at the bottom of a lake,' wrote the very same Berdiaev. Out of this faith in the incontrovertibility of the existence of this City, the logical conclusion naturally flowed: reality, which with its grimaces obscures this utterly beautiful mirage, must be repealed, rejected, detonated. The starry-eyed and seemingly innocent aspirations of the idealists to 'leap out' of historical time were transformed for the country into a chain of bloody disturbances, wars, revolutions and shocks, stretching from the remote past and extending through the present day into the unknown future. However, the 'Russian Idea' – though undoubtedly disastrous for the state, the individual and the world – turned out to be unexpectedly fertile for culture, giving humanity the great literature and music of the nineteenth century, and the audacious impulses of the avant-garde.

National culture took great pains in attempting to unite the flesh and the spirit, the real and the sublime, 'earth' and 'heaven'. These heroic efforts brought about a catharsis, a salutary illumination of consciousness for the individual and society.

Culture was once divided into 'Russian' and 'Soviet'. It is now clear that the most outstanding works of the Soviet period in many respects follow pre-Revolutionary traditions. The influence of Fedorov's philosophy is evident in Mayakovsky's poem 'About that', and shades of Dostoevsky's 'The Dream of a Ridiculous Man' can be divined in 'The Bedbug'. Pavel Korchagin represents the well-known type of the martyr in hagiography – the man who suffers for an idea. Books like *Quiet Flows the Don* and *The Golden Calf*,[2] though very different from each other, have inherited from the Russian classics the theme of the wandering 'superfluous man'. The philosophical dialogue between Ivan Denisovich and the sectarian Alesha – the high point of Solzhenitsyn's story – is an elevated parody of the discussion between the other Ivans and Aleshas on the value of harmony; the old Russian debate continues on the plank-beds of the camp to which our philosophers have been led by the inscrutable Utopian roads of that mirage which is the invisible City of Kitezh.

There are countless such examples, but the actual concept of the 'Russian Idea', which is integral to an analysis of our literature and philosophy, appears to be quite inapplicable to cinema. There is a reason for this.

The film-image is called upon to express the poetry of reality, of the terrestrial space which surrounds us, something that is evident in the achievements of American, Italian, Czech, Georgian and other prominent film schools. But the world of Russian culture is the world of the spirit, and it attempts to embody the non-material. The sensual nature of cinema is opposed to that; the true director deifies the rough matter of life.

Indeed, there are very few reflections of the 'Russian Idea' in pre-Revolutionary Russian cinema. It is obvious that our first feature film *Stenka Razin* [Ponizovaia vol'nitsa, 1908] was 'national': Razin, man of the people and Volga rebel handles his foreign beloved with great bravado, either in the name of a male brotherhood in arms, or of the struggle against the wealthy. But this is not some senseless trifle like *L'Arroseur arrosé* [France, Lumière, 1895]. However, 'Russianness' here was squeezed into the embryo of a *lubok*[3] theme, intended to entertain the public and not to set them on fire with a sermon. In the lavish screen adaptations of Russian classics, cinema sacrificed the philosophical meaning of the works of Pushkin, Gogol and Tolstoy, adapting them so that they became serial melodramas and didactic stories.

The high points of pre-Revolutionary cinema (for example, the school of Bauer) have more in common with a cosmopolitan modernist style than with the generic features of our national culture. The Golden Age of the 'Russian Idea' in cinema is, in fact, the Soviet period. From the tempestuous 1920s, the young art form, following on the heels of politics, was obsessed with cosmic schemes to re-create reality; to erect the Cathedral of the Holy Utopia on earth, which only the new man of the future deserved to enter. The authorities were quick to proclaim cinema as 'the most important art', something which implied a break with the religious and philosophical systems of the accursed past. From then on, every complex work of art that hit the screens was interpreted by the ideologues as exclusively Soviet and 'in line with Party policy'. This lie, which was monotonously drummed in, resulted in entire generations actually perceiving cinema as the worthy offspring of socialist realism. Because of this, the question of the link between our national cinema and the 'Russian Idea' was not posed until very recently.

The authorities sought to appropriate the works of every great artist and this destroyed many reputations. Hence the 'formalist' Eisenstein became the favourite whipping boy of the semi-official critics. However, during the 'Thaw' he became the 'banner of Soviet cinema', and then, for the 'children of perestroika', he was transformed into a symbol of the coarse kitsch of the totalitarian era.

Yet for the West, unerringly sensitive to the Russian origins of our culture, Eisenstein is, in fact, a *Russian* film director. That is why he is so popular there. Through the monumental images of his film frescoes he expressed the metaphysical immutability of the 'Russian Idea', not subject to the flow of historical time.

The Battleship Potemkin [Bronenosets Potemkin, 1925] opened with an impassioned Trotsky slogan; later this title was changed to a quote from Lenin. But there would also have been good reason to open the film with a dictum from the gospels, the epigraph to *The Brothers Karamazov*: 'Verily, verily I say unto you, except a corn of wheat fall into the ground and die, it abideth alone: but if it die, it bringeth forth much fruit.'[4] It is clear to the unprejudiced viewer that there is not a hint of Marxism in the film. The idealistic concept of the 'people's fate', shaped by the messianic religious origin of the 'Russian Idea', is here embodied with poster-like clarity: rivers of sacrificial blood flow for the sake of a sudden, logically inexplicable leap into a dazzlingly harmonious world of universal brotherhood. Vakulinchuk, wounded and dying, hangs on the yard-arm – a canonical pose of the martyr-Messiah which refers too openly to the source of the image to be ignored by the exasperated atheistic criticism of the 1920s. Historical facts are set out wrongly in the film; from the viewpoint of everyday logic there is much in the depiction of the everyday, the commonplace, that strains one's credulity, while, in terms of the messianic myth, everything is precise and accurate.

Eisenstein's film *The Old and the New* [Staroe i novoe, aka General'naia liniia, 1929] was formally devoted to village co-operatives (while it was being filmed 'total collectivisation' burst on the scene; the director had to mention collective farms in the credits and alter the tone of the film). Even here, however, beyond the topical issues it is the clearly evident dreamy meditativeness of the national

Weltanschauung, willingly taking flight from the uncomfortable earth, which in the final analysis quite obviously prevails. The actual village where Marfa Lapkina lives is characterised by darkness and dirt, whereas in the Utopian village commune there are bright buildings, stout herds and cascades of milk, which rush down straight from the heavens. The abundant future appears to Marfa only in a dream: the director significantly separates the real from the ideal. But how can one move from one to the other? The people know that the only way to a mirage is through a miracle. In Eisenstein's film the peasant pilgrims ecstatically beseech the heavens for beneficial rain. It goes without saying that in the film this is shown to be an absurd hangover from the old regime; Marfa Lapkina knows a different recipe for achieving this happy abundance – a separator. But this prosaic machine is slyly filmed like a magical, fairytale accessory, resembling Aladdin's lamp, which grants all wishes. A change of systems and civilisations does not change the popular consciousness with its inclination towards passive myth-making. It was thought that the title of the film emphasised the 'New', which is victorious over the 'Old'. But its graphic result speaks more of the inability of new ideas to break the age-old psychology.

In *Ivan the Terrible* [Ivan Groznyi, Part I, 1945], Tsar Ivan himself is literally ill with 'Russian' complexes. Fixing his eyes above the crowd he dreams obsessively of his 'Kitezh'– namely, the country's path towards the 'blue ocean, blue sea'. The idea is a fine one, and that is its misfortune: the ignoble human race does not value it. There remains only one thing to do to save the dream: to chop off all these irresponsible heads. Alongside the Tsar, Maliuta arises – a sadist and lackey paves the way to the Great Idea via base reality. The executioner here is the inevitable shadow of the pretentious idealist.

The rather loose first part of the film contains weaknesses in the acting, justly pointed out by Mikhail Chekhov,[5] and concessions to the dogmas of the times; but it also contains topical moments. The young Tsar Ivan, putting on airs, appears before the rebellious people. His political agenda is the universal platform of the populist demagogue: the struggle against sedition (this is the first thing to be announced and provokes particular exultation from the crowd) and domination by foreigners; the expansion of Russia's national borders; a concern for the working people and, of course, the promise – flavoured with appropriate popular wit – to 'cut off' the heads of those who disobey, something which provokes unbounded rapture. Part I is coated in the cold imperial style of late Stalinism, but in Eisenstein's epic system this style breaks down before our very eyes. Towards the end of Part II the film seems to return to the bosom of true piety, which repudiates the filth of the casuistic lies of earthly tsars. Metropolitan Filipp towers above Ivan's path; the fanatic of truth opposes the fanatic of the state and neither cedes one iota to the other. This is a fatally Russian condition: this insuperable contradiction cannot be solved by reason; it can either be resolved by blood (and Ivan executes Filipp), or avoided by slipping into an illusory, irrational space. What is startling is that, in keeping with the spirit of the 'Russian Idea', the bearer of a higher truth in the film is not Filipp, that ardent member of the opposition, but the meek fool, the weak-minded Prince Vladimir. The holy fool in Russia is a 'Man of God'; and people greedily seize upon his howlings as prophecies. That is why Eisenstein puts a candle in Vladimir's hands, radiating the quiet light of indisputable divine truth. The scene in which this ill, frightened child attempts to carry the warm flame through the surrounding thickening darkness is one of the high points of cinema art. Vladimir moves with uncertain gait, sensing death with his entire being. But the illumination which has descended upon his poor head wills him to go to the end, towards the knife of the fanatic hidden in the dark, because what is truth if it is not paid for by sacrificial blood?

Theorists who turned Eisenstein into a 'Socialist Realist' ignore the obviously religious meaning of the scene in the cathedral. Marie Seton spoke about the director's private acknowledgement of his deep faith, but a Soviet critic, denouncing her reminiscences, quoted this passage as obvious slander. Eisenstein was, of course, far removed from conformist church-going, but he undoubtedly carried within him the genes of a national spiritual outlook. The author of the brilliant scene inside the cathedral was, without doubt, overcome by a romantic fascination with the communist Utopia, but there is no contradiction here. This exalted dream struck root here thanks to the 'Russian Idea', which is the fermenting ground for the meaning of his films, independent of the extraneous features of the social epoch, taken here as something alien and unnecessary.

This is why *Bezhin Meadow* [Bezhin lug, 1935–37] sank into oblivion. The authorities wanted the director to make a propaganda film about the class war in the countryside. But the film, which, as it happened, reproduced the ferocious myths of the regime, was considered so unsuitable by that very regime that we have hitherto found no traces of it. In 1967, Kleiman and Yutkevich edited together a photo-film from the preserved bits of film, which totally explains the reasons for its suppression.[6]

The central episode in the film is the destruction of the church. The liberals, who knew of this episode by hearsay, were indignant; look at the barbarism the regime's lackey is glorifying. But it is absurd to accuse of cultural nihilism someone whose interest in the sources and phenomena of world culture was irrepressible in the extreme; Eisenstein was always willingly there at the Rabelaisian feast of culture. The destruction of a church could not delight someone who was so captivated by religious ceremonies in Mexico, who described the beauty of Russian cathedrals so poetically in his memoirs, and who created the majestic spirit of church ritual so accurately in *Ivan the Terrible*. True, in *Bezhin Meadow*, joyful villagers storm the church singing songs; but the scene is shot for the sake of its striking visual conclusion: the blasphemous crowd, inserted by the director into the world of the church, organically takes on the features of the biblical figures it had itself overthrown. The peasants here are grey-bearded prophets; the young men are broad-shouldered Renaissance apostles; the fleshy girls are earthly Madonnas; the peasant wrecking the iconostasis is a biblical Samson; the chubby young boy in the shirt, raised high under the cupola towards the slanting sun-ray which turns his locks golden, is the young Jesus ascending to the Heavenly Throne.

They carry out the church plate. The more the cathedral is stripped, the more actively, as if in defiance of this, reality becomes saturated with the features of that which is disappearing; it takes on the appearance of what is being exterminated; it is being ousted and substituted by the myth before our very eyes. What has been banished from icons takes up residence in life.

Vertov also filmed the destruction of a church in his film, *Enthusiasm* [Entuziazm, aka *Symphony of the Donbass*, 1930]: the bell-tower – lacking a top and decorated with plywood stars – was imprinted from a majestic angle, toppling over against a background of swiftly moving, whistling clouds; the spire soared and slashed through space and time, becoming resonant and cosmic, like a symbol of faith in general – without it being important to whom it is attributed and how.

Eisenstein depicts the episode that supposedly calls for the extermination of religion with the visual means of this self-same religious mythology. The common, human ideal is triumphant, even during the time of its extreme profanation, and soars above class excesses. The conflicts in the film are enveloped by the sphere of visual representations common to all mankind. Meaning derives not from the external subject matter, which is commonplace for the cinema of the 1930s, but from the very correlation of the old mythology with the new, social one.

Social mythology has pretensions to totality; the social myth was considered the highest and canonical expression of the most progressive views, which were mechanistically abolishing all others. In Eisenstein this myth seems not to be contested, but it is objectively belittled by being presented as an element, a particular manifestation of a certain old conformity to natural laws, not subject to decrees and private desires – a detail in a background, a link in a chain, a rosary bead, a stone in a mosaic. The presumptuous self-sufficiency of this new myth, measured against the principles of Eternity, is compromised: it appears deliberately imitative, transient. The social myth is a mere moment, and its pretensions are a historical imposture.

That is why the universal spirituality inherent in Russian culture was so persecuted by censorship, irrespective of whatever loyal 'casing' was found for it. The authorities coldly received even Vertov's film *Three Songs about Lenin* [Tri pesni o Lenine, 1934], where the wrong leader was celebrated and where the people's tradition of mourning was alive – rather than the new ideology. The film expressed a meditative grief for the Messiah, who sacrificially forsook this world in order to establish here a 'paradise for all'. This is what the Soviet Union announced itself as, in accordance with the already existing myth-making through song. Propaganda insisted that the way towards the radiant future lay through the sweated compulsion of the Five-Year Plans, urged on by the Stakhanovite movement. In the film, 'paradise' comes about by itself, through doleful idleness – a shedding of tears into cold space. Paradise, like grace from on high, is redeemed, pleaded for from a hollow emptiness, by the depth of sorrowful experience, which here the people literally aggravate in themselves. The more real the tears of the all-enveloping zeal, the more dazzling the mirage of Utopia. Grief and light are not in contrast here, their metaphysical wholeness does not correspond to the dull, bureaucratic optimism of the age, expressed by the slogan 'Life has become better, comrades. Life has become more cheerful.'[7]

The notorious 'optimism of the 1930s' is usually connected to entertainment films, like Aleksandrov's comedies.[8] But they have a worldly, real character and are very much oriented towards the achievements of Hollywood – an optimism of genre rather than of ideology is triumphant in them. In these self-same 1930s, films were created which painted Utopian pictures of a unified, accomplished, socialist paradise and therefore, it seems, they were bound to express a much more organic optimism: Room's *A Stern Young Man* [Strogii iunosha, 1936], Medvedkin's *The Miracle Worker* [Chudesnitsa, 1937] and *New Moscow* [Novaia Moskva, 1938], Dovzhenko's *Ivan* [1932], Vertov's *Lullaby* [Kolybel'naia, 1937]. The artists here, it seemed, were faithful to Gorky's instruction to emulate the 'third reality' – the radiant future, whose joyful features had to be bestowed upon the splendid present. But something in-explicable occurred: these works were met sourly, with 'certain reservations' and 'practical conclusions' on the part of the authorities. Their unenviable fate led to a situation in which this most interesting branch of our art of the 1930s has not only remained unassimilated by viewers and critics alike, but has also been driven out of the context of twentieth-century culture.

Cinema grew ever more closely knit with industry, business and propaganda. Experimental cinema was suppressed by Hitler's dictatorship in Germany and by the dictatorship of mass taste in France. And it is to the credit of the third country famous for artistic innovation that the avant-garde ferment in the arts in the USSR was so powerful that between the wars experimental films were made right up until 1938 (*New Moscow*), and, moreover, that they expressed and surpassed the 'last word' in aesthetics. *A Stern Young Man*, with its dream-like aura, is very close to surrealism, while the lyrical fantasies, the baroqueness and the philosophical irony contained in its shots presage the poetics of *8½* [Italy, 1962]. Its recent screening at the cinema of Gosfilmofond (State Film Archives) was enough to show that the old film was not only very much alive, but that it also became a cult film for the new avant-garde. They were delighted by the 'lyrical mockery', the total play on styles and stereotypes. There are paintings dedicated to this film, there is even a fashion salon called 'The Stern Young Man'. Generally speaking, these neo-Utopias are a phenomenon of neo-classicism, which in many ways determined and defined the face of modernism in the 1930s.

The beginning of the century was the epoch of 'Sturm und Drang' for avant-garde movements. The 1930s saw a return to classical tradition and concrete forms. Soviet cinema, which in the 1920s was intoxicated with a reckless re-creation of reality, returned, as it were, to a 'new integrity' in the 1930s. This should not be confused with the importunate official stance about the happy return of the lost sheep to the bosom of realism: the Soviet screen followed a long historical path, from little understood film epics to the simplicity of the popular *Chapayev* [Chapaev, 1934]. In practice, the organic development of artists by the 1930s led them almost to a reverse evolution.

The first sign of this is a very strange film, much misunderstood by its contemporaries, Pudovkin's *A Simple Case* [Prostoi sluchai, 1930–32]. Its plot was deliberately commonplace: while his wife Mashenka is away, a Red commander falls for another woman, but he soon repents and returns to his family. How could it be otherwise? After all, he and Masha are comrades-in-arms from the days of the Civil War. This fact was the main argument for the preservation of the marriage, but it did not really work within the system of the film. What if the commander's 'new love' had not been such an obvious flibbertigibbet, but a genuine proletarian – then what? Social rhetoric ceased to act as a universal magic wand for the artist.

Among the innovators of the 1920s, Pudovkin had the reputation of being the most 'moderate'; he did not reject the classics, but called on people to learn from nineteenth-century literature and the Moscow Arts Theatre. He worked with theatre actors, his film *The Mother* [Mat', 1926] overflowed with references to the New Testament, Russian literature, Rembrandt and Van Gogh. The film, announced as 'historical-revolutionary', in practice expressed the 'Russian Idea'. It did so not in 'stock' generalisations, as in Eisenstein, but unobtrusively, cultivating the 'Russian Idea' from daily life and subtle human relationships.

The workers in that film live lives worse than cattle, dividing their leisure time between the tavern and the police station (Pudovkin's particular merit was that he showed how the 'Black Hundred'[9] grows and operates, untrammelled, in these half-animal surroundings; the working class in Soviet cinema has always been monolithic, and has always given birth to thoroughly progressive ideas). These impassable Russian abysses seemed to serve no purpose; one could either have burned them to ashes or soared above them, spending one's life in a fevered dream. This densely hopeless reality is actually the condition for the transformation of Nilovna's life into the life of a saint. Having gone through a furnace of suffering, she and her revolutionary son unite and perish together for the sake of the mirage, arising above the suburb's loamy mud, of the new 'City of Kitezh' – embodied here in the image of the Kremlin battlements which dissolve into each other. The moment of happy union is here inevitably twinned with death, for it is absolute and in its highest triumph it aspires towards non-existence, which liberates us from precarious earthly fetters.

Nilovna's feat – standing with her flag in the path of the avalanche of punitive cavalry – is bereft of practical meaning. Like the martyrdom of a saint, it is a purely spiritual act of elevated self-immolation (it is not by chance that artistic intuition compelled Pudovkin to film long shots of her death against a background of an immense Temple of God). The film depicted the conversion to the new faith gently, with artistic tact and the authenticity of the everyday, and therefore more irresistibly than in a propagandist poster. The woman is led to her Golgotha not by reading Marx, but by her familial emotions: Nilovna raises the flag only because her son has chosen death in its name. The qualities of a realistic work are not here in contradiction with the irrational meaning of conversion as such: faith is attained not by reason, it is the fruit of a momentary illumination. *The Mother* is probably the most sincere and, therefore, the most organic embodiment on film of the 'Russian Idea'. The film is based on Gorky's novel, which is hailed as a classic of Socialist Realism, but this screen adaptation, which is almost independent of the text of the book, in essence returns Gorky to us as a God-builder and God-seeker.

The organic embodiment of the 'Russian Idea' gradually leaves Pudovkin's films. A born realist, he drove his heroes to inner conflicts, which were not solved by catharsis or catastrophe; rather, in keeping with the spirit of the times, they were revoked – by the storming of the Winter Palace (*The End of St Petersburg* [Konets Sankt-Peterburga, 1927]) or *Storm over Asia* (*The Heir to Genghis Khan* [Potomok Chingis-Khana, 1928]). The fissure between essence and idea in these films grew wider until it opened up into an unbridgeable abyss in *A Simple Case*.

Rzheshevsky's script[10] was written in rhythmical prose, almost in 'blank verse' (official criticism attributed the sins of *A Simple Case* and *Bezhin Meadow* to him; the spy from the avant-garde camp had beguiled honest Party workers). It was assumed that Pudovkin would overcome these peculiarities and return his plot to everyday sources and make a quality film closely depicting daily life. But the master of the realistic film-portrait attempted to express here the feelings and world view of a generalised and abstract 'universal man'. The film's visually static quality, stressed by slow-motion shots and ascetic interiors, exploded into eruptions of figurativeness, intended to communicate the very biology of unconscious processes. A revelation for the screen was the image of a vision of the world by a man who fell ill and recovered – it mattered not whether he was a Red or a White.

For dogmatists, the film became a favourite example of the cul-de-sac into which formalism leads. It was the director's good fortune that, blinded by various devices, they overlooked the true content, which was independent of the commonplace plot: the triumphant victors of the old world come into collision with a force which cannot be conquered by the usual blow of the sabre, nor abolished by a decree of the All-Union Central Executive Committee itself; a powerful biological source, to which everything is subordinated, imperiously and entirely. In the face of this internal enemy the soldier of the

October Revolution is helpless, Masha is left alone with her unusual experiences – knowing the language of rallies and commands, she cannot even find a name for the force which has destroyed her family life. The director, too, is perplexed, hesitating to acknowledge the conclusions of his work. In order to consolidate Masha ideologically, the ghosts of the dead soldiers are usually employed; but here they are totally out of place. The heroes' reconciliation is proclaimed as a victory of class-consciousness; however, their conflict is inserted into the greater scheme of things and, as it were, verified by eternity in such a way that next to it the truth of class battles and civil wars appears empty and transient.

The tone of the film is memorable for the obvious 'change of landmarks' in the consciousness of Soviet artists at the end of the decade. Dovzhenko's extraordinary film *The Earth* [Zemlia, 1930] appeared almost at the same time as *A Simple Case*. However hard critics tried to link it to the themes of the kolkhoz, Demian Bedny[11] accurately grasped the film's essence. His newspaper feuilleton about *The Earth* amazed people by its length, and was a unique denunciation in verse: for the director it is the 'eternal' that is sacred here, not collectivisation and the 'dirty tractor' but the 'juicy apple' and the woman's breast. Demian was angry but he understood the film with great perceptiveness. The same accusations could have been levelled against Eisenstein's film *The Old and the New*, made a little earlier, but at the time such a biased opinion was nowhere to be found. The sensuous urgency of the carnal origins of life, exuding from his unfinished masterpiece *Qué Viva Mexico!* [Da zdravstvuet Meksika!, 1931] is also felt in the frames of the equally unfinished *Bezhin Meadow*. It was no accident that the poeticisation of the biological sources of the life of the people coincided with bone-breaking collectivisation; the song to fertility was a reaction against this state genocide.

But Pudovkin, the singer of the 'Russian Idea', in seeking to renounce it, revealed self-sufficient values, in the light of which the struggle for universal happiness is somehow made to appear senseless. The images of revolt or the propagandist calls for revolution are not heterogeneous in the endings of the films of the 1920s, for they follow from the essence of the 'Russian Idea' which moulded them. The final call of the metaphysical film *A Simple Case* to strengthen the Red Army is utterly absurd, because it does not result from any of the pensive and meditative images of existence presented on screen, cloaked in white-foamed swirling clouds of resonant eternity. If not conveying the crisis of the 'Russian Idea', this spoke of the artist's alienated reflection on the ineradicability of life, which does not wish to succumb to wilful 'reforms'.

Part I

The Russian Idea:
A Historical and Cinematographic
Perspective

3. No Glory, No Majesty, or Honour: The Russian Idea and Inverse Value

Nancy Condee

1.

> The Russian Idea is eschatological; it is oriented to the end.
> It is this that accounts for Russian maximalism.
>
> Nikolai Berdiaev, *The Russian Idea*

> The visitor turned away from the saint and mocked at him:
> 'I came to see a prophet and you point out to me a needy-looking beggar.
> I see no glory, no majesty, or honour about him.'
>
> Epiphanius the Wise, describing St Sergius in
> *The Life, Acts, and Miracles of Our Blessed and Holy
> Father Sergius of Radonezh*

Nikolai Berdiaev, author of the 1946 treatise *The Russian Idea* [Russkaia ideia] is the best-known, but not the first, philosopher to write on the 'Russian Idea'. Among his famous predecessors was Vladimir Soloviev, whose 1888 Paris talk was first published in Russian posthumously in 1909.[1] My purpose is neither to elucidate the differences among these and other philosophers, nor to summarise their views, but to suggest that each pointed to a much older set of cultural oppositions that remain productive to this day. These oppositions derive not from a transhistorical 'Russian soul', but rather are a response to the historical experience of estrangement from Byzantium, a process that unfolded over a two-century period of imperial crumbling from the mid-fourteenth to the mid-sixteenth centuries, known in Russia as the monastic revival.

The term 'Russian Idea' suggests nationalism and logic (a strange juxtaposition in itself), yet it aspires above all to universality and faith.[2] Centuries-old, but known only recently as the 'Russian Idea', this cultural pattern is Russian only in a very specific sense. In the years leading up to and extending a century beyond the collapse of Constantinople in 1453, Russian Orthodoxy found itself cut off from the mother church and left, through no impulse of its own, as a national church. This 'involuntary nationalism', so to speak, is a key feature of an identity built on passive acceptance, non-compulsion, the refusal to assert one's will. Paradox, contradiction and inversion (such as, it might be argued, St Sergius's 'unsaintly' appearance in the epigraph above) are major reflexes of the Russian Idea. One of its chief 'mascots' – the holy fool or *iurodivyi* – operates by a similar strategy, confounding convention by acquiescence in, rather than resistance to, his own humiliation.

Berdiaev suggests that the 'Russian Idea' is a manifestation of the 'twofold nature of the Russian messianic consciousness'.[3] That twofold nature is expressed in (apparently contradictory) iconography as the pantocratic and kenotic Christs: Christ the Judge, who gazes down from the ceiling of the church dome, and Christ the Redeemer, who suffers on the cross that hangs on the church wall. Of these two representations, the kenotic Christ is more relevant to a discussion of the 'Russian Idea', although without the Pantocrat, his twin and opposite, he lacks the very stuff that renders this 'sadomasochistic' dynamic meaningful. The difference between these two Christs might be captured in the simplest of spatial terms. The pantocratic Christ is a vertical saviour; the kenotic, a lateral saviour – he is, so to speak, across from us, potentially a more immediate source of identification. While the 'Russian Idea' is, in Berdiaev's analysis, the interplay of many diverse opposites ('humility and arrogance; slavery and revolt'), the term is nevertheless weighted in favour of humility and slavery as the more deeply Russian trend. 'The exploit of non-resistance', writes Berdiaev, ' – *that* is the Russian exploit. Simplicity and humility – *these* are Russian traits.'[4]

The 'Russian Idea' is a belief system that reveres endurance, powerlessness and sacrifice in this historical world as necessary, even holy, elements in life's anticipation of a future (and 'therefore' transhistorical) Utopia. It is deeply anti-rational and, to paraphrase a polite scholar of Berdiaev's writings, unobstructed in its eschatology.[5] Yet the very term 'Russian Idea' bears a secular, modern tone, anachronistic to its fundamentally pre-secular concerns. It is odd, therefore, that Berdiaev constructs his major argument around the philosophical debates of the nineteenth century, a period (he claims) 'especially illustrative of the character of the Russian idea and the Russian vocation'.[6] He chooses this strategy, I suspect, in order to make the case for a 'Russian Renaissance', or post-Enlightenment revival of Orthodox mysticism, of which Berdiaev himself is a key figure, in the early twentieth century. In so doing, however, he becomes hopelessly entangled in oppositions (foreign versus Russian; West versus East) that lie not *within* the 'Russian Idea', but outside it, and in a historical sense *after* it.

2.

> While he delineated and painted all these things, no one ever saw him
> looking at models, as some of our painters do.
>
> Epiphanius the Wise, describing Theophanes the Greek at work

In the introductory passages of *The Russian Idea*, Berdiaev deals glancingly with
two major antagonists in the monastic revival, Joseph Volotsky (c. 1439–1515)
and Nil Sorsky (c. 1433–1508), 'symbolic figures in the history of Russian
Christianity':

> The clash between them arose out of the question of monastic property ... But
> the difference of type between the two men went a great deal deeper than that.
> Joseph Volotsky was a representative of ... a state Orthodoxy that later became
> an imperial Orthodoxy ... Nil Sorsky took the side of a more spiritual and
> mystical interpretation of Christianity.[7]

At issue here is not the difference between two men, but the difference
between models of power, sanctity and salvation. Nil Sorsky's mystical interpretation of Christianity followed in an already well-established tradition of
spiritual intensity and silent meditation known as Hesychasm (from the Greek
hesychia, inner quietude or calm), a trend brought northward from Mount Athos
to Russia by Orthodox monks fleeing an empire overrun by Islam. This tradition, originally associated with Byzantine monks led by St Gregory Palamas
(c. 1296–1359),[8] included such Russian figures as St Sergius of Radonezh,
founder of the Holy Trinity Monastery (1337); Epiphanius the Wise, author of
the fluid 'word-weaving' found in his *vita* of St Stephen of Perm (early fifteenth
century); Theophanes the Greek, whose equally fluid frescoes (1378) adorned
Novgorod's Church of the Transfiguration on Elijah Street [Spas na Il'ine];
Andrei Rublev, the most famous of Russia's icon-painters; the anonymous 'belt-
weavers' who adorned illuminated manuscripts; and Maxim the Greek, the
prolific translator and teacher (literally or figuratively) of Prince Andrei Kurbsky.[9]

While any general characterisation of these diverse cultural elements is
tenuous at best, many of the works associated with hesychast thought share a
tendency towards intense, rhythmical or repetitive abstraction, dynamic aural
or visual patterning away from fixed, detailed image or semantics. We see this
in Epiphanius's incantational prose, divested of specific historical detail ('Shall
I call you a prophet, since you prophesied prophetic prophesies ... ?');[10] in the
abstract ornamental 'belts' of the patterned manuscripts; and in the impression-
istic style of Theophanes's Novgorod frescoes, painted not from 'models, as
some of our painters do', but freehand.[11] This patterning mimics the technique
of repetitive hesychast prayer that will receive greater discussion later in this
argument.

The Russian Idea

At its core, hesychast thought strove for a direct connection with God through silent meditation, fasting and other ascetic practices, and an inner search for divine light.[12] Hesychast practices eschewed spoken prayer, strict observance of ritual, and much of the communal regimentation of monastery life. In contrast to a stable communal organisation within a large parent monastery [*lavra*], the hesychast movement was reclusive, peripatetic, and hermit-like. Its leader was not the *hegumen* or archimandrite, appointed to administrative power, but the spiritual elder [*starets*], revered for wisdom. Its structure was not the *lavra* but the *skit*, a small cell (usually no more than twelve monks) existing under conditions of deprivation and hard physical labour. While both models of monastic life, the *lavra* and the *skit*, had long existed in Kievan Rus' and Byzantium,[13] hesychast teachings extended far beyond these structural issues in their cultural and philosophical expression.

As the hermit movement associated with Hesychasm looked northwards to increasingly remote areas such as the St Cyril Monastery (1397) or the Solovki Monastery (1436), it provided an alternative to institutional faith. Hesychasm's alternative was a faith both beyond and indifferent to institutional boundaries, guided by choice rather than compulsion (in Cherniavsky's words, 'faith not religion').[14] If the manifest trappings of wealth in the large parent monastery were intended as analogous to the glory of the Kingdom of God, then hesychast logic was based not on analogy but on inversion: apostolic poverty in this world signalled wealth in the world to come.

The same kinds of competing logic in *lavra* and *skit* held force with respect to church and monastic ritual. If the large, coenobitic monasteries held to a stricter performance of ritual and external sanctity as directly indicative of internal sanctity (a reasoning by analogy), then the hermit cell was anti-ritualist, proceeding by an inverted model that avoided the distractions of external form in favour of a meditative quietude. Less visible, external sanctity equalled greater invisible, internal sanctity. In these two competing logics – analogy and in-version – we can find the major philosophic debates of monastic revival.

This debate came to a head with the conflict between Joseph Volotsky and Nil Sorsky in the early fifteenth century.[15] The final two decades of Joseph's life were devoted to the ordering of coenobitic life. His major work on this subject was written over many years and is referred to as the Extended Rule,[16] an ongoing document that governed the ranks, duties, discipline, penance system, schedules, protocol and procedural details of a large monasterial institution. While Nil had written his own 'Tradition' [*Predanie*] and a theoretical 'Statute' [*Ustav*] for monks, they described a 'small collective of artisan-mendicant hesychasts', avoiding routine, hierarchy and worldly analogues.[17] By contrast, for example, Joseph's recommended etiquette style for the monastery's ruling council, whose members were drawn from Moscow's wealthy families, was modelled on Kremlin court etiquette.[18]

While historians generally contend that the Josephites 'won' the debate,[19] the victory was eventually a diluted and compromised Josephitism that prevailed, one that incorporated the non-possessors' tolerance. In this sense, the hesychast legacy was not so much defeated as fragmented. It both tempered the Josephite ardour and provided an enduring mystical alternative to *any* institutional power, becoming identified with the people, the Russian land and Holy Russia. While it cannot be argued that the term 'Holy Russia' ('Helles Russland' and 'Holy Russia' are the terms used by Cherniavsky and Alexander Soloviev), which has been traced by some scholars from Maxim the Greek to Andrei Kurbsky,[20] is interchangeable with the Russian Idea,[21] both connote a mystical quality of sanctified, 'unincorporated' nationhood that resists embodiment in institutional form, *whether sacred or secular, Josephite or Muscovite.* As Cherniavsky has pointed out in his seminal essay, it tended to distinguish 'the myth of the nation ... [from] the myth of the ruler'.[22] Kurbsky's own affiliation both with Maxim the Greek and with the boyar opposition to Ivan IV, though not providing conclusive evidence, supports the notion of 'Holy Russia' as an anti-*institutional* slogan (not simply an anti-state slogan), a transcendental antidote to Moscow the Third Rome.

At stake here, therefore, is not a debate about the sacred versus secular, but something earlier, a debate about institutionalised belief *as such*. Originating in competing models of sanctity, it is then projected on to the secular/sacred divide precisely in the period (Ivan III–Vasili III–Ivan IV) when the secular state emerges as a powerful and distinct entity. One might argue further that, centuries later, as the early Soviet state sought to eradicate religion as such, the debate (transformed) nevertheless remained intact. Now *apparently* secular, it became a 'sacred choice' for the intelligentsia between affiliation with the (symbolically coenobitic) institutions of Party and state, accompanied by ritual, wealth and external display versus holy wandering: a peripatetic, solitary, reclusive existence of poverty, physical labour and masochistic denial. The fact that Berdiaev was himself exiled in 1922 and lived the rest of his life outside Russian society lends a kind of mystical legitimacy to this productive myth.

One could, of course, argue that the cultural pattern only recently dubbed the 'Russian Idea' long pre-dates even the hesychast movement. It might be seen as early as Illarion's 'Sermon on Law and Grace', with its emphasis on *freedom* over obedience, *grace* over law, an *alternative* Orthodoxy that comes late but spectacularly into the Byzantine world. What this argument ignores, however, is the Russian Idea's internal interdependence of two *national* systems of thought. The holy fool both subverts and supports the autocrat; the imaginary kingdom debunks and empowers the kingdom revealed; Kurbsky's Holy Russia fuels Ivan's Muscovite absolutism. Unlike the polemic of Illarion's time, which was conceived as a debate between Russia and a dominant, foreign (if Orthodox) outsider, the 'Russian Idea' is one half of an internal Russian dialogue: its conjoined twin and interlocutor is, among other instantiations, the Third Rome.

Nor could one convincingly argue that the cultural pattern of the 'Russian

Idea' emerges with the martyrdom of Russia's first saints, Boris and Gleb. Sviatopolk, their murderer-brother, was, after all, only an evil man. He carried no special, corporate power other than his own iniquity. Only in the cultural conflict of the hesychast mysticism first with Joseph, then with the ideology of the Third Rome and Ivan IV's absolutism do we find acted out a national performance of the kenotic and pantocratic Christs, twin nightmares of sacrifice and terror, alternately promising and threatening to destabilise the other. The transcendent, invisible Idea risks substantiation as Muscovite absolutism. The practical deployment of absolutism's terror is reined in not by the conventional institutions of Western democracy, but only by the anarchic impulses of Holy Russia.

In the historical context of the debates of these two centuries one may see competing models for both belief and salvation that have an evolving relevance for twentieth-century debates. Cast in various modes and presented by various pseudonyms, what is consistently at risk is a viable identity in opposition to any institution of the official, dominant culture, be it autocracy, the Soviet apparatus, or a newly 'corporate' Russia. Despite the veneer of secularisation, the 'Russian Idea' is in essence a sacred debate about the path to salvation, for which *hesychia*, a search for inner quietude, is not so arcane a task.

3.

The Russian people, in accordance with its eternal Idea, has no love for
the ordering of this earthly city and struggles towards a city that is to come.
Russian communism is a distortion of the Russian messianic idea.

Nikolai Berdiaev, *The Russian Idea*

From the mid-sixteenth to the late eighteenth centuries, little interest was evident in the mystical traditions of Hesychasm. Its revival at the end of the eighteenth century is attributed in part to the activities of Russian émigré monk Paisius Velichkovsky (1722–94), who lived for some time on Mount Athos and in Romania. In 1793, Paisius produced the first Slavonic translation of the Greek mystical compilation *Philocalia*. This compendium, whose contents were familiar to Nil Sorsky, was probably compiled by Nicodemus of Mount Athos.[23] On Russian soil, Paisius's traditions were continued through the nineteenth century in the Optina Pustyn Monastery (Kaluga), revered for its long tradition of elders.

A renewed scholarly and religious interest in the cult of Nil Sorsky and the Trans-Volga Elders was further enhanced by the appearance of the anonymous 'Candid Narrations of a Pilgrim to His Spiritual Father', dating from approximately 1860. This 'spiritual autobiography' of a devoted Russian wanderer [*skitalets*] tells of personal salvation through study of the *Philocalia* and constant repetition in hesychast fashion of the Jesus prayer. Published in 1884 (four years before Vladimir Soloviev's Paris lecture), the 'Pilgrim' became a treasured work in the late nineteenth- and early twentieth-century revival of interest in Orthodox mysticism that Berdiaev calls the Russian Renaissance.

The late nineteenth- and early twentieth-century philosophical movement that centred round Vladimir Soloviev and his intellectual interlocutors – Sergei Bulgakov, Nikolai Fedorov, Pavel Florensky, Semen Frank, Konstantin Leontiev, Vasili Rozanov, Lev Shestov, Gustav Shpet, Sergei and Evgeni Trubetskoi and, of course, Nikolai Berdiaev – was brought to an abrupt end in the early 1920s shortly after the Revolution. Berdiaev and other 'White professors' were expelled from the country for their religious and philosophical views, although interest in mystical idealism and Berdiaev's philosophical categories in particular continued in the West.[24] It was not until the mid-*perestroika* years (1988–91), however, that interest in turn-of-the-century mystical philosophy could again take published form in the Soviet Union.[25]

Berdiaev's *The Russian Idea*, a relatively late work of emigration, saw publication in his homeland only one year before the demise of the Soviet Union itself, an appropriate moment, given Berdiaev's late fascination with eschatology.[26] Since that time, a virtual avalanche of publications devoted to various glosses on the 'Russian Idea' have appeared in Russia,[27] testifying to the extreme productivity of the concept (in all the inevitable distortions that accompanied that popularity) in post-communist Russia.

What accounts for this appeal? A substantial answer to this question would have to account for interpretations of the 'Russian Idea' that range politically from free-market capitalism to conservative monarchism. A decent, partial answer, however, would suggest that the appeal of the 'Russian Idea' lies in its promise of national identity simultaneously nostalgic and new; indebted to its expatriate custodians and still 'patriate' without being patriotic; twentieth-century yet untainted by Bolshevik urbanism. In a culture long given to visionary and totalising concepts, the 'Russian Idea' is both of these. It offers an analysis of the Soviet period that does not so much annihilate its history as subsume it under larger cultural patterns indifferent to the good or evil of particular institutions as such. It thus points up institutional similarities (autocracy and Bolshevism; institutionalised Orthodoxy and Marxism–Leninism) while reserving a space of dignity for national consciousness beyond the boundaries of earthly institutions. This space might, however anachronistically, still be called Holy Russia, but its holiness is at times less sanctimonious than subversive, the holiness of the fool-in-Christ. Madness, religious vision, delirium, drunken frenzy, dreaming, illness, hallucination, song, hysteria, all reverberate with the anti-institutionalist intensity of Holy Russia.

This is not merely a debate over a renewed Russian messianism, for both Christs, after all, are messianic. Only the kenotic Christ, however, is adequate to express the idea that, by powerful identification with suffering, one becomes deserving of everything – of mistreatment, humiliation and, therefore, in the logic of Hesychasm, salvation and glory.

The Russian Idea

4.

> But the Russian Idea was always prone to the imperial temptation, as if you could simply create an earthly kingdom and from there, in one short leap, reach the Kingdom of God. The Russian Communists, completely in accordance with the Russian Idea, started with the destruction of the state, but hardly had they destroyed it than they set about rebuilding it ... The Russian Idea had been overshadowed by the imperial temptation.
>
> Oleg Kovalov, *The Russian Idea*

In their 1996 film *The Russian Idea*, Sergei Selianov and Oleg Kovalov suggest that the fateful moment for its post-Revolutionary citizens was their misapprehension of the Bolsheviks' Radiant Future as the long-awaited Kingdom. In their eager tearing down of 'this world' – autocracy and the official church – post-Revolutionary visionaries performed an invaluable service for its successor, replacing, in Berdiaev's words, the Third Rome with the Third International. This process, carried out at large throughout post-October Russia, was also manifest in the history of its early cinema.

I will not recapitulate Selianov's and Kovalov's argument further here, since it is above all a visual argument, not a verbal one. In their polemical response to the British Film Institute's invitation to produce a history of Russian cinema, the director and scriptwriter were keenly aware of early Soviet film-makers' deep complicity in building cultural institutions that acted contrary to their own conscious aspirations. Unlike Berdiaev, Selianov and Kovalov are highly ambivalent towards their subject matter; that is to say, not towards the cultural results, but towards a philosophy so intimately and paradoxically intertwined with terror. If their history of Russian film is a tribute to the extraordinary gifts of early Soviet film-makers, it is also a rueful recognition of the human cost. 'The "Russian Idea", undoubtedly disastrous for the state, the individual, and the world,' writes Kovalov in his synopsis to the film, 'turned out to be unexpectedly fertile for culture.'[28] Underscoring exactly this conundrum, the film returns again and again to Eisenstein's late masterpiece *Ivan the Terrible, Part Two* [Ivan Groznyi, II, 1946; released 1958].

Vast generalisations of the order contained in this article, cutting across centuries and cultural texts, run the risk of abstraction so great that they threaten to become emptied of meaning. Let me briefly in closing, however, address at least one recent cinematic text in this artistic lineage. Do we not find strong elements of this mystical world view in Alexander Sokurov's *Mother and Son* [Mat' i syn, 1997], with its emphasis on the exquisite powerlessness of self-sacrifice, its peripatetic isolation, its unrelievedly desolate setting, its insistent spiritual tone, its stubborn abstraction and introspection? The hesychast tradition is felt in its emphasis on voluntary compliance rather than compulsion, its subdued sense of impending eschatological catastrophe, the altered dreamlike consciousness, the film's transcendental *mise-en-scène*: What century is it? What country? What illness is this? Who are these characters? What are their names? The film stubbornly resists all spatial and temporal co-ordinates. We can catch the echoes of the old debates even in its most evident device, the inversion of the *pietà* of grieving mother and dying son.

Towards the end of *The Russian Idea*, Selianov and Kovalov present the viewer with a curious, intentional contradiction. Dubbing Sergei Eisenstein's *Ivan the Terrible, Part II* 'the last film of the Russian Idea', they visually characterise subsequent cinema as obeisant to state power, following the models set forth by Grigori Aleksandrov's *The Circus* [Tsirk, 1936]. Their Epilogue, however, cites Andrei Tarkovsky's 1980 film *Stalker* [1979], a visual tribute to the survival of the 'Russian Idea' beyond the period of Stalinist aesthetics, with its unremitting celebration of institutional power. Through the ancient device of negative parallelism, the film argues that Eisenstein's *Ivan* was merely *at first glance* the last film of the 'Russian Idea'. The 'Russian Idea', always an elusive and unreliable presence, re-emerges in the late Soviet work of Tarkovsky (another modern-day exile and wanderer) and his descendants. By now, the educated viewer can read this as both homage and warning.

One might well add that Tarkovsky's *Andrei Rublev* [1966] is the unnamed key text in this argument, built on the thematics of adept and elder, set in a spiritual environment that values ineffable essence over external pomp. It is Andrei Rublev, the fifteenth-century heir to Theophanes and the Palæologan tradition within monastic revival, who points to his twentieth-century spiritual cohorts – Alexander Kaidanovsky, Konstantin Lopushansky, Sergei Selianov and Alexander Sokurov – heirs to Tarkovsky's complex style.[29] *The Russian Idea*, whether the philosophical or cinematic text, attempts an ambitious leap backwards in order to understand the cultural patterns of the twentieth century. Andrei Rublev, whether the historical or cinematic figure, plays a pivotal role in the modern-day extension of hesychast mysticism, one of the most enduring cultural patterns of Russian society.

4. Now that the Party's Over: Soviet Cinema and Its Legacy

Richard Taylor

The notion that there can be such a thing as a 'legacy' of Soviet cinema presupposes of course that we can identify a distinctively separate or even unique construct that we might call 'Soviet cinema' or even '"Soviet" cinema'. The Georgian director Otar Ioseliani once recalled a conversation with the veteran film-maker Boris Barnet:

> He asked me: 'Who are you?' I said: 'A director.' ... 'Soviet,' he corrected, 'you must always say "Soviet director". It is a very special profession.' 'In what way?' I asked. 'Because if you ever manage to become honest, which would surprise me, you can remove the word "Soviet". Now I am a "Soviet director", although I only became one recently.'[1]

The identification of Soviet cinema with dishonesty as a defining characteristic is naturally provocative, in this case perhaps also ironic, but nevertheless rather too much of an oversimplification. Of course, for most of its existence Soviet cinema was expected to subordinate artistic considerations to ideological ones and for much of that time it did so, sometimes with scant regard for the artistic and moral integrity of the individual or the collective. Given the nature of the political system within which they were working, Soviet film-makers often had little alternative. But film-making is a complex and collective process and the braver spirits among them were frequently involved in a complicated web of negotiation and compromise, which sometimes enabled them to produce films that were original, thought-provoking and even subversive of the prevailing ideological hegemony: the names of Eisenstein, Paradzhanov and Tarkovsky immediately spring to mind.[2] Furthermore, the nature of that hegemony, as expressed in the doctrine of Socialist Realism, changed and developed over time: what was unacceptable in the 1930s might, for instance, be taken for granted in the 1960s.

It is difficult to determine specific dates for the beginning and end of the phenomenon known as 'Soviet cinema': for the purposes of this argument I shall take the 1919 paper nationalisation of the industry as the start date and the tumultuous V Congress of the Union of Soviet Film-makers in May 1986 as the end date. Both dates are problematic, even controversial, since absolute caesuras occur in cultural history even less frequently than they do in political history, but these parameters are probably less arbitrary than the alternatives. Hence these dates should be seen as commas in the sentence of cinema history rather than full stops; the very notion of a 'post-Soviet' cinema helps us to understand that the continuities are often at least as important as the discontinuities. Here the disintegration of the USSR and the end to the Cold War have given us an opportunity to re-evaluate the canonic view of Soviet cinema on both sides of the former iron curtain.

The original Western attraction to Soviet cinema depended in part on the lure of the exotic and the faith or hope in the possibility of an alternative model of cinema to the commercial exploitation associated with Hollywood.[3] At the opposite end of the political spectrum the fear of subversion from the East assumed a power on the part of Soviet cinema that it may not actually have had. It seems incredible now that Eisenstein's masterpiece *The Battleship Potemkin* [Bronenosets Potemkin, 1926], widely acknowledged as one of the most important films in the history of cinema, could not be shown publicly in the United Kingdom until the early 1950s. The vicious personal attacks that greeted Eisenstein on his forays into the West, especially in the USA, suggest also that intolerance of difference was not the exclusive prerogative of Stalin and his cultural commissars. Either way, Western criticism has traditionally emphasised the differences between Soviet cinema and the Western model(s) at the expense of the similarities. Hence a canon of great names (all from the silent era) was promulgated and remained largely static, even if Eisenstein and Pudovkin changed places at a certain stage and Tarkovsky and Paradzhanov were added later as token dissidents: Pudovkin, Eisenstein, Vertov, Dovzhenko. That there were such things as musical comedies in the Stalin era, that they were massively popular with audiences all over the USSR, and that they might be of some inherent interest, still come to many incredulous readers as a blinding revelation.[4]

Equally, the traditional Soviet approach to Soviet cinema has been governed by ideological rectitude and even puritanism, which has sometimes mirrored concerns expressed in the West and sometimes contradicted them. While there is no doubt that the attitude of Soviet critics was initially stimulated by a genuine faith or hope in a possible alternative model to Hollywood, paralleling the enthusiasm felt in left-wing circles in the West, there can equally be absolutely no doubt that this initial stimulation rapidly turned to a real and genuine fear of deviating from an approved official line, confirmed by the increasing impossibility of so doing as the screws of censorship and central Party/state control were tightened. Here the classic canon was reinforced by official approval (which could be given or taken away at a moment's notice)

The Russian Idea

and therefore fossilised: Eisenstein, Pudovkin, Vertov, Dovzhenko, and this time also Kuleshov. For political reasons there was a parallel emphasis on the differences rather than the similarities between Soviet and Western cinema and, in particular, an insistence that there was no continuity whatsoever between pre-Revolutionary Russian cinema (which remained almost completely un-known or 'forgotten' in the West) and the Soviet period. This petrified (in both senses) view obscured the bread-and-butter of what much Soviet cinema actually consisted of.

The official canon represented an élite cinema functioning in the name of a mass ideology, whereas there was in fact a mass cinema, notably but far from exclusively the musical comedies of Aleksandrov and Pyriev, which also func-tioned, indeed functioned more effectively, in the name of that mass ideology. The pioneering Russian cinema critic and historian Maya Turovskaya has recalled how intellectuals of her generation regarded this mass cinema as 'poor taste' and how she herself had subsequently come to see it as representing instead a 'different taste' that helped the mass audience to survive the rigours of the attempt to impose socialism in one country: 'The wheel of culture turns in the course of one generation: some names are left out, some brought in, and a third lot come back, sometimes more than once.'[5]

In this essay I want to identify some problems and to raise some questions for further research, rather than to provide any answers. First of all I want to identify the categories through which we might meaningfully distinguish the phenomenon that we call 'Soviet cinema', and then I hope to revisit those categories as they might be applied to the post-Soviet period.

Soviet cinema: a framework for analysis

1. Ideology and identity

We need first of all to examine the *rationale* for Soviet cinema, the *why?* As far as the authorities who for most of the Soviet period controlled and funded the cinema industry were concerned, the purpose of the exercise was ideological and political. This is true from the opening scenes of the *agitki* in the post-Revolutionary civil war, 1917–21, to the final curtain of *glasnost* and *perestroika*, 1985–91. In the intervening years the actors on the cinema stage – principally the directors, but also of course the scriptwriters, the actual actors, cameramen and so on – were to varying degrees moved by the same impetus, intermingled with an individual mixture of other driving passions, artistic and otherwise. Some became disillusioned (Eisenstein, Vertov, Kuleshov), others cynical (Barnet, Aleksandrov and Chiaureli in different ways), while others worked within the system to broaden its base (Kozintsev and Trauberg, Abram Room, Mikhail Romm, Raizman among many), and we should not forget that a director's career, in particular, should not be judged merely by the end product, the films themselves.

Many are the obstacles *en route*; many too are the failed or aborted projects, many more the banned or shelved films. Eisenstein's *Bezhin Meadow* [Bezhin lug, 1935–37] and many of his other projects fall into the first category; Part Two of his *Ivan the Terrible* [Ivan Groznyi, 1946], Kuleshov's *Theft of Sight* [Krazha zreniia, 1934] and *We from the Urals* [My s Urala, 1943], Barnet's *The Old Jockey* [Staryi naezdnik, 1940] and his musical comedy *A Good Chap* [Slavnyi malyi, 1942],[6] Aleksandrov's co-directed *One Family* [Odna sem'ia, 1943], Kozintsev and Trauberg's *Young Fritz* [Iunyi Frits, 1943] and *Simple People* [Prostye liudi, 1945], Abram Room's *A Stern Young Man* [Strogii iunosha, 1936], Mikhail Romm's *Dream* [Mechta, 1942][7] and the many shelved films from the Brezhnev 'period of stagnation', fall into the second.[8]

The reasons for delaying, banning and shelving both projected and completed films were many and varied, sometimes obvious and sometimes quite inscrutable. But those reasons are as much part of the ideological identity – the *negative* identity, if you like – as are the reasons for permitting and promoting other films – representing the *positive* identity of Soviet cinema – from *Potemkin* through *Chapayev* [Chapaev, 1934] and *The Fall of Berlin* [Padenie Berlina, 1950] to *The Cranes Are Flying* [Letiat zhuravli, 1957] or *Repentance* [Pokaianie/ Monanieba, 1984; release 1986] – indeed, this last film fell into both categories. Nor should we forget that politically 'difficult' film-makers were more often than not entrusted with the training of the next generation: Eisenstein, Kuleshov and Vertov are prime examples of this phenomenon. What applied to directors applied equally to the other cinematic professions, above all to scriptwriting, where the written text was all too easy to criticise, censor or condemn. Hence the ideological and political identity of Soviet cinema is a rather more complex matter than might first appear, and than it has appeared to generations of scholars, East and West.

How much more complex that identity appears when we consider broader contextual notions of 'national' and 'cultural' identity. The Soviet Union was a self-proclaimed 'single multi-national' [*edinoe mnogonatsional'noe*] state, but with Russians constituting more than half the population and rather more than half the geographical space. To what extent was the Soviet Union a 'Russian' state, perhaps a 'Russian Empire' in disguise? To what extent were Soviet films 'Soviet' rather than Russian, Ukrainian, Georgian and so on? How much validity is there in Oleg Kovalov's assertion that 'The golden age of the "Russian idea" in cinema is precisely the Soviet era'?[9] What was the national identity of Sergei Eisenstein, a man born in the Russian Empire in a predominantly German-speaking Hanseatic port of mixed Russian and German–Jewish ancestry? (Conversely, now that the same city is the predominantly Russian-speaking capital of independent Latvia, does that make Eisenstein a Latvian director?) Or was he purely and simply a 'Soviet' director, and does that designation make him either deracinated, on the one hand, or cosmopolitan (and I do not mean to use this word in the sense of the sinister Stalinist

The Russian Idea

euphemism), on the other? In a more recent period, Paradzhanov offers a similar complex of ethnic identities. There are countless other examples: to take just one, are Dovzhenko, Vertov, Savchenko, Chukhrai (or Muratova?) 'Ukrainian', 'Soviet' or 'Ukrainian Soviet' artists? Do they reflect different identities at different times and in different films? If we take the output of particular studios the question of identity becomes more complicated still: when Pyriev, a deeply 'Russian' director, made two musical comedies in the Kiev studios was he making Ukrainian, Russian or Soviet films? Was the Belorussian studio, Belgoskino, in any real sense 'Belorussian' when it was based in Leningrad?[10]

Perhaps the path to a solution to this particular problem of national identity might in fact lie with the official slogan 'single, multi-national'. We might see 'Soviet' identity as something closely related to ideology, and to the notion of class upon which that ideology was based, as something overlaid (or imposed) upon a sense of ethnic identity, so that a director, a film or studio might in fact be best described, at least at a certain period, as 'Soviet' (Eisenstein), or 'Georgian' (Shengelaia's *Pirosmani* [1969]) or 'Ukrainian Soviet' (VUFKU/ Ukrainfilm). This 'solution', ironically, at least facilitates an explanation of the resurgence of national, as opposed to Soviet, identity in the 1980s, as for instance in Jūris Podnieks' *Is It Easy to Be Young?* [Legko li byt' molodym?, 1986].[11]

2. Industry and structure

We need also to look at the *organisation* of Soviet cinema, the *how* – in the sense of where and when? To what extent did the centralisation of production, distribution and exhibition give Soviet cinema a uniform identity? How far was that uniformity deliberately modified to provide a varied diet for film-goers, for instance by providing a range of genres? How rigid and influential were the annual 'thematic plans' that studios had to produce for much of the Soviet period? To what extent were there regional or sub-Soviet national differences? How far was the assumption valid that, the further the film-maker was from centralised control in Moscow, the more creative freedom he or she had, or was it better to be a small fish in a big pool? To what extent were formal structures modified, or even underlined by informal structures, close friendships and personal animosities, even brief encounters? What were the censorship mechanisms, how effective were they and how did they alter over time?

Were there different studio styles? Did the officially promulgated change of name from 'film factories' to 'film studios' have any practical significance? Or the earlier change of gender in the Russian word for 'film'?[12] Were the products of Ukrainian or Georgian studios necessarily more 'folkloric' than those of Moscow or Leningrad? Within each studio how influential were men 'behind the scenes' like Adrian Piotrovsky, the artistic director of the Leningrad studio from 1928 to 1937, or his successors? What did the creative workshops associated with leading directors like Mikhail Romm or Sergei Yutkevich contribute to the creation or evolution of a studio style? How significant was the organisation of training? Or the influence of teachers? How far did it matter that most leading film-workers (apart from actors whose careers often followed a different, theatrical path) were trained at VGIK, or that breakaway 'higher courses' were later established as a reaction against the VGIK hegemony? At a higher political level, what real influence did men like Boris Shumiatsky, Ivan Bolshakov or Filipp Ermash exercise? What were the mechanisms by which they exerted that influence?[13] And how did film-makers both individually and as a group react to it: what was the significance of first the absence and later the existence, both shadow and real, of the Union of Soviet Film-makers, whose V Congress in May 1986 proved to be such a turning-point in cultural and political life?[14]

Were particular films specifically targeted at particular audiences? If not, why were there several categories of release? How were the films regarded as ideologically sound promoted and 'sold' to audiences? What precisely was the role of conventional film criticism in Soviet cinema and how did it evolve over time?

3. Economics and finance

Of course the consequences of the organisation of Soviet cinema have no meaning unless we look at the *funding* of what was, after all, an industry as well as an art form and a weapon of political agitation and propaganda. This also involves an examination of the *how* – in the sense of what with? Very little work has been done on this aspect of Soviet cinema, probably because most historians and critics are not accountants. How centrally controlled was funding? Was it a matter of a block grant distributed from the centre to be used as the peripheries saw fit, or were there controls at all levels? If so, how effective were they? To what extent was cinema affected by taxation, or did it have a privileged, exempt status?

Were there any other sources of income? Were there box-office receipts in any meaningful sense of the term? If so, how were they distributed? Did the system give film-makers and/or studios or work collectives any incentive to make films that were popular in the sense that they would make money? Was there a creeping commercialisation of Soviet cinema even before the advent of *glasnost* and *perestroika*? How were resources distributed within studios and within thematic plans? Was there any special funding for particular projects and, if so, what criteria were applied to identify those projects? Did particular film-makers have privileged access to funding and were the criteria applied political, artistic or commercial, or a mix of all three? Was money earmarked for film-making on a geographically weighted basis? Was cinema more generously funded in political priority areas where it might exert a particular effect? How did the system produce so many films that it was thought necessary to withhold from distribution? Were 'art' films, such as the works of Eisenstein,

Paradzhanov, Tarkovsky or Sokurov, in some ways privileged over mass-market films?

Consideration of finances also raises the question of technical resources. How advanced was Soviet cinema in the silent period? How widely spread was the cinema network at various stages in the 'cinefication' process and what were the implications of this for film production and distribution? How technologically backward did Soviet cinema later become in comparison with Western Europe or North America? How did it cope with new technology, from sound and colour to wide-screen processes?

4. Content and traditions

The examination of the output of Soviet cinema finally brings us to the *what*, to the *kolbasa* at the end of the sausage machine of the film production line. Was that output distinctive? Was it distinctively '*Soviet*'? Were there particular genres that predominated? Outsiders might assume that in its early period Soviet cinema concentrated on historical-revolutionary films and that later these gave way to re-enactments of the sacrifices and heroism of the war, and later still to screen versions of literary classics. How far was this the case? Did the legitimating myths change over time, for instance from the Revolution (Lenin) to the Great Patriotic War (Stalin to Brezhnev)? To what extent was the civil war film the Eastern equivalent of the Hollywood western? How was the musical genre translated to the Soviet Union, what was its function, and how effective was it? To what extent did Socialist Realism, which was supposed to show not 'reality as it really is' but reality 'as it will be'[15] in fact constitute an escapist flight from the problems of the present into the future, or even the past? Were there specifically Soviet film genres, emerging from any of the factors outlined above, that have not translated into other film cultures, including the post-Soviet cinemas of former Soviet Union republics or the former socialist states of central and Eastern Europe?

Do Soviet films have a particular 'look' and, if so, what constitutes that look? Does it derive from artistic, political or technical considerations, or is it influenced by all three? Similarly, do Soviet films have a particular 'sound' or 'texture'? Was the 1934 *Pravda* headline, 'The whole country is watching *Chapaev*'[16] justified and, if so, how and why? Can we assume that a film seen by millions of viewers was necessarily 'popular' in any meaningful sense of the word, or merely that it had been successfully promoted from above?[17] Was there such a thing as a collective Soviet audience 'gaze'? Was there a generational difference in the responses of Soviet audiences? How were audience reactions influenced by gender stereotypes or even gender transmigration? Or ethnic stereotypes and the attempt to create a model Soviet citizen? Or even typecasting, as in the depiction of enemies of the state? How did these stereotypes evolve? What was the cultural and political significance of dubbing, as opposed to subtitling, and what were the political effects of showing films in

Russian to non-Russian audiences in the national republics? Were educational or non-fiction films in any way privileged under the Soviet system? How important were newsreels, in both war and peace?

These are just some of the questions by which we might eventually definitively identify what has been called the phenomenon of Soviet cinema.[18] It is only then that we shall truly be able, with the benefit of by then considerable hindsight, to specify more precisely the legacy of Soviet cinema.

Post-Soviet cinema: legacy, disinheritance or renunciation?

The very term 'post-Soviet' is of course a loaded one, because it already implies and possibly defines a specific relationship with what preceded it. But there can be no legacy, no disinheritance or renunciation unless there is some relationship between the past and the present, as there must be, even if only for reasons of chronology. Russian cinema in the 1990s was not still-born, even if it may have to go back to the pre-Soviet period to rediscover some of its Russian roots, or at least those not adopted or subsumed by Sovietisation. Here, as in so much else, Russian cinema shares the experience of Russia itself, emerging from the seventy-four years of the Soviet experiment. Let us revisit the categories outlined above and ask some preliminary questions about how Russian cinema in the 1990s and beyond into the new millennium may confront and overcome its legacy, whether it accepts or renounces it.

The ideology and identity of Russian cinema in the 1990s is clearly different from that of the Soviet period: there is no single dominant ideology that is centrally directed and promulgated by an elaborate political machine and, although Russia is now closer to being an ethnically homogeneous nation-state in the Western sense than ever before, there is no real agreement as to what its 'Russianness' consists of. There is no real agreement even over the Russian word that should be used to describe the country and its culture, let alone its cinema: is it *russkii*, the word used to describe the Russian language, or *rossiiskii*, the word used officially to describe the federation 'of the Russias'? The choice has important political and cultural implications because the 'Russian Idea' is not the same as the 'idea of the Russias'. What are the sources for this Russianness, however defined? How far back do Russians have to go? Does this sense of Russianness comprise elements that require a reaction *for* or *against* them? Which brings us back to that core question: can we distinguish Russian cinema from Soviet cinema, or was the Soviet period really 'the golden age of the Russian Idea'?

Because of the collapse of centralised Soviet state structures, the organisation and financing of Russian cinema have also had to change. Has private finance, whether from domestic (respectable or Mafia-originated) or foreign sources, largely replaced state funding? What have been the implications of this for the

The Russian Idea

relationship between government, state and cinema? Or for the relationship be-tween cinema and other media such as the press or television? Or that between Russian and world cinema? How has censorship changed? How has the video revolution affected film production and distribution? How has privatisation affected the internal organisation of studios and their attitude and relationship towards audiences and distribution outlets? Has Russian cinema been swamped by the once forbidden fruit of imported films? Is Russian cinema becoming a colony of Western film companies? Is the distribution network catering for the lowest common denominator in the audience? To what extent is the audience, or assumptions made about it, a major factor in film production? What is happening to the education and training of new generations of film-makers? Are individual film-makers making profits at the expense of the film-making community as a whole? Is emigration a major problem, or is there a beneficial cross-fertilisation with Western ideas and practices?

Lastly we need to look at the films themselves, with all the caveats that I have already made. Is Russia in the 1990s now producing a wide variety of films that are broadly accessible to domestic audiences, either through cinemas or television, and sometimes exhibited and acclaimed abroad? Are these reason-able criteria for judging the health of Russian cinema? In short, if the 'Russian Idea' had its golden age in Soviet cinema, can we at least say that in the post-Soviet period, the 'Russian Idea' is alive and well, if not necessarily actually kicking, in Russian cinema? Has the 'Russian Idea' been born again, resurrected, or merely half-heartedly resuscitated?

It will be a long time before we can answer these questions with confidence and conviction and with proper historical hindsight, but the essays in this volume will at least provide a start. We should not be too downhearted if the path to knowledge is strewn with obstacles but should draw comfort from the famous exchange between two French film-makers:

'Movies should have a beginning, a middle and an end,' harrumphed French film maker Georges Franju ... 'Certainly,' replied Jean-Luc Godard. 'But not necessarily in that order.'[19]

5. Russian Cinema – National Cinema? Three Views

The three speeches gathered here all address the question of the role which Russian cinema plays in defining a national identity; they were given between October 1997 and May 1998.

1. 'Cinema and Life', *Sergei Selianov*

It was suggested I should talk about the changes in Russian cinema in recent years. This is a legitimate question, since life in Russia has changed with *perestroika* and the other reforms that followed. But the question is whether in this context cinema's imagery and style have changed. Do the changes in life influence art?

There are various theories about this. The first theory argues that cinema is a mirror reflection of life. If the spectator says 'It's just like in real life', this means that it is good. Normally the spectator makes such comments about Latin American soap operas. The second theory argues that the art of cinema has, and can have, no connection with real life. The artist sits, as they say, in his ivory tower and ignores the signals that emanate from the external world (that is, from life) but listens only to some kind of divine messages and signs.

I am a practitioner, not a theorist, and for me this question is akin to 'Is there life on Mars?' That is to say, my attitude to the question of the connection between life and art is quite ironic, because artists – directors in this case – understand that they *are* the link between cinema and life. The director deciphers or relays, i.e. there is an 'input' into him and then an 'output' from him, which is how a work of art comes about. In other words, the director feels that he himself stands behind this question of the relationship between life and art; he takes it upon himself to reply, and not everybody can do this without irony.

However, in recent years such great changes have occurred in Russia that even the least thoughtful practitioner has been thinking about a great many things. After all, life has not just changed, it has changed radically. In this context cinema has changed too, and some kind of link has been uncovered between these changes. Those artists who thought that they conversed directly

The Russian Idea

with God now feel humiliated, insulted and distraught. Nobody in Russia is really interested in that sort of art at the present time.

I have a very simple thesis which sums up my understanding and explanation of what has happened in Russia: in the past, cinema in Russia was greater than life, whereas nowadays in Russia life is infinitely greater than cinema.

You are all familiar with recent Russian history so that this thesis probably does not require any proof. I had certainly not anticipated that I would live under any another system than a totalitarian one. I had not foreseen or anticipated anything, and was sure that there were enough General Secretaries around to outlast my lifetime. I was not depressed by this, since my real life took place in the bosom of art and cinema. I felt an immense inner freedom. In 1980 my friends and I made the film *Angel's Day* [Den' angela, 1988], slightly infringing the state's monopoly on film production (which was rather like forging money or making *samogon*).[1] I had grandiose plans in the area of cinema, and all my ideas were connected with the creation of my own worlds, since the real world was dead, sterile and unnatural. Socialism, after all, is also a work of art; it is invented, but without talent. And there is nothing more dead than a talentless work of art.

Life in Russia under socialism was extremely impoverished, sanitised and sterilised, with a great number of restrictions. Yet any kind of prohibition passionately stimulates the creative imagination – not only the imagination of directors, but of spectators, too. Our audiences were the most advanced in the world. They did not just enjoy art, but drank that freedom from books and films. It was not social freedom, but a great and genuine freedom of an almost religious nature. Clearly, this created a unique paradox: it was, in a certain sense, easier for real artists to create serious films working with this audience and these restrictions. Generally speaking, totalitarianism assists a genius by clearing away the superfluous. The great talented artists were more than mere artists; they were prophets and teachers. For instance, people came to ask Tarkovsky how to live, where to go, where to find the truth. And he was not shocked by these questions, because he acknowledged his teaching mission as his duty.

In other words, in those days, art was greater than life.

I am convinced that any sort of restriction benefits art, and that art cannot exist without restrictions. These may be external, or they may be internal, i.e. the artist must act as a self-censor. There are also natural limitations, like natural monopolies. For example, there is a very powerful limitation to which nobody attaches any significance, nobody even acknowledges its existence: this is the format of the frame, which is always standard (1:1.33) or wide frame (1:1.66). In short, it is some sort of rectangle, and it has never occurred to anyone to challenge this terrible limitation and make the frame round, for instance, or somehow vertical. Another classic and well-known example is that of the canon in icon-painting, which prescribed which colour to use for which

Russian Cinema – National Cinema?

object. Yet under these strict limitations, the art of icon-painting (if one considers icon-painting here merely as an art) was one of the most piercing, clear, radiant and completely unlimited art forms, where no external limitations are to be felt. It is clear what I am suggesting: when 'the prison walls have crashed, and freedom met us joyfully at the door', none of us was prepared for it.[2]

Then *perestroika* burst upon us. Suddenly things from a life that was healthy and natural appeared, which we had forgotten about in Russia. Life itself became more natural, an elemental force that knows no limits. But art is all about limits, about conventionality. Our artists were not ready to assimilate, process and evaluate this new elemental force. In our daily life such things appeared as money, when for decades prices and salaries had not changed; starving people emerged who had been hidden away; sex was spoken about as though it had never existed before. These features of everyday reality had not existed in the consciousness of directors, audiences or the Soviet people as a whole. Money, hunger and sex became the building blocks of art. At the same time, other features slipped away for good: the country opened up and the powerful myth of abroad collapsed. It was not so much that Russians had been unable to go abroad in the past, but 'abroad' was a different world. Living in Russia, it was very important to know that somewhere out there was such a different world. Suddenly it transpired that there is no other world. This is what we have lost.

The ideological state, which for artists had been the main creative irritant 'of opposites', that is, something to react against, disappeared.

At the same time, people received an enormous amount of information about their own history and about all sorts of current events throughout the world. New sources for this visual information also emerged: video recorders, new television channels, computers and so on. These dealt the 'final blow' to cinema: artists did not know what to film, and audiences stopped watching. because they had access to all sorts of new, brilliant and striking images. The existential condition of the artist in Soviet Russia had vanished. In those days one could have paraphrased Dostoevsky: 'Why art, if everything is permissible?' On the whole, this situation has not been overcome even today. Perhaps this is a harsh and simple view, but I reckon that in recent years not one *genuinely* worthy film has been made in Russia. A number of good films have been made, but for the last twelve years there have been no great *events* in cinema of the sort that we used to have before. Directors of the standing of Tarkovsky, Ioseliani or Paradzhanov[3] – I could continue this list – have not emerged. I shall not discuss what has emerged in their place: it is a kind of '*chernukha-pornukha*'[4] and a number of directors have taken the commercial route, which is not a very easy route, and almost none of them has been successful. At best, magical realism has turned into fantasy.

It is worth adding in parentheses that, strangely enough, in contemporary European cinema films have started to appear which we would never have expected from Europe, but rather from our own film-makers. We had thought that this was our exclusive territory. Such is the case with *Breaking the Waves* [Denmark/Netherlands/Sweden/France, 1996], a film which is very Russian in its concern with the tremendous force that naïve faith can have; or with American films, such as *Forrest Gump* [USA, 1994] with its Ivan-the-Fool type character[5] of Russian history.

Now that things are fine in Russia there are no longer any great films. I began with the premise that the director represents the link between cinema and life. He changes, things happen to him, and this filters through to the screen. Unfortunately, nothing is happening to us at present, and that is our misfortune. We are making some rational moves and are building a new life, sometimes quite successfully.

In cinema a lot has been achieved, too; the establishment of a national film market in Russia means that films will get produced and will break even financially. Since 1997 film production in Russia has been rising. But sadly, there is no will to be artistically creative in Russia at the moment; there is no motivating force. In a rather comic way, this has been understood at a high political level, and political advisers have been given the task of creating a national idea through the medium of film.

We Russians are zoological optimists: it would be impossible for us to be anything else. It goes without saying that I have not the slightest regret about the passing of those totalitarian years, which were dead and stale. It will be quite normal, perhaps even remarkable, if, with time, Russian cinema can take the same place that cinema takes throughout the world: somewhere between entertainment and light intellectual challenge. Any serious discussions about Russian cinema would then come to an end. We will make films, you will either watch them or not watch them, and basta! But for some reason we keep expecting more of cinema, as we did in the past.

Bristol, 17 October 1997

2. 'The State of the National Cinema', *Daniil Dondurei*

Sergei Soloviev[6] has delivered a gripping and inspiring thesis about the irreversible resurrection of our cinema. Indeed, all the signs speak for such a resurrection: in 1997 production has risen by 250 per cent; fifty-two full-length feature films have been completed, and seventy are in production; television companies are producing seven serials for a total of 100 hours of transmission time. Russian-language films and serials accounted for 45.5 per cent (4,110 of 9,073 hours) of film screenings on television. Moreover, there was a completely new phenomenon: an increase in the percentage of Russian films to 43.6 per cent, which includes a rise by 15–20 per cent of Russian films shown at primetime. For the first time, three Russian titles figured in the top ten charts of the Russian video market, which is the main source of recouping production costs.

The success of the Kodak-Kinomir cinema where the evening ticket prices are among the most expensive in the whole of Europe, and the revamping of cinemas like the Pushkin, the Arts Cinema (Khudozhestvenny), the Cine-Centre (Kinotsentr), have led to a situation where three powerful financial groups are preparing to invest $100 million each into the construction of multiplexes and into the Russian film industry. This is the situation at the moment.

The government will certainly bring into effect the Law on Cinema,[7] which gives some hope for additional investments in production. But it will not guarantee the key factor in the development of our film industry: the return of the money invested into film production. This will not be guaranteed even by multiplexes with Dolby-stereo systems; it can only be achieved if audiences respond to films that appeal to them. Here, the most acute problem arises: the question of our national repertoire.

First, we face a catastrophic shortage of films that can survive twelve television screenings in one year, such as Sakharov's *The Lady-Peasant* [Baryshnia-krestianka, 1995].[8]

Second, we have to stand up to competition with world cinema. It is no longer possible to say, as it was five years ago, that the cinemas and television are full of third-class films. Moscow premières of some of the best-known blockbusters run parallel to premières in other capitals; and, with television screening four or five masterpieces of world cinema per week, Russia stands, in the opinion of experts, among the world leaders.

For six years we have refrained from any discussion of the repertoire, content and quality of our films; our concern was just to survive, and hope that 'there may be no war'. But now, on the threshold of a film boom, we must at last be decisive and face up to the new situation.

I do not intend to speak about the artistic quality of films made in the 1990s, some 800 titles altogether. The directors themselves are better equipped to do this. I shall only point out that our film-makers still act as their own clients. The absence of state censorship, of any 'social command', the weakness and confusion about the producer's profession have allowed directors throughout the entire Yeltsin period to screen their own ideas and their own readings of events exclusively.

This has had two consequences: (1) The creators of what is essentially mass production have ignored its function, and oriented themselves towards foreign festival organisers. (2) In practice, almost the entire body of films relayed to the audience images that contradict the aims of the modernisation of Russia.

We all know perfectly well that the heroes of a commercially successful cinema cannot be cynics, defeatists, failures or unmotivated killers. A national inferiority complex cannot be cultivated in cinema. Mass audiences throughout the world deny such subject matter the possibility of financial support.

The Russian Idea

Hollywood, which controls almost 70 per cent of world screen time with 4 per cent of world production, means not just fantastic sums of money, stars and technology. Above all, Hollywood is the most important myth-maker, producing ideologically regulated films with an extremely stable value system. Confusion, despair, heroes who have no belief in themselves, their fatherland or the future are ruled out; 'doom and gloom' are absolutely forbidden. During the Great Depression this principle applied more than ever. After ten years of exposure, our Russian spectators are proud of American heroes, American detectives, American dogs and, especially, the American government.

I have randomly selected some programme notes from festival catalogues and from reviews that provide simple, basic, primitive plot summaries of our films. Apologies in advance for their primitiveness.[9]

The Year of the Dog by Aranovich: 'The brief happiness of an ex-prisoner united with a lonely woman in a village that has been exposed to radiation.'

Limits by Evstigneev: 'Friendship turns into treachery, love into an illusion.'

Peshawar Waltz by Bekmambetov and Kaiumov: 'Russian helicopters shoot their own soldiers held hostage by the enemy. All the Russian prisoners of war in Afghanistan die.'

Life with an Idiot by Rogozhkin: 'An intellectual from a madhouse seduces the hero's wife, then the hero himself, and then together they chop off the ex-wife's head.'

Riaba la poule by Konchalovsky: 'The son of the heroine is a "new Russian" who comes from the city. At home he naturally lands in the shit; meanwhile, the village "new Russian" burns his own model house.'

The Muslim by Khotinenko: 'The hero returns from captivity in Afghanistan and reviews his relationship with his family, his village and his own past; after that, he is killed.'

Schizophrenia by Sergeev: 'As a result of two acts of provocation the KGB takes the hero on "special duty" – as a killer. The bank, whose chairman of the Board of Directors is to be "eliminated", is "protected" by a powerful criminal group, subordinated, of course, to a high-ranking official of the Ministry of Internal Affairs. And the gentleman who has ordered the murders turns out to be the deputy prime minister of the government. All in line with the political momentum.'

Brother by Balabanov: 'A typical modern family. The father – a recidivist thief; the brother – a degenerate character, a hired killer. The charming hero does not like "black arses" and "Jews", but he adores the songs of Nautilus Pompilius;[10] and, without the slightest doubt – having become a killer – he decides who to "off" and who to spare.'

Situational and existential killers, 'new Russians', power and comradeship – it's all the same, our cinema asserts to its audience which does not understand high art.

Thus, cinema refrains from laying the foundations for a new life, hopes and success. Together with television, we seem to be trying to persuade the population: 'Dear fellow-countrymen, look and don't forget, you're living in a real hell.'

But surely we cannot seriously think that films immersed in an ocean of unpunished violence will arouse delight and identification in any sensible spectator. Who likes to see the hero defeated, or all government structures shown as totally criminal? The tradition of which culture are we developing here?

Here are some, in my view, symptomatic titles of the very latest, most recent works: *The Vampire, The Cutter, Good Trash – Bad Trash*, and so on.[11]

Some 25,000 years ago our ancestors – amateur artists – drew on the walls of their caves scenes of their triumph over dangerous beasts before they went out to hunt. The following day, in real life, they naturally achieved what they had aspired to in their own imagination. Why do we so stubbornly ignore the wise counsel of the masters of that primitive era? [...]

You may argue that such analysis is unfounded, since we are talking about 'auteur' cinema. But I should like to remind you that the 800 films made in the 1990s cannot all be 'auteur' films. We understand perfectly well that the main clients – Gilles Jacob, Moritz de Hadeln, Marco Müller[12] and other directors of well-known international festivals – take between five and ten films per year, no more. That is the first point.

Second, in terms of world-wide statistics, only between 3 to 5 per cent of the audiences understand 'auteur' cinema. Our films are screened on television for millions of viewers. Third, 'auteur' cinema cannot develop without a good-quality mass culture. And fourth, how can we recoup the money if all production is such as described in the annotations above. I am not speaking here of the aesthetic, artistic quality (that would be dangerous) but simply about the plot.

The communists on the one hand and the bankers on the other do not want genuine, fast and effective reforms in Russia. They benefit from preserving the vast ideologically protected zones of socialism. Their sluttish business tricks rely on retrograde steps, on the intimidation of the country, and on swindling.

But why have we, the creative intelligentsia, for the past few years, bowed to the cult of feigned poverty and hopelessness and served with such spiritual enthusiasm (such unanimity has never been before, even in the terrible years of the Stalin era) the interests of the communists and financial oligarchs? Not for the applause of intellectuals at international festivals who will say, 'Of course, this is remarkable, this is the real truth: Russia is a very dangerous and utterly unpredictable country.'

Everybody, except our producers, understands that the predominance of sorrow over happiness, of poverty over well-being, relishing the details of the hero's defeat, the absence of miracles eventually condemn films to oblivion. Nowhere and never has a cinema for the spectator grown on such soil. The most ordinary human psyche protests: art, above all, is a means to model the future successfully.

I view the prospects for our cinema with optimism. Alongside non-returnable state subsidies the film industry will soon attract large investments. The entrepreneurs behind these investments will no longer be part of the old-boy network; they will want to understand the nature of the project in which they are planning to invest, and they will aim at the creation of a truly marketable film. In contrast to our beloved Goskino (State Department for Cinematography), they will not be afraid to talk about the social command, since they know that the best film of all time and all countries, *The Battleship Potemkin*, was made to order. There is nothing reprehensible in this. The ineradicable desire to recoup investments will eventually prompt us to do what we did so well in Soviet times: make films that appeal to mass audiences. The investors will certainly ask us to renounce our long-standing obsession with despair, and will first and foremost reassure us that we are already living in a beautiful and very active country that is about to blossom forth.

III Congress of the Film-makers' Union,
22–23 December 1997, Moscow

3. 'The Function of a National Cinema', *Nikita Mikhalkov*

You may think what you like about the personality and actions of Vladimir Ilyich Lenin, but almost nobody would dream of questioning his political acumen and the precision of his formulations. Cinema was nominated as the most important of all the arts because it was capable of shaping the consciousness of the masses. It was an art, because it was clear even then that it was not only a document, but an artistic illusion, a myth, if you like, capable of facilitating the creation of a model for a new society, and for a hero which the state and the authorities needed at a particular time.

I deliberately expose the issue in such an almost cynical way, because we all know how ideology has manipulated this most powerful weapon.

But to serve the Fatherland does not necessarily mean to serve the regime. That is why today we can state so openly: cinema has betrayed its audience, has left it to the mercy of fate, has rejected its love! When did this happen? At that very moment when cinema could have helped those same people to live through difficult times, to feel themselves part of a whole, to sow some sort of hope. [...]

Have many of our fellow countrymen have been in the USA? I imagine some 5 per cent; maybe even less, 3 per cent. Yet do many people know about the USA? Almost everybody does. But they know the America that cinema has shown them.[13] America has forced the world to perceive it through cinema. Moreover, American cinema has actually become the most important of all arts for the American audience, and not just for them. Nowadays only France has managed to restrict the screenings of American films to 60 per cent of the total. Everywhere else that percentage is higher: in Russia it is over 80 per cent, while in America it is 92 per cent. How talented you must be to make your audience watch your own national cinema to such a degree! This would have been impossible if the film industry was not profit-making. Otherwise a film like the $250 million *Titanic* would never have recouped over two weekends; currently its profit is approaching $1.5 billion.

But for what do we want to get money from our spectator? What should he take out of the cinema with him? What should be going on in his soul when he leaves the cinema, having bought a ticket from a salary he received four months late? Do we want recognition here or somewhere far away? Can we count on anybody else's respect when we do not respect one another? Who will become a hero to our children? Who will be a folk hero? Who will be the subject of anecdotes, as Vasili Chapayev or Stirlitz[14] were? Yet without this kind of folklore, there can be no cinema. Man cannot exist without a hero. He has to have a model, a symbol. I do not mean the varnished model of a superman. This is not the only important thing. But look around you: all over the children know who Stallone and Schwarzenegger are, because it is through these heroes that American cinema teaches its children the concepts of honour, justice, and so on.

What do we have? We are film-makers, and we can make use of this opportunity. […] (*A film with clips from the latest Russian movies is shown on the screen.*)

What will become of our children? What will they know about their own country? Why should they love their country? What should keep them in this land? What can help them to survive in such hard conditions?

You may argue that there are also many American films with violence, sex, prostitutes and killers. Probably more than ours, because the volume of American film production is several times larger than ours. But the concept of justice and law, respect for these ideas, for the flag, for the national anthem, for the President are unshakeable. An American who suffers a misfortune in another country will expect help from his own country, will anticipate it, even if that help never arrives. […]

A badly made, empty film provokes anger and vexation. But if a film lacking creative principles and artistic compassion loses touch with roots, but is made competently, professionally and skilfully, then it is even more painful and frightening, because the talent, intelligence and potential of many young directors are directed towards evil and destruction.

Only one thing gives us reason for hope: with the upturn in the film industry and film distribution the spectator may point them in the right direction, because the film industry cannot exist on subsidies alone. To demand state privileges for cinema means to draw on funds needed by the health service, education,

The Russian Idea

the army and even the miners. The industry can be reborn only by the spectator, who will, however, pay only for a cinema in which he recognises himself. This certainly does not mean that we must lie and varnish our reality; such thoughts are far from my mind. But it means that dignity and faith must be at the foundation of human existence, however cruel the subject matter may be. A wise man once said: 'A cruel truth without love is a lie.' Cinema has no right to take oxygen from the air that we breathe, for this air already lacks oxygen. The issue at stake is not just one of our present times, but of our future. If we are to be really serious: it is a question of our national security.

This is why I appeal to our President, to our government and to all those on whom we depend, to turn their attention to the problems of cinema. We are not asking for money, but for attention. Cinema is the most powerful weapon; if we let go of this weapon, it may be seized by our enemies and work against us. If our present situation does not change then in fifteen years' time we shall have a government and people who know nothing about their own country. The unique cultural bridge between East and West that Russia has traditionally formed will collapse. [...]

What do we suggest? As I explained, we are not asking for money, that is to say we shall not be asking for the state to finance the film industry. We are asking for additional measures to regulate the industry which rely upon clear political decisions and the will of the state.

We suggest enlarging the number of licensing activities by introducing licences for the retail trade with videos and for film screenings on aerial, cable and satellite television; this is in the interest of film and television.

At the same time, we suggest licensing the production and sale of equipment, tapes and disks for copying audio-visual works for private purposes without permission from the author.

The Russian State Extra-Budgetary Fund for the Development of Cinema, which we are proposing to establish, must be in charge of licensing and define the conditions of licences.

By licensing the video retail trade we shall create the conditions for a radical eradication of the illegal trade with video production, and raise the income of those companies which legally acquire licences and copy the films. At the same time the income for authors will rise.

By introducing licensing of film screenings on television we shall abolish the completely phantasmagorical situation of the present system when on a Friday, Saturday and Sunday films take up over 300 hours of screen time on all the Russian channels together. This will in turn raise the interest of the television channels in the production of home-grown national television.

All this will create the conditions for a limited and balanced co-existence between television and the film industry, as is the case in the rest of the civilised world.

But all this would be pointless without the resurrection of film distribution, i.e. the construction and reconstruction of film theatres. The means for such a development can be found through the compulsory labelling of equipment and tapes used for copying film and video production for private purposes without the agreement of the author.

Estimates show that the price of one dollar per duty stamp would enable us to build over 500 modern cinemas within ten years; their profit would form the basic path for the return of the production cost of Russian films, and fully satisfy the interest of the spectator. According to estimates, the first results of this process would be visible within the first and second year.

This mechanism is not as simple as it seems at first sight. It demands a huge amount of work and legislative support. The political will of the state is most important.

IV (Extraordinary) Congress of the Film-makers' Union,
29–30 May 1998, Moscow

Part II

Remapping, Fragmenting, Myth-making: In Search of the Russian Idea

6. Tinkling Symbols: Fragmented Society – Fragmented Cinema?

Nina Tsyrkun

When dealing with post-Soviet Russian cinema, we should first and foremost focus our attention on young film-makers and their films. Although the landmark of the new age in cinema was Tengiz Abuladze's *Repentance* [Pokaianie/Monanieba, 1984; released 1986], this film still addressed the past to settle the final account with totalitarianism. Later on, several more films about the Stalinist epoch appeared sporadically, such as *Ten Years Without Correspondence* [Desiat' let bez prava perepiski, 1990] by Vladimir Naumov, but they could no longer draw on an overwhelming public interest.

It was high time for debuts: in 1990 and 1992 the first two festivals of 'Debuts' took place; their programmes included about 600 films, and the main body of the festival crowd was formed by brat-packers. As is commonly known, water starts to boil around the edge; the most provocative and innovative pictures were shot by debutants from the periphery, the former Soviet republics, especially Kazakhstan. A 'new wave' of Kazakh film sprang up, in which Rashid Nugmanov with *The Needle* [Igla, 1988] became the cult figure. Young cinema in search of new heroes and a fresh language met with rock culture. The protagonist of *The Needle* was played by rock-singer Viktor Tsoi.[1] Hot issues, such as drug-dealing and the Mafia, gaining more and more control over the young generation, were addressed frankly and clearly in the film.

Cinema and rock music promoted a new consciousness. Alexander Khvan's *Diuba-Diuba* [1992] became emblematic, a sort of self-meta-description. Its main character is a scriptwriter, a student of the Film School, who is drafting the story of his life as a scenario in the genre of a fairytale. He plans 'to rescue a princess from a charmed castle': the 'princess' – his ex-girlfriend – is a nurse involved in drug-pushing; 'the charmed castle' is a jail. The fictitious life on screen seemed more real than reality itself; it looked palpable and easy to manipulate. But it turned out to be just an illusion: the death of the hero was just as inevitable as the death on screen of Viktor Tsoi's romantic hero, which coincided with Tsoi's death in real life. Igor Alimpiev's *The Shell* [Pantsir',

Remapping, Fragmenting, Myth-making

1990] anticipated the romanticism of the first post-Soviet years, depicting a rock-band transforming into a criminal gang. The period of naïve romanticism would come to an end by the mid-1990s.

The 1990s also saw the end of attempts to mythologise the new reality as moulded by the young subculture, and the end of the dominance of the periphery in film art following the collapse of the inter-republican union (USSR). From that time on, myth-making in Russian film limited itself to easily recognisable mythologemes known as components of the 'Russian Idea' and of the well-trodden territory of cinema production. These myths are: the image-myth; the myth of heaven-turned-hell (crime and the underworld); the myth of the Fatherland; and the myth of abroad and other lands.

By that time, the situation in Russian cinema had radically changed. The older generation attacked the younger one, accusing it of the betrayal of national, spiritual values. The young generation argued that 'the ball is not in the oldies' corner and that there is no demand either for daddy's cinema or its worn-out mythology', as the key figure of the young generation, Sergei Livnev, pointed out.[2] The ideological vacuum, the lack of some all-uniting idea, and the mythological void became a commonplace in the rhetoric of the 'chattering classes', the intelligentsia, traditionally concerned with guiding the nation, which is perceived as the mission of this specifically Russian social stratum. These notions of ideology, mythology and national unity are referred to as something desirable, which should be invented and induced, since their old versions have been exhausted and condemned as rotten, but no actual background for their natural source can be traced. Yet these notions are crucial for a strategy of revival in all spheres of culture. It is remarkable that the general idea, or, more exactly, the 'Russian Idea', is actually inextricably tied up with national mythology. The question arises whether such an idea, such a myth, could be voluntarily fabricated. Anyhow, as one of the most prolific young film-makers Maxim Pezhemsky remarked at his press conference during the film festival 'Debuts', the new body of myths and ideas is being created from the ruins of old ones. He supported this thesis with his vanguard *Comrade Chkalov's Crossing of the North Pole* [Perekhod tovarishcha Chkalova cherez severnyi polius, 1990], exploring one of the most popular myths about the legendary pilot who dared to travel to America.[3] Charity begins at home; the field where mythologising is most effectively yielding is self-image-making.

Image-making became the starting point of the typical career in cinema. Traditional blue jeans and leather coats were replaced by fashionable jackets and exquisite coiffures. There is the taciturn and reserved Sergei Livnev, the refined, oriental-looking, mysterious Alexander Khvan, the simpleton with provincial naïveté, Petr Lutsik, the 'good fellas' Oleg Boretsky and Alexander Negreba, the 'femme fatale' Renata Litvinova, the intellectual eccentric Ivan Okhlobystin, the Manchurian Buddhist whose body is covered with ritual scars and tattoos, Andrei I;[4] a great many business-like young men work for television commercials and spend their leisure time in posh night-clubs. These are *dramatis personae* on the *avant-scène* of present-day Russian cinema. It should be noted that any self-image is a transient category. In the turbulent year 1994 Ivan Okhlobystin called himself a 'son of the sun', a subject of his own desires, or simply a 'madman';[5] four years later he was the host of the religious programme 'Canon' on TV 6 (the Moscow channel).

Generally speaking, 'kitchen sink' realism, characteristic of the dawn of post-Soviet film production, has given way to the clip-like dandyism of the new 'yuppies', aiming not only at self-expression but at making a 'green harvest' (dollars), too. The film-maker with a pragmatic frame of mind and a calculating self-interest has succeeded the figure of the director who was ostentatiously distant from material problems and fully engaged in the problems of art. Now and then young directors work also as producers. Suffice it to say, that Sergei Livnev, an actively working screenplay-writer, director, producer and head of the Gorky Studio, is also a successful estate agent; scriptwriter and director Sergei Selianov is currently running the film studio STW in St Petersburg; film-maker Karen Shakhnazarov has taken over Mosfilm while his colleague Viktor Sergeev has taken over Lenfilm.

Nobody wants to shake up the world; the goals have become quite moderate and absolutely concrete. Instead of prophecy, the search for a suitable mask or a popular image concerns today's film-makers. Instead of creating a message for mankind, participation in international festivals is their main concern.

Sober-minded film-makers draw their attention to the needs of their compatriots. Here the problem of financing arises. The golden years of movie boom, when criminal money was being laundered through the film industry, have gone for ever. State support is enough only to launch, not fully produce, about ten pictures a year. Thus a revolutionary turnover was created by a group of enthusiasts headed by Sergei Livnev. The 'Manifesto of 14' declared at the 1997 Sochi Film Festival states a new policy for film production: to make low-budget films at about $200,000, which will recoup the production cost even in the case of a flop. This strategy is shaped like a perpetuum mobile, solving two major problems while providing a cure for the national cinema: it engages professionals and accustoms viewers to home-grown movies.[6]

The question arising from this strategy of low-budget films is that of the target audience. Young film-makers are ideologically and aesthetically oriented towards young audiences, who, in turn, prefer blockbusters with special effects screened at the more fashionable movie theatres in town. Chamber films are preferred by the older generation. Thus, there is a vicious circle. The Gorky Studio devised a witty strategy: the limited financial resources in low-budget cinema mean that the visual side, the special effects, are secondary to the subject matter. The low-budget films therefore either draw on popular genres such as melodrama, detective story, or thriller; or they are released on important holidays, such as New Year, Women's Day; Victory Day.[7] The project is

Remapping, Fragmenting, Myth-making

designed to acquaint the audience with the films largely through video release; the revenue from the sales will go towards the production of more new films. This project aims at the reconstruction of the film industry by turning it into a conveyor belt, a strategy that places the director in second place behind the producer, who is in charge of the schedules and programmes, and relies very much on audience taste and demand.

The myth of the criminal world soon began to fascinate young film-makers. When asked about cinema's obsession with criminal motives at the press release of his feature *Diuba-Diuba* in the summer of 1992, Alexander Khvan referred to Shakespeare, saying that we are undergoing a shift of epoch, and a new realm of passions advances itself. The same happened during the decline of the Renaissance, and Shakespeare's world was thus built on criminal motives, he commented. Criminal themes dominate the contemporary screen. Whereas most films depict bloody crimes, Pavel Chukhrai tried to trace the genesis of crime in Soviet history. *The Thief* [Vor, 1997] is a story about the childhood of Chukhrai's own generation, which was brought up in the immediate post-war years under the influence of overwhelming violence. Chukhrai stresses that the profession of his protagonist is of no importance: he could be not a thief, but a plumber, a carpenter or whatever – the main point is that he believes in mental and physical power as a kernel of existence. The three main characters in the film are a man, a woman and a child. They form a model of a family in society, a cell from which new generations will emerge. The theme of fatherhood is prominent in the film: it is not without reason that the thief Tolian calls himself Stalin's illegitimate son. He alludes to male impotence by referring to a substitute father. The prevailing role of women, traditionally associated with the female image of Russia itself, is typical for the thinkers of the 'Russian Idea' and for the poets of the Silver Age, such as Alexander Blok: 'Oh my Rus! my wife!' he wrote in his poem 'On the Field of Kulikovo' (1908). The fact that the boy Sania has lost his real father in the war is not just a problem for the post-war period, it is a reality of Russia today. There are not only real orphans, but millions of people feel fatherless as their fatherland is going to pieces. Hence the craving for a master, which is a conductive factor for the revival of totalitarianism and for the search for a shelter in the shadow of the Mafia.

In the absence of a father-figure the relationship between mother and son becomes central. It also serves as an additional colouring of a social shift. According to Nikolai Berdiaev, crucial social changes in Russia unleash obscure chaotic forces, which in turn cannot but remind one of the pre-oedipal female.[8] Men's voluntary retreat from domineering positions is the theme also of Alexander Sokurov's debut feature film *The Lonely Voice of a Man* [Odinokii golos cheloveka, 1978–87], which treats the problem of man's impotence, linked to the theme of wasting energy during a war. In his latest film *Mother and Son* [Mat' i syn, 1997], Sokurov pictures the relation of a mother and a son, isolated from the whole world and fully plunged into a situation of an impending permanent separation. It easily reads as a metaphor of a dying Russia, which is traditionally conceived as a maternal figure (Mother Russia) and her disabled son, unwilling to live any longer. The culminating scene of the film is composed as a reversed Pietà – the son mourning over his dying mother.

I would agree with Maxim Pezhemsky that the mythology of recent cinema reverses the old, familiar mythologies, both the Soviet and orthodox Russian one. Andrei I's *Scientific Section of Pilots* [Nauchnaia sektsiia pilotov, 1996] may be an apposite example. The scene is set in the Moscow metro: a gorgeous network of underground palaces, the metro used to be a symbol of Soviet omnipotence. It represented the industrial and architectural achievements, embodied effectiveness and safety, and, moreover, it symbolised the future communist paradise. There was a special irony in the fact that this paradise was located underground. At the same time the underground palaces remind us of Byzantine temples in their architecture: Komsomolskaya station is a genuine basilica with a mosaic ceiling, representing stages in the development of the Russian and Soviet state, and crowned with sparkling red stars. This symbol of Soviet power alludes to the star of Bethlehem, a point of orientation for pilgrims, deemed to be following the same point of reference as the Magi on their way to their divine destination.[9]

One of the first things to deteriorate after the collapse of the Soviet system was the Moscow metro. Terrible stories about true underground life were spread through the mass media: we were told about armies of rats, the damaged sewerage system, monstrous diggers in the tunnels; to crown it all we very soon experienced the horrors of stopping trains, which caused panic. We noticed the decay of the marble panels, the bronze sculptures and the luxurious chandeliers. The metro became the favourite haven of beggars. Furthermore, a series of terrorist acts occurred in the underground. Thus, a would-be communist paradise had turned into post-communist hell.

This is the background to Andrei I's *Scientific Section of Pilots*. The director, who calls himself a Manchurian god, claimed that he had wrought out the script before terrorist acts started to occur on the metro, and found out that the entire system could be paralysed by a single person. His invisible subversive gang is a monstrous degeneration of the system itself, in the clutches of deterioration. Andrei I showed the dense transport system as an impersonal terminal of death. He visually contrasted opposing textures: soft, pliant flesh with the mechanical toughness of trains, tunnels and rails. Men and women seem especially vulnerable, even lifeless; their eyes are always semi-closed, and they never look into camera, so we never meet them eye to eye, as if they are leaving for some other reality, or already belong to it. The former paradise has become a domain of malice, and blood is shed here as an ominous sign of overwhelming crime. Sleepwalking creatures resemble the whimsical canvases of the mysterious pre-Revolutionary painter Borisov-Musatov,[10] which are populated with strange maidens with downcast eyes. Persistent motives of the eternal dream are also characteristic of Igor Alimpiev's *The Shell*. It should be noted that cinema appears as a 'fatal attraction' for film-makers due to its dreamy nature. As Alexander Khvan put it, 'Dream is a model of reality *sui generis*, which is more real and truthful than reality itself, since it is reality summed up.'[11]

Promoting his *Comrade Chkalov*, vanguard film-maker Maxim Pezhemsky commented that new mythology is built from the ruins of the old mythology. The most appropriate example here would be Vilen Novak's *Princess on Beans* [Printsessa na bobakh, 1997]. There is a pun in the title: the princess on a pea (a fairytale about a spoilt maiden who happened to get into a jam, and the idiom 'to stay on the beans' (to be left with nothing). The logic of the film is that of a fairytale: it is the story of a New Russian depicting not a national character, but a national idea. The story is quite typical in that a number of rich Russians long for nobility and buy titles in England. The tough business-man Dima wants to marry a woman with an aristocratic surname. Nina is a descendant of the Sheremetiev family, who cannot be seduced with a washing machine, or a luxurious life of parties. Offspring of the former Russian aristo-cracy willingly accept alliances with the new Russians. After a series of films in which national pride was humiliated, the public now welcomes such films as *The Princess on Beans* which, with its dream-like quality, flatters national self-esteem. This play with the audience reminds me of Zizek's thesis that there is a silent agreement between Western countries and Russia: Russia preserves its status as a great power on condition that this power should not be exploited.[12] Cinema audiences are happy to delve into virtual reality where they encounter a terrible, but comforting, figure of the master while they need not submit to his power in reality. This is where all the fragments of society consolidate – those who bewail the past, those who hate it, and those who have never experienced it. Identifying themselves with a noble, attractive and independent heroine makes them happy in spite of the fact that nobody is going to bargain this illusory nobility for any tangible means.

Emigration to some nondescript land and digging into one's native land are the two furthest poles of attraction for film-makers. A comparison of two films with an inner rhyme in the titles – *In That Land* [V toi strane, 1997] by Lydia Bobrova and *The Land of the Deaf* [Strana glukhikh, 1997] by Valeri Todorovsky – may elucidate the point.

While Bobrova's film carries a personal message (her brother plays the lead), Todorovsky's is a refined study in West European cinema. *In That Land* is a film by a woman director, an adaptation of short stories written by a male writer Boris Ekimov, concentrating on male protagonists. *The Land of the Deaf* is a film by a male director, based on a story by a trendy woman scriptwriter, Renata Litvinova, focusing on female characters. Bobrova's film is mainly shot in 'cinema vérité' manner, depicting a typical Russian village with its everyday life. Todorovsky's film plunges into the realm of an extraordinary community, an 'alien nation' with a girl dreaming of an imaginary 'land of the deaf' as a

1. Valeri Todorovsky. *The Land of the Deaf*. Film poster: YaYa and Rita (Dina Korzun and Chulpan Khamatova).

paradise on earth. Finally, *In That Land* is a sober sociological survey, while *The Land of the Deaf* is a playful psychological sketch.

It should be noted that the use of the phrase 'that land' (meaning Russia, the motherland) instead of the habitual and standard 'our country', alienates the author from the scene, making it a sort of a dreamland, whereas 'the land of the deaf' is an imaginary locus, a promised land.

Remapping, Fragmenting, Myth-making

Lydia Bobrova pictures a traditional patriarchal world on the verge of its natural death. The decay of male dominance takes shape in the figures of three characters of traditional national colouring: a holy fool, a merry drunkard, and a thug. Except for the thug (who is a stranger here), the male population bears signs of degeneracy. The parts are played not by professionals, but by natives of Northern Russia, who are presumed to be the purest national breed – hence their physical disability as visual evidence of their miserable condition looks particularly striking. Moreover, the men of the village seem to be obsessed with a suicidal syndrome: the manager summarises the accidents of the year – an overturned tractor, a burnt stable and so on.

The decay of male dominance takes shape in the characters: there is a sharp contrast between the physical characteristics of men and women. Fragile, worn-out and passive men with faint hair and somewhat guilty eyes are juxtaposed with plump, muscled, steady-eyed women. It is none the less a society with strongly marked gender roles. Though weak men suffer under the strong hand of their wives, the latter fundamentally depend on the men, since wives cannot do without their husbands under the hard living conditions of the Russian countryside. Ironically enough, the problem of male dominance is reshaped into the dominance of the disabled male in Bobrova's film.

Nevertheless, it is still a patriarchal society untouched by the stormy winds of social change. Urban life discloses the same disability, disguised by pretentious toughness. The male body of *The Land of the Deaf* consists exclusively of gangsters, deaf men among them; the male protagonist is a gambler-loser, ready to live off his girlfriend Rita and turn her in at the first hint of danger. A treacherous lover, he forces Rita to find money to repay his debt, when a deaf mobster hires her to function as 'his ears' for negotiations with other bandits. The same suicidal syndrome here takes other, much more aggressive forms of male self-extermination. In big cities men prefer to annihilate each other; Macedonian duels in John Woo's style have become a favourite national sport in recent years. By the end of *The Land of the Deaf* none of the male characters has survived; all they have left are the chalk traces drawn by the investigators around their corpses on the spot of the last 'countdown'.

Todorovsky's film is based on Litvinova's story entitled 'To Possess and To Belong', which sounds like a basic formula for male/female opposition. The heroine called YaYa (a name repeating the Russian word for 'I' – 'ya') works in a striptease bar and literally embodies the notion of a woman as an object of desire and possession. Unwilling to belong to anyone, she breaks away, symbolically cutting herself off from male dominance by slapping her former lover who had told her to have sexual intercourse with her manager (or rather owner). Her name, which she invented, stresses her striving for independence: it is easy to pronounce for a deaf girl, who speaks only with difficulty. Her tongue and voice are special: YaYa speaks like a mechanical creature. Her dance against the background of a multi-armed sculpture in an artist's studio equates her to an automaton of the eighteenth century, and makes her a sex-partner of Casanova in Fellini's *Casanova* [Italy, 1976]. As such she remains an object, though a rebellious one.

There is a key episode in Fellini's film, when Casanova dances in Venice with a woman-mannequin, which follows the scene of Casanova's encounter with his dead mother in the theatre. This sequence is not arbitrary: the woman-mannequin substitutes the figure of the mother; she is her meek shadow. Casanova fell in love with an automaton, the ideal image of his dream. The perfection of the mechanical subject in this case is emphasised by transition of coitus into dance. At the same time the possibility of conception is excluded, and thus the sexual partner is attached to the world of the dead. It leads to the conclusion that female emigration or dislocation to some other world is a reciprocal desire of both sexes, tired of mutual elation.

In *The Land of the Deaf* YaYa asks Rita to escape with her from the men's world to the land of the deaf, a mirage, which seems quite real to her. Rita, in turn, is not inclined to follow YaYa; she has to go through a process of initiation before she becomes fully convinced that men are unreliable. Ironically enough, she 'gets the message' (becomes deaf) through a shock caused by a man's gunshot. At one point YaYa suggests that they should earn the fare for the trip to the land of the deaf through prostitution; the women still act in keeping with the rules established by men. Rita's dotty smile when she realises that she has lost her hearing is telling: from now on, she is to play a part of a holy fool, a blissful inhabitant of the promised land. The escape from male dominance turns out to be the materialisation of a traditional pattern, since patriarchal women dream of absolute leisure and seek for shelter in the same way that is predetermined in a male-dominated world. In this respect, the female protagonists of *The Land of the Deaf* serve as social reflectors of the present-day situation in Russia, undergoing a quick shift from feudal socialist state to capitalist order, when individual consciousness lags behind the economic changes. Female ideals hover between the outdated self-esteem of patriarchal creatures on the one hand, and the attractive new opportunities of bourgeois glamour, which has been unattainable for the majority of women in generations, on the other. At the same time, heroines stand for a great majority of the nation, in the most difficult moments of life seeking for 'another kingdom' – an inseparable component of the 'Russian Idea' in its mystical Utopian pathos of the revelation of 'a parallel world'. As a prominent ideologist of the 'Russian Idea', Vladimir Soloviev, put it: 'The target of Russia is elsewhere.'[13]

7. Viewed from Below: Subverting the Myths of the Soviet Landscape

Emma Widdis

'The Russian soul', wrote Nikolai Berdiaev in *The Fate of Russia* in 1915, is 'oppressed by the boundless Russian lands'.[1] The sheer scale of the Russian and Soviet territory is at the centre of any 'Russian Idea': a defining feature of the nation's self-perception, and a key historical factor.[2] 'Wide is my native land', the proud words of the refrain from Grigori Aleksandrov's film, *The Circus* [Tsirk, 1936], were as much Russian as Soviet. The mapping of the territory was a crucial political task through the Soviet period. Maps, real and imaginary, defined the contours of the new state, and the extent of its power. Under Stalin, the map became an alternative icon. In 1935, the NKVD assumed control of national cartography, and the largest map of the Soviet Union was completed, to enormous acclaim, in 1947.

The Soviet imaginary map pictured a tamed and knowable space, with Moscow – the red star – as the organising centre of a space which was conquered [*osvoeno*]. In 1991, the collapse of the Soviet Union shattered these coherent visions of the territory. The map was fragmented, and Russia no longer the centre of an empire. In addition, the explosion of historical 'truth' under *glasnost* challenged Soviet ideology at its core, debunking the key myths that had sustained the totalitarian system. Russian national identity was fundamentally *dislocated*. By the early 1990s, therefore, the post-Soviet space was a decentred, disorientating vortex, pictured in the chaotic city spaces of films such as Pavel Lungin's *Taxi Blues* [Taksi Bliuz, 1990].[3]

In this context, redrawing the national map became a vital cultural and social task. In the face of the collapse of empire and the loss of familiar co-ordinates, post-Soviet cinema sought a knowable space, a firm ground from which to reconstruct a post-Soviet Russian Idea. This chapter will identify one way in which this task was confronted. Looking in detail at one film, *The Time for Sadness Has Not Yet Come* [Vremia pechali eshche ne prishlo, 1995], directed by Sergei Selianov, it will explore some key Soviet myths of landscape, and the ways in which they are used, subverted and ultimately appropriated. In this film, as in his earlier films, *Angel's Day* [Den' angela, 1988] and *All Souls' Day* [Dukhov den', 1990], Selianov grapples with the search for an alternative map.[4]

Selianov is a self-appointed spokesman of the new Russian Idea in cinema, and his early films offer a clear line of development towards *The Russian Idea* [Russkaia ideia, 1996], directed by Selianov to a script by Oleg Kovalov. Immediately preceding *The Russian Idea, The Time for Sadness* was one of several films in the mid-1990s which began to engage with the icons of Sovietness in a new way. In *The Russian Idea*, Selianov and Kovalov explore Berdiaev's concept of Russian identity through fragments taken from a century of Soviet cinema. Thus they explicitly link identity with cultural image. Taking cinema seriously, the film suggests that the myths of Sovietness – created, interrogated and ultimately sustained by cinema – are a very real part of contemporary identity. Any 'Russian' idea must necessarily take account of a 'Soviet' idea. This is not, of course, to validate the Soviet period, but to recognise its role as a constituent part of contemporary Russianness. In this respect, Selianov is not unique. Irony, blended with resignation and reconciliation, was a key factor in a new sensibility in 1990s cinema.

The central character of *The Time for Sadness* is Ivanov, a forger of money. He is a creator of image *par excellence*; his livelihood depends upon blurring the real and the false. In the opening sequences of the film, Ivanov runs away from the grim urban reality of Petersburg, escaping the ties of convention, his job, his apartment and his girlfriend. His escape prompts a flashback, returning the viewer in time to Ivanov's childhood, and to his encounter with a semi-mythical *zemlemer*, or land surveyor, Methodius. While the young Ivanov and his companions eke out their existence in a nameless village, somewhere in the middle of the boundless Russian territory, Methodius arrives as if from nowhere. His arrival challenges and changes the lives of six key protagonists.

Methodius's first appearance in the village establishes him unambiguously as explorer and map-maker. The camera focuses on him, fixing a 'typical' village scene (the slaughter of a pig) through his theodolite, and standing, spread-eagled, surrounded by all his 'measuring equipment'. Silently, he places a stake in the centre of the unkempt yard. Immediately, Methodius is labelled: 'So, you're carrying out some surveying?' one character asks. 'Yes,' he replies, 'for railways.' 'Oh, they've tried that here before,' comes the cynical reply. 'But this time it's for real,' Methodius retorts. Although the film is set in the contemporary period, the phrase 'road surveying' [*dorozhnoe izyskanie*] evokes a central myth of the Soviet landscape. Infrastructural and transport systems were to provide the basis for the unified and homogeneous space that was central to the union of Soviet peoples. In particular, the railway was at the heart of these projects of integration, providing a skeleton of interconnection which reached across the boundless territory.

Methodius's image as land surveyor [*zemlemer*] recalls the semi-mythical status of explorers and map-makers during the Stalinist period. Mapping and

2a. Sergei Selianov. *The Time for Sadness Has Not Yet Come*. The villagers.

2b. Sergei Selianov. *The Time for Sadness Has Not Yet Come*. The surveyor (Petr Mamonov).

measuring the territory was part of the process of *osvoenie* (conquering the space) that developed under Stalin. In Andrei Platonov's story of 1929, 'Citizen of the State' ['Gosudarstvennyi zhitel''], for example, a surveyor is found sleeping in the woods, the magical tools of his trade (a theodolite and a measuring rod) laid carefully at his side; the protagonist of the tale, an ageing and fervent enthusiast of the state, carefully places a pillow beneath his head and continues on his way, proud to have been able to aid the nation.[5] Similarly, documentary and feature films of the 1930s and 1940s featured these heroic *razvedchiki piatiletki* (scouts of the Five-Year Plan), whose role was to uncover the vast riches of the Soviet territory. Vladimir Erofeev's travelogues, for example, followed expeditions of film-makers and geologists, united on a mission of exploration.[6] Sergei Gerasimov's blockbuster, *The Brave Seven* [Semero smelykh, 1936], told of the Arctic adventures of an expedition of young Komsomol-geologists. And, as the territory was discovered, so it was conquered.

Through Methodius, therefore, the film interrogates the key Soviet project: the creation of a single, unified 'national' space. The village, into which he enters as a catalytic 'outsider', is at once a traditional Russian village [*derevnia*], firmly situated within a rural idyll, and a typically Soviet settlement [*poselok*], neither rural nor urban, industrial nor agricultural. It is a lacklustre example of the success of *smychka*, the powerful 1920s policy which called for the harmonious unification of town and village, peasant and worker. As a result, it lacks clear identity. In part, its wooden houses, curious individuals, women in windows, and pastoral setting are exaggerated archetypes of the folkloric village. Like the folkloric space, it is unmapped, located outside a coherent geographical framework. In the Russian folktale [*skazka*], the narrative is traditionally unlocated: 'In some kingdom or other, in some nation or other.' At the same time, however, the village is part of the Soviet space, with poorly constructed and disused factories at its edge, and its characters emerge clearly as products of the Soviet era.

It is through the juxtaposition of these two spaces, both archetypally Russian and prosaically Soviet, that Selianov explores the contemporary landscape. The settlement 'discovered' by Methodius appears to have been bypassed by Sovietisation and integration. A single, broken rail track has been left, overgrown, in the middle of the *poselok*. It is *unconnected*, not part of the national network. In Soviet films of the 1920s and 1930s, the laying and linking of rail tracks became a symbol of the new society, linking the diverse places and peoples of the Soviet Union.[7] Through this single image, therefore, the film deconstructs Soviet industrial mythology. The heroic mapping of the territory was represented first and foremost by the development of infrastructure, the creation of a communications skeleton that was to structure a space hitherto vast and unformed in the public imagination. This village is located on a fault-line in that infrastructure, and is left unmapped.

At the same time, cinematic images of rail tracks during the Soviet period

Remapping, Fragmenting, Myth-making

celebrated the industrial might of the new state, and *The Time for Sadness* satirises this trope directly. In one sequence, a railway worker is hammering tracks together in the countryside near the village, laying down the lines of communication. In a kind of mass orgasm, which Methodius himself affects by the sheer will of his imagination while describing the Kama Sutra to his assembled 'disciples', the railway worker begins to hammer his tracks in a kind of frenzy, increasing with the momentum of Methodius's chant. This explosion of energy carries satirical overtones of the Stakhanovite shock work of the Five-Year Plans. Soviet industrial energy is, implicitly, sexualised: a national orgasm.

This ironic take on Sovietness recalls another film of the period, *Hammer and Sickle* [Serp i molot, 1994], directed by Sergei Livnev.[8] *Hammer and Sickle* was one of the earliest examples of what might be called post-Soviet kitsch, a blend of irony and humour through which the horrors of Stalinism are mocked, and to some extent neutralised. In *Hammer and Sickle*, a sex change creates the perfect man, who goes on to become the perfect Soviet shock worker, icon of national achievement. Thus a subversive and divergent experiment becomes the bedrock of industrial mythology. In a similar vein, the more recent film, *Scientific Section of Pilots* [Nauchnaia sektsiia pilotov, 1996], directed by Andrei I, uses the Moscow metro, icon of Soviet construction and 'the peoples' paradise', as the setting for a gruesome series of deaths. In this curious blend of thriller and black comedy, the metro, revered for its efficiency, is transformed into a nightmarish space of transgression. In this way, *The Time for Sadness* is part of a new tradition in post-Soviet cinema which uses irony as a means of reappropriating the Soviet past. All of these directors reveal the key myths of the Soviet landscape. Drawing on familiar images, they recall a common mythology which is fundamental to post-Soviet consciousness. Using humour, they rescue image from historical context, and so liberate a national heritage, without excusing it.

The question of integration and the creation of a unified Soviet space is the thematic centre of *The Time for Sadness*. Methodius's first meeting with his six 'disciples' in the village raises fundamental questions about identity. The characters introduce themselves: a German, a Gypsy, a Russian, a Tatar (Sania), a Jew (Zhibaev) and young Ivanov. Methodius functions as a kind of universal figure, who is himself non-national, but can speak in every tongue and knows the songs and the stories of every culture. By contrast, those whom he meets have lost their heritage; they know little of their cultures, do not speak the language, and have forgotten the words to their folk songs. Methodius tries to engage with all of them on their particular national terms, with language, or with song; they respond with initial enthusiasm, and with emotion, to his encouragement, but it becomes clear that their 'national identity' is pure decoration. At an emotional level, for example, Zhibaev proudly believes himself to be a Jew, but he speaks no Hebrew, and has forgotten even the songs that his mother used to sing him.

This picture of lost identity is implicitly the result of the Soviet nationalities policy. Just as the national pavilions in the Exhibition of Economic Achievements in Moscow (VDNKh) were modelled on a single style of classically inspired architecture, decorated by national 'symbols', so these characters have a national identity which has been reduced to folk costume and poorly recalled songs. They define themselves according to a nationality which has no reality for them. They are, implicitly, 'Soviet', existing in a curious non-national space. The tragedy, of course, is that this Sovietness no longer exists, and the film has equally revealed its fault-lines. These characters are isolated within a national space that has collapsed. Through this single group of rather ridiculous characters, in their unconnected village, we discover both the power and the failure of the Soviet project.

For Selianov, this combination of the success and failure of Sovietness is a key problem. The search for an authentic new Russian identity is a serious one, explored through Methodius's ambiguous preaching on national identity. The figure of Methodius unites religious symbolism with Soviet: the Saint whose name he carries was named Apostle to the Slavs in the ninth century. His name, etymologically, implies literally a 'going after' (from *meta* – after, and *hodus* – path), and he is thus as much land-surveyor (literally creating a new path through the space) as spiritual leader.

At one level, Methodius is responsible, in the course of the film, for teaching these characters about themselves, revealing to them the identities that they have lost through the blanket of Sovietness. At the same time, he is himself a non-national figure, preaching a common identity and a common world. His role throughout the film embodies this curious duality. Questioned about religion, for example, he replies that his faith is 'general' [*obshchii*]. Later, he preaches a vision of the world as a 'single organism' [*edinyi organizm*]. The ambiguity of Methodius's position on national identity points to a central problem in Selianov's formulation of the new 'Russian Idea'. He seeks to offer a positive vision of a global space, in which a sense of national authenticity is a crucial precondition for harmony. In the film, however, this is unresolved. The success of *The Time for Sadness* lies rather in offering an alternative kind of solution, and a reconciliation with everyday life.

The key to this reconciliation is the debunking of myth, and it is not only Stalinist myths that Selianov challenges: those of *glasnost* are similarly under scrutiny. Lalia, the film's single heroine, jokes about her longing for Paris; Ivanov hijacks the plane, takes her hostage, and demands that they are taken to the City of Love. His fellow travellers applaud him for seemingly fulfilling their dreams; the myth of foreign travel, a sustaining dream throughout the Soviet period, and developed in the first period of *glasnost*, was encapsulated in Paris. By the early 1990s, however, that myth had been revealed as false. The West, as imagined from the East, was a just another fantasy. In *The Time for Sadness*, the plane seems to land in 'Paris', and the Eiffel Tower is visible from

Remapping, Fragmenting, Myth-making

the window. Ivanov and his hostage get out, seemingly preparing for a romantic adventure. Suddenly, she disappears, and his Eiffel Tower is revealed to be no more than a cardboard model, concealing policemen who arrest him. The 'Paris' of dreams does not exist.

This interrogation of the idea of travel as salvation was common to several films of the period. Yuri Mamin's *Window on Paris* [Okno v Parizh, 1993] showed a Petersburg apartment in which the back of a wardrobe opened, miraculously, into Paris. In Vladimir Khotinenko's *Patriotic Comedy* [Patrioticheskaia komediia, 1992], characters were astounded to discover an underground network of tunnels which transported them across the world, to emerge, startled, through manholes into New York and Paris. These characters do not even get out to explore, however. The myth of foreignness holds no more appeal; Russia is reinstated as the central 'home'. Escape is devalued; the myth of travel is revealed to be essentially a chimera. The key to contentment is reconciliation with your immediate, local environment.

Often, however, this reconciliation is achieved through the injection of magic into the banal everyday. The supernatural, or mystical, was a common feature of Russian film in the first half of the 1990s. But it was a peculiarly ordinary kind of mystique. In *The Time for Sadness,* Selianov blends post-Soviet *byt* with a semi-mystical supernatural. He creates a curiously decontextualised space within which he can explore key human themes. As part of Ivanov's memory, the village exists out of space and time. The mysterious Methodius is himself part of this semi-mystical world, arriving from nowhere and vanishing just as suddenly. Similarly, Khotinenko's *Patriotic Comedy* is a blend of farce and thriller, tracking the encounter between Andrei, a member of the new Russian Mafia, and Penia, a lovable house spirit [*domovoi*], comfortingly represented as a bearded little fat man. Post-Soviet urban reality blends with the Old Russian supernatural. In the end, it is the element of magic that defines Russia, teaching the protagonists to value their home: 'We have our own spirits – home-made.' It is a recognition of this uniquely Russian magic that enables a rejection of the myth of escape and foreign travel.

A similar blend of the mystical and the prosaic marks Methodius. In practice, his work as surveyor offers something other than surveying for railways. Methodius and the young Ivanov set off for what he describes as a very important day: 'Today I will bring [tie] all the ends together.' In this sequence, 'mapping' assumes an aim very different from that which it may have had in Soviet times. It is given metaphysical dimensions, as Methodius, using his theodolite, searches for a mystic 'centre' to the world, the point of a solar eclipse from which, he says, on this same day in thirty years, a new and marvellous life will begin. It is this, he claims, that will bring salvation to the dislocated, confused characters in the village. The organising centre is represented as a kind of alternative *omphalos*, a new centre for a disorientated national space.

In some ways, the supernatural 'centre' fulfils Methodius's predictions. His central stake, so carefully placed, grows into a venerable tree. The process of measuring is harmoniously blended with the processes of nature. The solar eclipse does come to pass. It does not seem, however, as though any new life will begin. Rather, the characters from the village have created their own new lives. All of them have taken significant steps over the last thirty years to change their lives. Grisha, the Russian, has fulfilled the truly Russian dream of 'going to Moscow' – even to the Bolshoi, the centre of the centre – and has become a middle-rate opera singer; he has an African wife. Sania and Zhibaev, Tatar and Jew, have both emigrated to Israel. The young 'gypsy' Yasha has tracked his gypsy roots to India. There, rather than discovering his original identity, he has assumed a new one, becoming a Hindu. Identity, it seems, is unrecoverable, and confused; none of the characters has discovered a pure 'essence'.

The protagonists return to Methodius's *omphalos* for the eclipse, but the event functions more as a reckoning and evaluation, a reunion, than as a beginning. Methodius's role in their lives, therefore, was not as prophet of a new life, but rather as having, in some sense, persuaded them all to take a form of action. It is ironic that it is in the end not Methodius's profound lessons, his preaching of a new world order, that propels the protagonists into action. It is, rather, his romantic success with Lalia, the single woman and heart's desire of the village. At a feast they all, one by one, see his hand on her knee under the table, and thus find resolve. After this, we might add, he disappears, his role complete. In this way, *The Time for Sadness* is a fundamentally existential film. It is not the cause of the decisive existential action that matters, but the fact of it – the individual accepting responsibility for his own fate and creating a life.

Thus there is no 'organising centre', and Methodius does not find the 'single point' where everything comes together. Indeed, the quest is itself flawed. The future Utopia is rendered almost irrelevant. Instead, the film offers a kind of salvation in minor key – a reconciliation with the everyday. This is echoed at the level of spatial imagery. The surveyor constructs no railway, no Soviet 'path' to a shining future. The 'centre', framed by the viewing glass, is in fact merely a tree in some abandoned and unmapped corner of the former Soviet space. Throughout the film, Selianov undermines the quest for coherent maps, or visions, of space. The search for narrative centre is continually frustrated.

Methodius's search for the centre identifies a place where, he says, everything 'like in cinema, meets in a single point'. This raises a key question in the film, which contrasts the 'mapping' of space, with the experience of real space. Throughout the film, Methodius's viewing glass intervenes in the cinematic frame, forcing the chaotic flux of 'real' space into a contained, centred view. It creates the artificial impression of an organising centre, a point at which 'everything meets in a single point'.

Cinematically, this is expressed through the opposition of the static view, exemplified by the telescopic frames offered by Methodius's theodolite, and the mobile shots which accompany moments of decisive action during the film. In the opening sequence of the film, Ivanov focuses his own viewing glass (a version of Methodius's surveying equipment, in this case a device for forgery) out of the window of his Petersburg apartment, creating a still image. He then turns to a pile of bank notes which he has forged. Using them, he constructs an improvised flick-book, where the succession of frames creates the illusion of movement, causing the flag to wave above the Kremlin. Here Selianov creates an interesting comment on the nature of cinematic representation. The flick-book, which creates what Henri Bergson called, in his comments on cinema, 'false movement', disrupts the centred, static image of the viewing lens, the photograph. Bergson saw the flick-book as a metaphor for cinema as a whole; the film shot, he believed, is merely a single shot (an instant in time) to which an abstract idea of succession is added in order to simulate movement. Real movement, by contrast, has a 'concrete duration' – that is, it takes place in the present and is heterogeneous. It cannot be broken down into instants.[9] Ivanov's scrutiny of the flick-book and Methodius's statement that in cinema everything 'comes to a single point' question the way in which cinema represents the world, and the opposition between still image and mobile image.

In *The Time for Sadness* this is expressed through the use of aerial shots and maps. In the opening sequences of the film, the camera tracks along a relief map, hung on the wall of Ivanov's Petersburg appartment. The shots of the map gradually and almost imperceptibly become an aerial view, accompanied by the growl of an aeroplane, such that the viewer shifts between the representation of landscape and a 'view' of landscape. Later in the film, when the mature Ivanov is travelling on the plane that he will later hijack, these aerial views return, thus framing the flashback narrative. This use of the aerial perspective is important: the space, seen from above, is mapped and controlled. It is for this reason that the aerial view was central to Stalinist cinema of the heroic 1930s and 1940s, and the pilot was a central Soviet hero. In this film, however, the narrative of the film subverts this tradition. The aerial view, which appears to give Ivanov knowledge of, and even control of, his destination, in fact deceives him: that which was Paris, is not Paris.

Selianov's use of the aerial shot raises questions of representation and reality. Cinema, one might suggest, offers a different vision of space from that which is presupposed by mapping. It pictures a mobile space, in which the relationship between the individual and space is one of action and 'experience'. There is no fixed 'reality', but only experience. This is the key theme of the film. Ivanov's escape at the beginning of the film, and his subsequent hijack of a plane, is in a sense the ultimate consequence of this: a quintessential existential act of life creation. It is accomplished with a gun, made from magic clay given to him by Methodius, who tells him: 'The whole world can be moulded and re-moulded.'

Through the figure of the surveyor-prophet, *The Time for Sadness* dismantles the Soviet landscape, replacing it with a mouldable, existential world. *Izyskanie*, mapping, and the creation of networks of communication, so central to the Soviet homogenising project, are revealed as fruitless tasks. Furthermore, the single Soviet national space, in which all nationalities co-exist within a supra-national sense of Sovietness, is interrogated. Methodius, a new kind of land-surveyor, offers a new kind of map for the national space. That map is first global, picturing Russia and, more importantly, the individual village and the individual character, as part of a larger 'single' global space. Second, it is experiential. The knowable space is the space of action, as it occurs in everyday life. Thus it is not through maps, or through aerial perspectives, or through measuring, that the physical world can be known. It is, rather, through experience. This, in a sense, although by no means valedictory, is what all the characters achieve. Methodius, in an early sequence, sums up Selianov's positive vision of the new Russian Idea. Drawing on the old Russian term *strannik*, or wanderer, he states: 'We are all wanderers' (*Vse my stranniki*). It is not where we wander, but simply the fact that we wander, that is salvation.

8. To Moscow! To Moscow? The Russian Hero and the Loss of the Centre

Birgit Beumers

Over the last decade the 'Soviet nation' has had to remap its territory, literally in the redesignation of streets and cities by their pre-Revolutionary names, but also in coming to terms with the fragmentation of the Soviet Empire into small, independent states. This search for a name, an identity, disclosed the illusory and artificial nature of Soviet values, and left both the individual and the nation without an immediate point of reference. The search for an identity led back to the past, to pre-Revolutionary Russia. Selianov's *The Russian Idea* [Russkaia ideia, 1996] ends with extracts from Eisenstein's *Ivan the Terrible, Part II* [Ivan Groznyi, 1946], made in the year that Berdiaev's *The Russian Idea* was published; in terms of cultural history, Russianness was superseded thereafter by the spirit of unity achieved in the sacrifice that the Soviet nation had made during the fight against fascism in the Great Patriotic War, which, along with Party celebrations and anniversaries of the Revolution, at least superficially bonded the Soviet people.

With the demise of the communist state, and more importantly with the collapse of the Soviet dream of socialism, an entire value system disintegrated. The fairytale that socialist utopian dreamers wanted to make come true in the 1930s had suddenly evaporated; Livnev thoroughly deconstructed this myth in *Hammer and Sickle* [Serp i molot, 1994], proving the symbol of socialist perfection (Vera Mukhina's statue of 'The Worker and the Peasant') unsuitable for real life. Man and the masses had suddenly lost any sense of location, direction or centre.[1] In the turmoil of trying to establish a democratic system, to conduct major economic reforms, and to bring in new legislation, the state forgot about the people, who lost not only their ideals of a bright future but also the sense of direction of where this all would lead; they were deprived of any ideals to believe in, any hope for a better future (in the grander sense), and finally of any positive portrayal of the country in which they lived.

Cinema had always provided models to follow: the positive hero of early Soviet cinema had been a Revolutionary leader who rose against oppression and sacrificed himself for the cause of the Revolution and for greater justice (the Vakulinchuk figure of *The Battleship Potemkin*, Chapayev, or Shchors). In the 1940s the hero became an ordinary human being who sacrificed personal happiness for a political cause. In the 1950s the official version represented the war as a heroic act of the collective rather than the individual, and the hero lost his individual stamp in favour of a mass heroic celebration. This view is contested in a number of films throughout the Thaw, and at this point two types of hero emerged: the hero who resists the system, and the hero who is created by the system, who is heroic because he is part of the mainstream.[2] The rebellious hero resists, and preserves his individuality in opposing the official, patriotic cause, and places his personal life above the political (socialist) cause – his representation in film was often in conflict with the official views and such films were therefore prone to be banned (for example, *Asya's Happiness* [Asino schast'e, 1967; released 1987]). The socialist, conformist hero is a product of the social system, and achieves personal happiness only after a contribution to the greater social cause (Katia of *Moscow Does Not Believe in Tears* [Moskva slezam ne verit, 1980]).

This second type of hero collapsed with the disintegration of a value system created artificially by the state and Party (although he reappears in a subverted form as the war hero), while the rebellious type led to the emergence of cult figures of the former underground movement on the post-*glasnost* screen. These cult figures often represented romantic ideals associated with the pacifist cause; they fought drugs and bribery while essentially rejecting officialdom and society (Bananan, played by Sergei Bugaev in Sergei Soloviev's *Assa* [1988], or Moro, played by Viktor Tsoi in Rashid Nugmanov's *The Needle* [Igla, 1988]). They continued in their resistance to social, political and moral standards and sought to create their own set of moral standards, preparing the path for a new type of hero in the 1990s, a hero who defends his own 'moral code' without following a social or legal normative pattern: the killer.[3]

When Party and state no longer provide an ideal, and social developments have no perspective, the hero escapes from a reality in which he cannot establish himself; he becomes destructive, aggressive, in an almost childish and playful way, while his actions seem to have a dream-like quality.

Three distinctive types of heroes emerge: the escapist (the successor of the non-conformist hero); the soldier (the successor of the conformist hero, but challenging the ideal of the Fatherland); and the new killer-hero.

1. The escapist hero

In a setting which offers a bleak everyday reality, the most basic pattern of behaviour is the escape into another world, imagined or real. In the films of

Remapping, Fragmenting and Myth-making

the period immediately following the collapse of the Soviet Union, the dream world offers basic and simple happiness for the heroes, in this world, as is the case in *Paradise-Cloud* [Oblako-rai, 1991] and *Diuba-Diuba* [1991]. In the second phase the escape into a dream world is induced by alcohol; it leads to a surreal world (*Drum Roll* [Barabaniada, 1993], *Window on Paris* [aka *Salade russe*, Okno v Parizh, 1993]), or to the destruction in this world of any social hierarchy (*Peculiarities of the National Hunt* [Osobennosti natsional'noi okhoty, 1995]). Finally, in the most recent films, the 'other world' is marked by a physical difference to this world: it is either the world after death, or life in a physically different state.

In Nikolai Dostal's *Paradise-Cloud* the hero, a retarded young man called Kolia, is teased and provoked by his friends into declaring his plans for the future. Tired of being asked a question to which he has no answer, he makes up a story: he claims to be leaving shortly for Siberia to live with a friend. His evasive response is turned into reality; but it is not a dream which becomes true, but rather – a lie. His friends urge him to depart, sell his room and his belongings, and arrange everything for him, while he is in love with a local girl, and really wishes for nothing more than to stay. His dreams are shattered when he leaves at the end of the film, almost against his own will, but he has to persist to the end with his lie of another life that awaits him beyond the limits of his provincial home town. Void of any direction in life, the 'hero' is forced along a path which, in reality, leads nowhere. In fact, he is far from being a hero.

A similar blurring of the borderline between the real and the imaginary occurs in Alexander Khvan's *Diuba-Diuba*. The 'hero' Andrei is a student of scriptwriting at the Film Institute in Moscow. Although he lives in the capital, the centre of activity, he has no role, no function in this context. Yet he seeks to give his life meaning and content. It is important that he has chosen a creative path for his profession: as he invents plots for films, he creates a scenario for the escape of his former girlfriend, Tania, from prison, and carries out his plan right to the end. When he has seized her from prison, it becomes clear that he did not act out of love, and Tania rightly challenges the reason for his action. Andrei meddles in Tania's life without any right to do so. Only afterwards does he realise that his action was based on a false premise, and that Tania does not love him, and he probably does not love her any longer. Like a scriptwriter, like an author, he has taken control of her life. As such, he must execute his plan, and he resorts to violence without having any qualms about the ethical issues relating to his action. In the end Andrei is on his own, at an airport, possibly in the USA. As if nothing had ever happened, he embarks on what seems to be the training course in the USA for which he had been nominated at the beginning of the film. For Khvan, cinema is a 'collective dream vision, more real and true than reality, because it is a reality in which conclusions are drawn'.[4] Andrei is a hero in that he acts perhaps for unselfish

To Moscow! To Moscow?

3. Sergei Ovcharov. *Drum Roll*. Alexander Polovtsev.

reasons; yet at the same time, he satisfies merely his creative impulse by his action, whereas in reality he is passive, introverted and lonely.

In Sergei Ovcharov's *Drum Roll* the 'hero' has no incentive or will of his own. As the film begins a drummer, a naïve, good young man, a Buster Keaton type character, is getting drunk with his colleagues from the funeral orchestra. During the funeral the dead man rises and leads the drummer away into another world, where objects rule; the drum Stradivarius takes command over the drummer's life. The drummer never resists evil; he does not protest when all his belongings are gradually taken away from him but he defends the drum, which is being misused as a frying pan, flowerpot and wash basin. He wanders aimlessly through Russia, exposing in a grotesque manner its social degradation: the homeless, the beggars, the criminals and the corrupt. *Drum Roll* is an allegory of man in Russian society: the drummer does not know where he is going, nor whom he is following; he has no orientation. In the end, though, maybe this was all the dream of a drunken man; there are no borders between reality and imagination.

Yuri Mamin's *Window on Paris* portrays the inhabitants of a communal flat in St Petersburg, who, under the influence of alcohol, discover that at certain times (and for a limited period only) the back of a wardrobe opens on to the roof of a Parisian apartment block. The inhabitants soon begin to seize from the capitalist West what they can bring back into Russian reality. Russia is not

Remapping, Fragmenting and Myth-making

a place where anyone would want to live: a Russian émigré dreams of returning to St Petersburg and is horrified when facing it in reality; a Parisian artist (who accidentally walks through the wardrobe) witnesses chaos and destruction in Petersburg. The hero of the film, the music teacher Nikolai, is an exception to this; he embodies all the values of a Russian hero: he is a 'bearer of spirituality and hopes of Russian culture'.[5] He appeals to his pupils to change Russia, having found in the West only the corruption of his ideals, which he is not prepared to give up. He eventually rejects the opportunity of staying in Paris, and convinces the children to return with him to build their future in Russia. And back in Russia he takes action to build that future: he starts digging a hole into a wall behind which a cat has mysteriously disappeared, just as through the wardrobe.

The film stresses two points: the action of the hero consists of building a castle in the air (or digging a window to Paris); and the creative stimulus generated through alcoholic intoxication. In both *Drum Roll* and *Window on Paris*, the other world opens up after an 'alcohol consciousness' is induced which blurs the borderline between the real and the imagined.[6] Indeed, at the end of *Diuba-Diuba*, the hero orders a glass of vodka, having just awoken from the nightmare of his scenario.

Rogozhkin's film *Peculiarities of the National Hunt* uses the notorious love of Russians for vodka as a motif for a comedy of social reality. A Finn researches the traditions of the Russian hunt from the time of the tsars to the present day. He joins a group of five Russians from the military and police forces who take him to the hunt. This consists for them of drinking vodka, exploring the Russian sauna and drinking yet more vodka, which is not what the Finn expects: he initially refuses to drink, tidies up after the drinking bouts, and persistently pesters the Russians with his request to go out to hunt animals or go 'fishing' (instead he is taken to some Russian peasant women-prostitutes), while he dreams all the time, in his visions, of the imperial hunting party of the late nineteenth century, stylishly hunting down a fox with their dogs, elegantly riding horses, and, of course, conversing in French (whereas he is marginalised as a non-Russian-speaker). Reality and imagination do not correspond and, moreover, the breakdown of social order in contemporary Russia is treated with self-irony. At the same time, no animal is killed on this Russian hunt: the cow – illegally transported on a bomber plane – is not dropped from the plane when the bribery of the pilots is discovered, and it later survives when shot accidentally by the hunters; the baby bear gets drunk on vodka; and the fish which the Finn catches is thrown back into the water. Drinking may be without a purpose, but it is a habit which makes social and national differences disappear, which lifts temporal boundaries in bringing together past and present, and annihilates the borders between animals and humans. The world returns to its purest form, without any boundaries or limits. 'The film is as good for the soul as 250 grams of vodka in good company.'[7]

Many films presented at the 1998 Sochi Film Festival showed a concern with the 'other' world: imaginary journeys into the 'other' world, unburied corpses, and revenge by the dead featured prominently. An escape into a different world forms part of the plot of Valeri Todorovsky's *The Land of the Deaf* [Strana glukhikh, 1997]. Rita dreams of simple happiness with her boyfriend Alesha, who is a gambler and has lost the Mafia's money at the casino; unless he repays, he is a target for the Mafia. YaYa is a deaf girl, who dreams of taking Rita with her into the happy land of the deaf. The two women become involved with the Mafia in order to make money to realise their respective dreams; they survive a shoot-out of rival gangs, when Rita turns deaf. Rita's dream is a manifest illusion, while the (unreal) journey to the land of the deaf comes true for her: Rita has joined YaYa in the land of the deaf. The everyday reality of Moscow is mainly represented in images of the city at night, while its daylight depiction in the last frames turns the buzzing city, in which YaYa is always at risk, into a quiet sea of movement under the sound of the ocean which is all that Rita can now hear.[8] Deafness is a retreat from reality.

'Heroes' are motivated by a series of ideas – self-created myths – which are, one by one, exposed and debunked: the invented idea (the friend in Siberia); the hollow idea (the drum); the creative-imaginative idea (rewrite life); the false idea (the hunt of the past); and the idea of another land ('physical' escape into deafness). The next step for film-makers was to dismantle the myth of the Fatherland.

2. The war hero

The hero's loss of direction and meaning is extended to another area which holds the potential for heroic action: the war. Yet the Soviet-type heroism associated with the Great Patriotic War was connected with an idea, with patriotism, with the sense of collective spirit (responsibility for each other), and often with victory and sacrifice. The recent wars in Afghanistan and Chechnia follow the inverse principle of the Great Patriotic War: 'forget, do not look back' instead of 'remember, do not forget'. No *hero* had returned from Afghanistan or Chechnia; no memory of victorious deeds could be evoked. In *Is it Easy to be Young* [Legko li byt' molodym?], the 1986 documentary by Jūris Podnieks, the returnees from Afghanistan do not wear their medals; in Balabanov's *Brother* [Brat, 1997] Danila claims never to have been in a war zone (although he has clearly not served in the military headquarters either). The wars form the underlying theme for a number of films, such as *Peshawar Waltz* [Peshavarskii val's, 1994], *The Prisoner of the Mountains* [Kavkazskii plennik, 1996], discussed in Chapter 11, and *The Muslim* [Musul'manin, 1995]. In all these films Russian soldiers are deprived of an ideal to fight for, and are let down by their own army.

In *The Muslim* the Russian soldier Kolia returns home as a Muslim, after

Remapping, Fragmenting and Myth-making

4. Vladimir Khotinenko.
   The Muslim. Kolia Ivanov
   (Evgeni Mironov).

seven years as a prisoner in Afghanistan. The history of the Afghan war is remote, it is brought to life through a television report, while the impact it has made on an individual life is immediate: the life of Kolia and his family has been uprooted as much as that of the Afghan family who used Kolia as a substitute for the son they had lost in the war. Kolia had refused to shoot three Afghan soldiers who had been captured, and offered instead to fight in the front line, to sacrifice his own life like a hero. While the other soldiers took flight, believing it was better to retreat and die than to fall into captivity, Kolia surrendered; he lacks the ideal of the Soviet Fatherland, and has little interest in the medal he receives upon his return. Kolia has seen the reality of war (rather than the abstract ideal of the defence of the Fatherland) and the human lives involved, the human suffering caused by a war of ideas. He surrendered in the war as he surrenders at home to the hostility of his family and friends, when he merely states what he cannot do according to his beliefs. Kolia returns to his roots, his village, a Russian village in the Russian countryside, where drinking, bribing and stealing are the order of the day. Yet he refuses to participate in these activities and excludes himself from the life to which he once belonged. Kolia is an outsider, who is excluded because he maintains moral values in a society where others have none rather than because of the values he holds. His heroic qualities are dissociated from the epithet Russian, while his self-sacrificing attitude and passivity clearly emphasise the spiritual side of his character.

Russia as a state offers no ideal to fight and die for; no father-figure in the political or military leadership; ideas may be the cause of the conflict, but the lives of individuals are more important than abstract ideals in a society which has lost its values, in a country which has lost its ideals.

3. The killer-hero

The myth of the Soviet hero has been debunked; the modern hero has nothing to live for – other than hollow dreams and imagined love – and nothing to die for in the absence of patriotic values. The new hero which emerges against this background is the killer-hero, exemplified by Danila Bagrov of *Brother*.

Brother defines a new type of hero who upholds no moral standards at all. On the one hand, Danila possesses skill, strength and courage; he knows how to work guns, is physically fit to fight and his actions display a sense of military logistics; he helps the poor (he defends an old man – Hoffmann, the German – on the street against a racketeer, helps the conductor collect a fine from two Caucasians – 'black arses' – travelling on a tram without a ticket, and shoots at his girlfriend Sveta's violent husband). Yet he is ruthless to his enemies, he leads a dangerous, adventurous life, and is a man of action. In the tradition of the romantic hero, he is a knight,[9] who keeps his word; but he is also a killer. He combines within himself the contradictions at the heart of the 'Russian Idea': self-assertion and self-effacement, the right to judge and the compassion to redeem, West and East.

Balabanov debunks the myth of socialism which sees the hero as part of a historical process: Danila has no role in society at large. A true killer, he is a loner, an individual, acting without a reason.[10] At the same time, Balabanov rejects the *chernukha* model which perceives man as a victim of circumstance and is therefore essentially non-heroic. The new hero makes no choices, but lives on the spur of the moment.

The title of the film is parodic in two ways. First, in its reference to the substitution of the brotherhood theme for the father-figure in Stalinist culture; and second, in the way of film narrative, where the elder brother replaces the father for Danila who, at the end of the film, protects the elder brother and father-figure, and saves his life by rescuing him from the hands of the Mafia bosses who employ him as a killer, having successfully carried out the killing which his brother was paid for in the first instance. Danila reverses the relation-

Remapping, Fragmenting and Myth-making

5. Alexei Balabanov. *Brother*. Viktor (Viktor Sukhorukov) and Danila (Sergei Bodrov jr).

ship of authority and respect for his elder brother – he sends him back home to look after his mother, while Danila moves on to Moscow to become a professional killer.

Danila sets no model to follow; he does not offer a lead to the future, yet nor does he have a past. Or, if he does have one, it can only be a fictional past, of Bodrov's previous hero, the soldier of the Chechen war, Vania Zhilin. At the beginning of the film Danila Bagrov has just returned home from service in the army, claiming that he has merely worked as a scribe in some office. It soon becomes clear that this is a myth: he has a very good knowledge of firearms, and his manoeuvres are much too carefully planned.[11] It is much more likely that Danila has served in a belligerent region (Chechnia?), and is hardened to the realities of life by his experience of war. Indeed, Danila's personality and background are like a blank page, on to which any story could be written. This is reflected in the technique of black-outs after each episode, which fragment the film and almost allow it to be reassembled in any order. Danila is deprived of any psychological depth, and the choice of a non-professional actor reflects the director's need for a façade rather than a character.

Each episode concludes with a straight, direct, forceful action. Then – a blackout. Exactly at the point when the frame needs to continue to allow for an analysis and explanation of the basic parameters of existence and its features. But instead, a deaf, black sheet, like a wall, a sign of non-existence, of death.

Each episode in fact begins as if from a blank sheet. The snowy road at the end is like a director's prompt for the next action. The hero completes one more action, a deed, a heroic feat, but he remains innerly unchanged, as if he were born again in the following episode, dying thus in the previous episode and dissolving himself in any action he completes. [...] The absence of temporal duration [...] the clip-like treatment of frames in the epoch of video, is masterfully turned into a sign of the hero's blindness, or, more broadly, the blindness of that type of conscience.[12]

Danila accidentally walks into the location of a clip for the rock-group Nautilus Pompilius's latest album *Wings*, and later he literally marches into lead singer Butusov's flat; he seeks to identify with the group, but fails to realise that these are different worlds. In both cases, he crashes back into reality: at the police station, bruised and beaten, and into a murder scene. Nautilus's music functions as a leitmotif for Danila's journey to St Petersburg. As the band is originally from Sverdlovsk, but moved to St Petersburg in the 1990s, so Danila comes from provincial Russia and arrives in St Petersburg where he finally acquires a compact disc of *Wings*. Danila plays Nautilus most of the time on his personal CD player – he lives in the world of the music and only partly perceives the reality that surrounds him.

The songs endow the film with a dream-like quality. Bagrov's movements are paced by the rhythm of the music, and thus appear as though they were performed under a spell or under the influence of drugs, but not by an in- dividual who reflects upon the surrounding reality. He acts almost from his subconscious.[13] Nautilus's songs are about another reality, daydreams, making this other reality a good one, and about the crippling effect of this reality – the wings that enable man to fly have been lost and all that remains are scars. The songs accompany Danila's arrival, his 'new life', the lead-up to the shootings at the market and in Viktor's flat. They are all from the albums *Atlantida* and *Yablokitai*, which, in fact, Danila fails to acquire in the music shop. In other words, the audience hears the music Danila wishes to hear on his CD player, but has actually not yet managed to acquire – the latest albums of Nautilus. The spectator is entangled in the illusionary quality of sound as much as Danila is entangled in the illusionary quality of his perception of reality. The hero lives under the sound-system of another world, in which he is immortal; the CD player saves his life when it deflects a bullet. Once the CD player has been destroyed, the music shifts to an older vinyl album, to which Danila listens while preparing the gun. His farewells to Kat and Hoffmann are set to a song warning not to wait until the morning for the 'beast' in man to appear; at this point, Danila prepares for his new image – the Moscow killer. After a black-out he will wear this image for the trip to Moscow, the centre, which he never reaches within the film.

The heroes of *Assa* and *The Needle* died in defence of their values and their integrity; they transgressed the borderlines between this world and an ideal

Remapping, Fragmenting and Myth-making

world with ease, as though their ideals lived on through the rock music of Viktor Tsoi whose songs 'Blood Type' and 'I Want Change' stand at the end of these two films. Bagrov walks into the world of music in the first, not last, shots of the film. Butusov's and Nautilus Pompilius's music may attract him, but he never tries to copy the lifestyle of his idols or the idealistic world of their music. He follows a different path, in the real world, from which he does not escape.

The film lacks an authorial moral stance, as does Balabanov's *Of Freaks and Men* [Pro urodov i liudei, 1998]. Here the hero, Johann, lacks moral values altogether. The film, set at the turn of the century, shows the subversion of social structures: servants dominate the bourgeoisie, the educated classes are replaced by the perverted and debased proletarian classes, freaks take over from people. Yet the film does not function as a social critique. Shot in black and white with silver halide tint and in the style of early twentieth-century photographs, its aesthetic perfection contrasts with the sadomasochistic motives chosen by the photographer in the film for his work: the pleasure of women's naked buttocks beaten as the object of photos. Balabanov comments on cinema as a medium which, from its beginning, was not merely a means of propaganda and education which offered moral guidance, but a medium that catered also for the masses, the sick taste of those rejoicing in the humiliation of others, of exploitation of abnormalities (Siamese twins). Amorality triumphs at the end, when Johann is seen standing statuesquely on an ice floe floating down the Neva river.

Balabanov refrains from moralising and preaching, a function which Soviet directors had taken on for such a long time; he no longer provides ideals to be followed, and no longer sets moral standards. He does not condemn or reject the amoral conduct of his protagonists, but portrays a new type.

> The significance [of *Brother*] lies in the conscious, consistent, and – for post-Soviet cinema – amazingly novel attempt to find a style in the environment. [...] An environment which excludes the ethical imperative not only from life, but from the vocabulary of generally used expressions; and which does not do so 'from above', from ideology, philosophy, or aesthetics, but 'from below', in the obvious connection with the devaluation of the rouble.[14]

Bagrov is an isolated individual with no friends, no family. In romantic terms, he is the lonely hero of the 1990s; in ethical terms, he is a ruthless, amoral killer. But there are already younger characters, children, representing this type on the Russian screen: in Muratova's *Three Stories* [Tri istorii, 1997], the evil in man turns him into a social, serial or natural killer – cast in the roles of man, woman and child, who kill without explanation.

The attempt artificially to create Soviet folklore, Soviet heroes, Soviet culture in the 1930s effaced the Russian traditions from cultural life, as Kovalov has argued in *The Russian Idea*. Film-makers of the 1990s have debunked the myth of Stalinist culture, explored the loss of direction, values and aims of a hero whose heroic qualities were deemed to consist in conformism to the ideological mainstream, and in cherishing the ideal of the Fatherland; they developed instead the model of the rebel-hero into the ruthless killer. Balabanov's film stands apart from the mainstream because of the detached and cool view which the director adopts towards his hero. The responses to the film are indicative of the audience's disorientation: the events in the film are not condemned by the director, and the audience remains in a state of shock at its own indifference, similar to the response to Tarantino's *Pulp Fiction* [USA, 1995], or more appropriately, perhaps, to Danny Boyle's parodic treatment of kidnapping in *A Life Less Ordinary* [UK, 1997], or murder in *Shallow Grave* [UK, 1995]. Balabanov here connects to the European mainstream while developing a character who is very Russian in the contradictions and polarities he harbours in his personality and conduct. The new Russian hero is a criminal knight.

A comparison with high Stalinist culture may be appropriate here: both the 1930s and the 1990s show a concern with shaping a Soviet and Russian national identity. If we compare the paradigm of the hero in *Brother* to Katerina Clark's definition of heroism in High Stalinist Culture of the 1930s,[15] we see a reversal of values. The brother-figure which had made way for the father-figure in the 1930s reverts in the 1990s to the brother-figure, for whom there are no longer any idols or models. In terms of the paradigm of time, the present has made way for the historical perspective in the 1930s; in the 1990s, ad hoc decisions are taken, there is no sense of a past (it is annihilated, destroyed, and biographies are invented) or future (Bagrov does not know where he is going at the end). Where the Stalinist hero sees higher reality, Balabanov's hero has no vision, no perspective. In Paperny's terms,[16] 'Kultura 2' is superseded once more by 'Kultura 1', the centrifugal pattern replaced by a centripetal one, the vertical substituted by the horizontal. The aviator's vision of space from above facilitated by steel wings that grow from man's hands is no longer possible; the hero of the 1990s is afraid of heights and open space, he is deprived of the wings that would allow him to fly, be it into another reality or to survey this world:

We were born to make a fairytale come true, / To conquer the distances and space, / Our minds made steel wings for our hands / And throbbing engines take the place of our hearts.

'Even Higher' (The Aviators' March), Pavel German and Yuli Khait (1920)

I can see the fresh scars on your spine which is as soft as velvet, / I want to cry with pain or forget myself in a dream / Where are your wings which I liked so much? [...] I see that you are afraid of open windows and upper floors, / And if tomorrow there is a fire and the whole building is in flames, / We will die without those wings which I liked so much.

'Wings', Viacheslav Butusov and Nautilus Pompilius (1997)

Part III

The Past of the Fatherland Reviewed

9. La Grande Illusion

Tatiana Moskvina

Time, Time! – and we are its children!

Thomas Mann, *The Magic Mountain*

Introduction

The formula of human existence: impossibility,
irrevocability, inevitability.

Nikita Mikhalkov[1]

At last I found these words. Everything fell into place – you will see later why. Impossibility, irrevocability, inevitability.

Three words, three golden fish caught in a stream of words, words, words ... words by Mikhalkov, words about Mikhalkov ... past enthusiasms, forgotten insults, former controversies, new insults, and new enthusiasms, new times ...

Television programmers have a unique way of amusing themselves. They schedule *I Walk Around Moscow* [Ia shagaiu po Moskve, 1963][2] on Monday, and *Burnt by the Sun* [Utomlennye solntsem, 1994] on Friday. 'Is he really me? Did mother really love this man – yellow-grey, almost white hair, wise like a serpent?'[3] It cannot be denied – he's lived a Great Life.[4] In 1995 every other journalist writing about Mikhalkov's birthday entitled his article 'Dear Nikita Sergeevich'. One descended into utter nonsense: 'His parents named him in honour of the great man – it could not have been otherwise.'[5]

It is hard not to envy such prophetic parents who named their child in 1945 in honour of the then little-known Nikita Khrushchev! But their sagacity is of a mythical nature: there was really nothing prophetic, but rather something in the mystical depths of the Russian psyche. To be born in the year of Victory and be given the name and patronymic of the future head of state is a good start for a legend-to-be.

The legend became true, and the battle for a Great Life is won. Mikhalkov gave clear and straight answers to all those damned Russian questions: 'Hey, mate, look at me! Do as I do!'

The myth of Nikita Mikhalkov is a completely rewritten *Hamlet*. The Prince acted decisively and energetically: he overthrew the pretender, assumed the throne, married Ophelia, and they had, let's say, four children. The link in a time that was out of joint was reinstated. Or, in another translation: 'The path of life is disrupted, and I am thrown into this hell to put things right again.'[6] The eternal prince never became king and was unable to make anything of his life apart from tragedy.

Mikhalkov made everything of his life apart from a tragedy. Lev Tolstoi's venomous comment comes to mind: 'Occasionally Turgenev would visit and go on and on: tra-agedy, tra-agedy ... '

Maybe the Russians by now have bored the entire world with their 'tra-agedy', and Creation, having plenty of infinity to spare, has decided to play, for our edification, this particular card?

Or perhaps the blinding surface of the Mikhalkov legend conceals a real story which is, if not tragic, then at any rate genuinely dramatic? [...]

I should warn my readers here: opinions are never simple and straight-forward, but ambiguous; this applies also to any given opinion on Mikhalkov. How could there be clarity when the author of this article too is a product of her time and all its grimaces?

Living on the magic mountain, the country's number-one director, the first Russian Oscar winner, the father of a thriving family, and the friend of the powers-that-be pronounces the formula for human life – impossibility, irrevoc-ability, inevitability – provoking my inquisitive consciousness to an experiment: to understand just *what* is impossible, irrevocable and inevitable in Mikhalkov's own life story.

1

> A man with such potential should be placed in harder
> circumstances ... he lacks a canon, perhaps a moral one.
>
> Konstantin Rudnitsky[7]

'Everything was fine until it all went wrong.' Over many years Mikhalkov has enjoyed the (almost) unreserved support of the progressive community, the liberal intelligentsia.

Mikhalkov's debut as an actor 'walking around Moscow' not only fascinated the thinking audience but created the impression that the young artist had a special and serious link with the time.

'The Mikhalkov of those years', wrote Vera Shitova, 'is the personification of youth ... content with everything in the world.' This youth was so 'self-sufficient', so perfect and complete in its natural appearance that Mikhalkov's hero was somehow deprived of any future development and remained for ever eighteen years of age, the actor's age. 'Stop, moment, you are beautiful!'[8] Mikhalkov's hero was more a state of the soul, a lyrical tune of the time, than a concrete 'somebody'.[9]

This lyrical tune of the time had the ideal qualities of fiction, even of a fairytale, albeit interwoven with elements of reality. The clever, kind, benevolent and rather mischievous boy Kolia, although singing that he might wander 'through tundra and taiga', remained in the idyllic space of Daneliya's lyrical comedy without any particular feats.

This does not apply to Mikhalkov himself. Those who wish to wipe away an uninvited tear should read the heart-rending story by Zori Balayan in *Literaturnaia gazeta* of 28 February 1996 about the heroic expedition to Kamchatka and Chukotka,[10] in which Mikhalkov took part in 1971–72 while serving in the navy on Kamchatka.

It is painful to read how, in temperatures of 50 degrees below zero, he crashed through an ice-hole and got frostbite in his hands and nose. However, the purpose of the expedition is noteworthy: it was organised to search for the traces of another Red Army expedition which perished in 1923. It is as if Mikhalkov had run away from his time and place into the place and time of a more heroic era. Not actually (alas, you cannot run away from time), but apparently. Here, I think, are the first signs of Mikhalkov's search for his 'Grande Illusion'.

An illusion, especially a great illusion, is not a dream or a mirage; it is not something sweet and hazy, spectral and shaky. An illusion is a fortress, for whose construction people may be willing to lay down their lives, and not merely get frostbite in their nose ...

There is no doubt in my mind that the principal myth of the New Age – the myth of Hamlet – contains within it all the subsequent history of the New Age.

Thus, if the father is destroyed or overthrown (the father of the Kingdom, the Father-creator) and Another, with whom the Mother carries on in a shameful way, usurps the throne, then the time is out of joint and any activity is illusory, including that of revenge.

The idea that it may be possible for a single person to reinstate the link in time is heroic, dangerous and comic at the same time.

Any person who proposes himself and his life as a universally valid lyrical Utopia is in danger of losing the understanding of his rational contemporaries.

I am not saying that Mikhalkov does this consciously or deliberately; he lives in accordance with his understanding of what is important and necessary. But in the mid-1980s something about Mikhalkov began to irritate, disturb and annoy many people – and not without reason: 'Let the Mikhalkov of today pose a bit with his thick moustache and his trained muscles, and with all his self-confident bearing,' wrote Shitova in 1984.[11] A bit, she said. In 1995 Sergei

Nikolaevich wrote differently: 'Mikhalkov behaves in life and on screen in a familiar, unceremonious manner which is rare even for our brazen times.'[12]

He has committed no specific 'offences'. When, after the row between Mikhalkov and the progressives, the latter tried to formulate their legitimate annoyance, it transpired that no specific charge could be made. 'Mikhalkov did not sign a single obsequiously loyal text,' confirmed Elena Stishova.[13] So what is the reason: the moustache, the muscles, the undue familiarity, the excessively self-confident tone? All these reasons seem trifling when viewed against the background of today's 'moral collapse' [...] The irritation was profoundly existential, as Nikolaevich explains: 'For members of our intelligentsia who have spent half their lives in communal apartments dreaming about foreign countries he is, without doubt, a strange and unpleasant figure.'[14]

The faith of Moscow journalists in the supreme power of the housing question is amazing. I know many people who have a problem neither with their living quarters nor with foreign travel, but for whom Mikhalkov is nevertheless a 'strange and unpleasant figure'.

It seems to me that the anti-Hamlet tendency of Mikhalkov's social conduct antagonises them: before his decision 'to be' there is not even a hint of reflection; moreover, this clear, direct, simple 'to be' is offered to all and sundry as a clear and direct lesson. In 1992 Yuri Bogomolov, participating in a discussion about whether to ban Mikhalkov's television programme 'Crossroads' [Perekrestok], commented: 'The core of the disagreement between the ideal director and actor and the cinematic community lies in his behaviour as a mentor. At that time, he reproached some with childishness, some with low moral standards. He spoke like a pastor.'[15]

He spoke like a pastor. He had an answer to everything. No reflection, no doubts, no subtext – all he offered was text.

Yet the heroic Utopia of society and family that he created in his life is not an absolute in Mikhalkov's artistic world.

In moments of inspired lucidity the master of life and the teacher of life becomes an ordinary pupil of life, a diligent observer; clear and direct answers to those damned questions vanish like smoke.

2

Fatherland, father's name, father. The refutation of the Hamlet myth, the myth of the replacement of the father and of the time which is out of joint, which the Son is incapable of restoring, this would in Mikhalkov's case be the myth about the Father, builder of the Fatherland, endowing the Son with his father's name. Any attempt to search for the Father or father-figures in Mikhalkov's artistic world proves fruitless.

Until Urga [Urga, territoriia liubvi, 1991] and Burnt by the Sun, fatherlessness reigns in Mikhalkov's cinematic world. Some old men doze in their armchairs.

6a. Nikita Mikhalkov. *Burnt by the Sun*. Mitia (Oleg Menshikov).

6b. Nikita Mikhalkov. *Burnt by the Sun*. Nadia (Nadia Mikhalkova) and Kotov (Nikita Mikhalkov).

The Past of the Fatherland Reviewed

'Dad, don't sleep!' The stern Stolz senior will not even embrace Stolz junior to say good-bye (*Oblomov* [Neskol'ko dnei iz zhizni Oblomova, 1979]); the pathetic Vovchik (Ivan Bortnik) from *Kinfolk* [Rodnia, 1982] and the really pitiable Tasik (Yuri Bogatyrev) are not even given serious, adult names; Mikhail Ulianov's monstrous hero in *Without Witnesses* [Bez svidetelei, 1983] continues this line; and Marcello Mastroianni's hero (*Dark Eyes* [Ochi chernye, 1987]) is no father, but a good-for-nothing.

These are pseudo-fathers, so-called fathers, dubious as human beings and dysfunctional as fathers. And the shadow of the evil Uncle Claudius is irrelevant here; the father has not been killed or replaced. He is simply absent, an empty space.

The longed-for positive father appears for the first time in the Far East, in the Chinese steppe, where 'urga' is the territory of love.[16] Outside historical time fathers exist, of course, but they exist outside the theme of time which is out of joint. Geographically and ethnographically they exist, but historically and mythologically they do not.

The fatherlessness of Mikhalkov's cinema until *Burnt by the Sun* corresponds to our reality in the 1970s and 1980s, and, of course, to the world of Russian literature in the nineteenth century.

With all the best intentions, where could Mikhalkov find a positive father-figure in the great Russian classics? Even the brilliant Pushkin made Eugene Onegin and Tatiana Larina orphans. Indeed, all the heroes of our great literature are wretched orphans or homeless children. In Lermontov's world there is not even a hint of a father-figure. Dostoevsky and his 'fathers' are better not remembered late at night; the best of them all is probably Semen Marmeladov: 'Sonia! My daughter! Forgive me!' – at least he asked for forgiveness. Simeonov-Pishchik, the poor fool of *The Cherry Orchard*, seems the only thoughtful father in the world of Chekhov's plays.

But 'of nothing comes nothing'. What sort of fatherland is conceivable if there are no fathers?

At this point Mikhalkov decides to correct the course of time. In life, and in art, he creates the figure of the father and lends this figure his own face; he fills the empty space himself. At one time he had himself filled the gap of the hero-lover in *A Cruel Romance* [Zhestokii romans, 1984]; towards the mid-1980s there was not a single accounts department in the USSR without his portrait. Why then not try to out-argue this sad Russian fatherlessness?

I do not know whether Mikhalkov managed to do so in life, but the image of the father, Sergei Petrovich Kotov, in *Burnt by the Sun* is a unique phenomenon in Russian cinema.

The solicitous parent, the loving husband, the war hero (even if not very illustrious – only the civil war) leads a fully bourgeois lifestyle, substituting, of course, football for cricket. The heroic past treats the divisional commander quite well, and adds elements of show and buffoonery to his present existence.

Sergei Kotov is a Soviet 'superstar', who is happy to play on the cult of his own personality. He is the master in another family's house; and he has added his own pictures – showing himself together with Stalin – to the collection of old family photographs. The decent divisional commander will pay cruelly for this sweet self-delusion, when, above his recently shiny but now brutally beaten face a grandiose portrait rises of the man who overthrew the father and became the Father of the people, and who could not stand petty comfortable illusions. The times, linked by a lie, again become out of joint.

In Mikhalkov's latest film, *The Barber of Siberia*, the hero (the cadet Andrei Tolstoi) is once more fatherless; moreover, he shares an obvious feature with Hamlet: after his father's death his mother lives with a nasty uncle. But in the new film the father of the Russian people features: Alexander III. And who else could play him than ... you have three guesses.

3

In the mid-summer of 1996, Russia's cultural sphere was permeated by two emanations from Mikhalkov. The *Nezavisimaia gazeta* published an open letter from him to the newly elected President, while Sergei Gazarov's film *The Government Inspector* [Revizor, 1996][17] in which Mikhalkov played the Mayor reached the screens (as we used to say when there were cinemas in the country). Both events were connected by the theme of Russian statehood.

The grandly serious, rhetorically high-flown letter from Mikhalkov contained the following definition of human personality: 'Personality in its collective symphonic incarnation is not a naked individuum, but a complex, hierarchical unity of man, family, society and state.'[18]

If, in this unique definition, we replace the word 'personality' with the word 'Mikhalkov', we come closer to the solution of this agonising secret: is it possible that the same man wrote this letter and played that role? For Mikhalkov's Mayor is a complete and total refutation of everything he wrote in the letter. Not because the Mayor is a 'pig's snout', as Gogol intended (Mikhalkov's Mayor is a completely positive character), but because fiction and reality are separate things. It may be possible to overcome that division within oneself, but only through the complex, hierarchical unity, and in no other way than in a collective symphonic incarnation.

'Fraternal service, the union of faith, honour and self-sacrifice on the part of the citizens and the president' is the path Mikhalkov suggests for the Fatherland, because 'this is the ancient tradition of Russian statehood'.

We will not point out here that, if the people *en masse* were capable of fraternal service, we would not need statehood ...

We will not point out that the tradition of the Russian state has always presumed an infinite sacrifice only in one direction, that is its 'citizens' ...

We will also not point out that the union of 'faith, honour and self-sacrifice'

The Past of the Fatherland Reviewed

has been imprinted in the people's memory on very few occasions: the second national army of 1612, the patriotic war of 1812, and – ?[19]

We will say instead that Nikita Mikhalkov's Mayor is a lively and convincing embodiment of the real and natural traditions of Russian statehood. He is deeply rooted in his native soil. He is firm in his faith. He adores his family. Only one single feature distinguishes him from the ideal image of Russian statehood: he indeed serves in a selfless and sacrificial manner – but he exclusively serves his own prosperity.

Having met a large number of First District Secretaries, later provincial governors, Mikhalkov knows very well how things are in real life.

And he wrote to the President about how things Should Be!

Actually, Mikhalkov did not write to the President. In fact, he never really got to like the current president. When, on his fiftieth birthday, he received the Presidential Award (Third Class) 'for Services to the Fatherland', a spark of dissatisfaction appeared in the eyes of the Oscar winner. Why 'Third Class'? 'It would have been better if they'd given me money for a film,' he muttered to the entire country.

'A task worthy of the former monarch and the current president,' Mikhalkov sums up his epistle, addressed to the former-present president-monarch, who exists solely in Mikhalkov's imagination.

It is quite incredible that this inconceivable man should have conspired to give his fellow citizens the impression that he had both common sense and sober reason. Just think what he proposes: he suggests that the addressee should become the director of the whole of Russia; that he should sketch in his mind the ideal image of the state, and with the help of fraternal service, faith, honour and self-sacrifice should realise this ideal in life.

He offers advice from his heart, as one director gives advice to another. And what is incredible here? That he, Mikhalkov, acts this way. The things he imagines are then turned into reality ... of course, not fully into reality, but nevertheless into something existing to a certain extent in a separate form of space.

But it works, doesn't it?

[...] Today, in Russia there is an ideal monarch, who, with the help of fraternal service, faith and self-sacrifice, governs the land of his own Imagination.

And we know the name of this monarch.

4

> For Nikita Mikhalkov a strong hero
> offers the only salvation from circumstances.
>
> Nina Zarkhi[20]

In any discussion about the principles of his work with actors and about his artistic methods Mikhalkov speaks only about love.

His love for his actors is fully reciprocated.

They would do anything for him! They even lose weight which, normally, for a Russian is a fate worse than death. Svetlana Kriuchkova in *Kinfolk* and Alexander Kaliagin in *Unfinished Piece for a Mechanical Piano* [Neokonchennaia p'iesa dlia mekhanicheskogo pianino, 1976][21] are not Svetlana Kriuchkova and Alexander Kaliagin; they are ideal phantoms living only in the space of Mikhalkov's films.

As I write this article a similar phantom is being created from Oleg Menshikov,[22] who is thirty-six years old. Any traces of an in-depth study of Shakespeare and Dostoevsky are erased from his face, and he becomes an eighteen-year-old cadet. Who among us would not give half a life to become half a life younger?! By contrast with the President, Mikhalkov chooses his population himself.

Not the other way round.

The actors' community looks with never-ending hope to its potential ruler: choose me! But here is a game of patience formed from a thousand packs of cards; there is an image of the imagined country (film), the people are chosen, and so is the civil servant for the ideal leadership. Between this moment and the last day of shooting something mysterious happens.

The participants in this mysterious something remember their experience for years to come with a haze of dreamy sorrow in their eyes. If Romeo had survived, he would probably, after many years, have remembered his first night with Juliet in that way.

It is impossible to make sense of this even from close by. Mikhalkov's ideal state, as always, lives in complete isolation, behind the walls of a news blackout, in silence and secrecy, which, as is well known, are necessary for love and magic. This method of total immersion in the particular circumstances derives from the early Arts Theatre when Stanislavsky and Nemirovich-Danchenko went into seclusion on their estates, in search of the keys to the mysteries of Chekhov's dramas.

This method is, of course, not universal; but it creates the especially charmed atmosphere of Mikhalkov's best films. The artists are adjusted to each other, adapted and blended in, as in a good theatre ensemble.

Of course, it would be simply wonderful to take the whole of Mother Russia away somewhere, and in peace and seclusion to adjust and adapt all Russians to each other.

A director for this could be found.

5

Berlin, February 1996. Nikita Mikhalkov is the president of the jury at the Berlin Film Festival.

He plays this honourable role conscientiously and seriously, appearing at

The Past of the Fatherland Reviewed

every screening with impeccable punctuality. His slight air of impatient boredom – the boredom of a forward observing someone else's game – may be discounted. This Mikhalkov is well-known. This Mikhalkov, like a barrister, delivers speeches on behalf of 'Mother Russia' in current affairs programmes – he is now invited exclusively on to discussion programmes on television, although he would also adorn any comedy show.

A year later, a somewhat different Mikhalkov strolls with the governor of Kostroma, trying to capture the attention of Russia's favourite 'dark eyes' (Menshikov) in the labyrinth of the Higher Military Academy for Chemical Warfare from which Menshikov should emerge appearing half a life younger and into a setting of the last century. Among the fairytale cadets and the real students of the Academy, a bewitched Menshikov diligently marches in step and undergoes a rigorous reincarnation.

This alchemy strikes one by its baroque abundance. Without any chemical defence, Menshikov, well known for his skills in artistic reincarnation, has already played a tsar's officer (*Moonsund*, 1987). And without daily English lessons in the Kostroma Higher Military Academy he has performed in English in a London production (Gogol's *The Gamblers*).[23]

Why is all this excellently organised, immense illusion necessary? An illusion with one huge flaw: if, for the reincarnation of the actor as an English-speaking cadet, such a considerable degree of imitation is required, then for the highly artistic performance of the love story the actor would need to fall in love with somebody at once. His English may be impeccable, but what about his emotions?

In any event, Mikhalkov is not interested solely in the artistic result. Of course, this result is necessary, but then the fairytale ends, and a new film begins: the routine schedule of festivals, distribution, television, reviews, critics (the devil take them all). When again will the occasion arise, if indeed it will ever arise, when he can command a parade, albeit an illusory one?

It cannot be said that Mikhalkov is more attracted by war than by peace. War brings death, which the director generally avoids (in his work), but he likes the military a lot more than he likes civil servants.

In peacetime the world is governed by tragi-comic muddle. The meaning of life, for example, is an utter mystery. Strange things happen. People permit themselves to lie around on their sofa for days on end. And in general they do a lot of stupid things. Yet the meaning of life is crystal clear for a valiant military man: he is to serve the Fatherland. And there is no place there for any Hamletism or Oblomovism.

So far, mankind has evolved only two archetypal lifestyles: Athens and Sparta. Athens means home, peace, a private life, democracy, family life, philosophy, art. Sparta stands for war, despotism, the state, military fraternity, marching songs, death for the Fatherland.

As a citizen, Mikhalkov, of course, fully supports 'Athens' – the home, peace, private life, family life and art. As far as democracy is concerned, things are somewhat worse; the film-maker cannot bring himself to love democracy. But if and when the home appears in his work, it is a place of warmth, light and comfort. With one single correction: it is doomed. Reviewing *Unfinished Piece for a Mechanical Piano*, Maya Turovskaya remarked that the film's main hero is the Voinitsevs' home. 'All of this still exists ... but it is doomed to be sold, demolished, removed, doomed to disappear.'[24]

The home in *Burnt by the Sun* is also doomed to disappear. In Mikhalkov's world there are no other homes, since one has to discount such kitschy closets as those in *Kinfolk* and *Without Witnesses*, Oblomov's den, the touchingly pathetic communal flat of *Five Evenings* [Piat' vecherov, 1978], or the dead and empty spaces in which Anna roams in *Dark Eyes*.

The one and only happy home we see in Mikhalkov's films is the home whose inhabitants sleep and dream an eternal and serene dream: Oblomov's dream of childhood ...

Athens is Athens. Yet something about this Athens is alarming and sad. Everything here is so equivocal and brittle, like the team in *Slave of Love* [Raba liubvi, 1975] which completed a film nobody needed with a childish bravery amid general chaos.

How much better is Sparta! Sailors, cossacks, cadets. 'For faith, the Tsar and the Fatherland!' The world is clear, honest, simple, just and, most important, rank is honoured properly.

Malicious tongues asserting that the image of the present governor of Kursk, General Rutskoi, was created in its time by Mikhalkov have captured a grain of truth. It seems that Mikhalkov here dreamt up some fantastic, imagined version of his own destiny ...

Sparta is Sparta. Yet Mikhalkov has shot only one 'Spartan' film so far: *At Home among Strangers, a Stranger at Home* [Svoi sredi chukhikh, chuzhoi sredi svoikh, 1974]. Now the atmosphere of the Spartan cadet community expertly re-created on the banks of the Volga serves only as a framework, an *entourage*, for the story that lies at the heart of *The Barber of Siberia*.

Both heroes of *The Barber*, the Russian cadet and his son, the American soldier, fight the entire hierarchical despotic world for the sake of their Mozart and their love.

6

In Mikhalkov's artistic world love is a rare and rather sorrowful guest.

Until *Dark Eyes*, love conflicts were peripheral in his films. The heated domain of military and sports portrayed in *At Home among Strangers* blissfully ignores this enchanted sphere of life, which any 'friend of mankind' explores with alarm and confusion. The love story in *Slave of Love* is conventional, even if picturesque. Oblomov has no answer to the turbulence of summer and the emotions of the youthful Olga Ilinskaya. More often than not Mikhalkov's heroes remember what once was and has now gone for ever. Impossible to repeat, to revive.

So what happened? Nothing, really. 'The branch of lilac, the crumpled kerchief … ' sings Shulzhenko.[25] The banks of a river, a steamboat, vows, a volume of Shakespeare, somebody's tears, promises, a letter – or maybe not even that – mist, 'dark eyes'. Then the girl leaves. Or the boy leaves. And when they meet again, the story begins; yet this is no love story, but a story of irrevocability and impossibility.

Mikhalkov himself, when acting for other film-makers, gladly and merrily played all sorts of evil conquerors, fast and smart in their pursuit of a certain goal (*The Stationmaster* [Stantsionnyi smotritel', 1972, dir. Sergei Soloviev], *Siberiade* [Sibiriada, 1978, dir. Andrei Konchalovsky], *A Cruel Romance* and *Station for Two* [Vokzal dlia dvoikh, 1982, dir. Eldar Riazanov]), usually endowing them with a cool irony. But he never admitted that type into his own films.

He himself has played successful and amoral (even if only partly so) victors, but, trusting his artistic intuition, in his own films he has introduced the figure of the gentle, sad, shy, unsuccessful hero, even to the extent of fatefully admitting into his artistic world, and by his own choice, the angel-destroyer as portrayed by Oleg Menshikov. Through the mid-1980s Mikhalkov was fascinated by this actor, but virtually nothing came of this fascination. It might seem that there he was, the ideal hero of Russia's national cinema, the answer to every dream. Together with Alexander Adabashian[26] Mikhalkov wrote the screenplay for the film *My Favourite Clown* [Moi liubimyi kloun, 1986, dir. Yuri Kushnerev] in which Menshikov selflessly created the convincing image of a fine and positive Soviet artist, the best friend of orphans, the defender of the injured and insulted. At that time, too, the first version of *The Barber of Siberia* was written with Rustam Ibragimbekov,[27] in which Menshikov was to create a fine and positive cadet, this time within a fairly elaborate love story.

But nothing happens, except that several years later comes *Burnt by the Sun*.

The gentle and sad boy, who went away somewhere some time ago, whose task it is to softly pluck the strings and grieve over a life unrealised and a love lost, over the time when 'I am thirty-five, and a nobody!' (Platonov in *Unfinished Piece for a Mechanical Piano*), over the song that will never be sung – this boy destroys not only Home and Father, but wreaks some large-scale existential destruction in Mikhalkov's entire created world. It is, of course, Mikhalkov himself who wreaks this destruction with the help of the character he conjured up.

Mikhalkov likes open spaces – fields, the steppe – but he had never previously ventured into such non-set open spaces as those in *Burnt by the Sun*. Doubt is cast over any intimate setting, every situation; everything reveals its shaky, mirage-like, spectral essence of existence, and all ties of kinship and social dependence will be destroyed. There is a certain justice in all this. This justice cannot be understood or fathomed by the 'pitiful, earthly' mind – for otherwise living would be impossible. And yet this justice exists. A life based on lies and illusions must come to an end. Into Mikhalkov's life-loving and life-affirming world death has come.

Death had never featured before: like love. It was there, somewhere, in the distance, after the film, or it was a necessity of the genre like cranberry juice in the fairbooth.[28]

In the last novella of her latest film *Three Stories* [Tri istorii, 1997] Kira Muratova – a totally different director from Mikhalkov – gives her audience an almost direct lyrical explanation of her own view of the world. Cruelly and clearly she says that old age is repulsive, and death inevitable; that the eternally young girl (life) who has no notion of any morality, will, one day, run away from us for ever.

It would have been legitimate to turn to the semi-fairytale world of *The Barber of Siberia* ten years ago, after or during *Dark Eyes*. But to return to this world now is rather surprising. It seems that the hero of the 'Grande Illusion' intends to fight reality once again, and in a decisive manner.

Artem Mikhalkov's appearance in Mikhalkov's illusion (he plays in *The Barber*) is understandable: in this way, almost the entire Mikhalkov family has become a collective character in Mikhalkov's film world. But forcing Menshikov to play to the end what he did not fully play in the past – is this a classic challenge to real time?

I see no rational explanation for this, except for one: if Menshikov is back to eighteen, then Mikhalkov is back to age thirty-three.

7

Happiness is found in overcoming oneself.

Nikita Mikhalkov[29]

The audacious single combat with time undertaken by Mikhalkov reaches its climax in *The Barber*.

In Mikhalkov's work there has been only one episode of an intense encounter with direct, immediate reality; this was at the beginning of the 1980s when he made *Kinfolk* and *Without Witnesses* and acted in some films set in that same present time. Both the films and the roles were overtly derisive. It was, after all, not difficult to triumph aesthetically over the temporary motley human trash. At the time, I was interested in Mikhalkov's 'romance with reality' and my analysis concluded with the following words: 'To laugh means to get rid of, to conquer, to be liberated ... but if despair (I meant despair about human degradation and imperfection) were to form the leitmotif of his films, then they would probably be great. For their time. For a time from which one cannot liberate oneself through an illusory, aesthetic victory.'[30]

The Past of the Fatherland Reviewed

In the final analysis, any aesthetic victory is illusory. If real time did not inspire Mikhalkov to a poetic vision but pushed him towards farce and sarcasm, then this is quite understandable.

He wants to live in his own time. He has invented his own civil war, his own 1936, his own Goncharov, his own Chekhov.

All his main heroes, except Kotov, have reached middle age and stopped there.

There are no elders above them; if any elders appear, then they know nothing and speak with no authority. 'Dad, don't sleep!'

But the boy has returned, the girl is weeping. The river is shallow, but if you cut your veins in warm water, the blood will not clot.

And yet Ophelia did not drown; she is an excellent swimmer. The mother did not marry the uncle. Rosencrantz and Guildenstern are alive. Everything in the garden is lovely.

For Faith, the Tsar and the Fatherland.

Hurrah, all you cadets.[31]

10. Fathers for the Fatherland: The Cult of the Leader in Russian Cinema

Natasha Zhuravkina

Daniel Defoe's Robinson Crusoe, while contemplating suicide on his desert island, finds a large tree, cuts it down and begins building a boat. He works long and hard on it, and constructs a perfect ocean-going vessel that has one major drawback: it is too far from the sea. Crusoe's ship remains on dry land: it is too heavy to be moved and not suited to the purpose for which it was built. This image of a ship constructed with considerable effort which proves to be totally useless is typical of the situations portrayed in post-*glasnost* and post-Soviet films on the theme of political leadership. These films have not been widely distributed outside Russia because they are firmly rooted in a specific Soviet or Russian context, but they remain major landmarks when considering the attempts of Russian culture to come to terms with the country's past.[1] This is a selective analysis of films of recent years that have one feature in common: they tackle the issues of tyranny and freedom that have fascinated, and bedevilled, Russian culture for decades.

The past few years have seen a series of convulsions in Russia's history: the decline of the Communist Party, leading to the collapse of the Soviet Union and the introduction of private enterprise in Russia, the establishment, at least on paper, of a strong presidency and a democratically elected Parliament. However, by the end of the 1980s many Russians realised that although History may be in the making before their very eyes, little had changed in their day-to-day lives. Political cataclysms were not followed by any real changes for ordinary people. Russian art became dominated by the idea that the most important aspect of any society or collective was the individual; at the same time, the individual consciousness had not changed. In practical terms this confirmed that the dominant artistic idea first enunciated by Lev Tolstoi more than a hundred years ago was still in place: social development could come about only as the result of the development of the individual. But people worn

The Past of the Fatherland Reviewed

down by the problems of everyday life all around them could not effect change.

The most significant film of the post-*perestroika* period which treats the theme of tyranny and dictatorship in an allegorical manner is Tengiz Abuladze's *Repentance* [Pokaianie/Monanieba, 1984, rel. 1986]. The dictator portrayed here combines features of the great dictators of the twentieth century: Mussolini, Hitler, Beria, Stalin. Yet Abuladze explores not so much the figure of the dictator, but rather the theme of non-resistance to evil, and the paralysing effect of tyranny and dictatorship on its survivors; Keti, whose parents fell victim to the dictator's purges, is capable of resistance only in her imagination, while in reality she is stifled, crippled by her fear of the past, and reduced to decorating cakes with churches made of icing sugar.

Another allegorical treatment of the theme of freedom and tyranny occurred in Mark Zakharov's film *To Kill the Dragon* [Ubit' drakona, 1988], which contains an uncomfortable truth: tyranny is not imposed on the people, but the need for tyranny emerges from the people. Dictatorship is not an abhorrence grafted on to the body politic from outside, but something born and nurtured within. Tyrants are often succeeded by mediocrities who prove to be even more terrible than the tyrant himself. Society becomes fragmented through the all-pervading need to hate, but the need to love becomes difficult to instil. Freedom cannot be taken for granted, and must be defended and developed. The central theme of *The Servant* [Sluga, 1988] by Vadim Abdrashitov and Alexander Mindadze, is all about the cult of the leader. The important official Gudionov carefully selects his chauffeur Pasha Kliuev and gradually turns him into his slave. Pasha's credo is, 'Your ideas are my actions', while Gudionov's idea is to destroy, rebuild and then destroy again in order to enslave a nation and erase their memory of the past and traditions. It is thus easier to rule. Gudionov encourages falsification and deceit to break down the bonds between people, and then puts them in prison. He calls virtue a vice, and turns vice into truth. All this he does consciously, and with the sole aim of depriving the nation of their ability to think and make decisions independently. People must become the slaves of his ideas. The resulting mob later features in Yuri Mamin's film *Window on Paris* [Okno v Parizh, 1993]. Abdrashitov and Mindadze show that through the microcosm of one individual, Pasha Kliuev, this experiment is successful: he becomes the slave of Gudionov, and is prepared to do anything to please him. Eventually he does not need to be ordered, as he can read his master's thoughts, and carries out all his wishes: he has become a mediocrity.

Leaders of the past, such as Lenin, Stalin, Beria and Hitler, dreamed of creating a new society and a new man, a 'positive hero' who would carry out his leader's and the Party's wishes without question. A society built on oblivion and the wholesale destruction of the past, on the disintegration of bonds between individuals and the physical extermination of its best people, engenders the likes of Pasha Kliuev, whose nickname is, significantly, the Jackal. Society is thus reduced to the level of an animal-like existence, both in terms of interpersonal relationships and the sheer visceral terror of power. Gudionov is likened to a wolf, and Pasha to a dog.

As a film of the post-*glasnost* period, *The Servant* is a psychological study of the mentality of the slave, and the function of a slave as a building block for tyranny. Pasha, a handsome, athletic man knows only fear. Even when he has not seen his master for some years, and has become a recognised conductor, he reverts to his former servitude as soon as Gudionov reappears in his life. He is once again ready to fulfil his master's every whim, and not only does not wish to leave him, but is prepared to carry on serving him. The film asks disturbing questions: where does man's desire to be a slave stem from; why does fear govern people's actions; and how long will it take to overcome this fear and vanquish the evil genius Gudionov?[2]

Yuri Mamin's film *Sideburns* [Bakenbardy, 1990] extends the theme of the leader to a cult figure of Russian literature: Alexander Pushkin. In the form of a long drawn-out joke the film subtly raises serious issues, and at the end the viewer realises that he is laughing through tears. A young man turns up in a small town, dressed like Pushkin, with sideburns and a walking cane. The town, seized with the impulse to create informal organisations and movements, is struck by the young man's idea of organising a Club for the Lovers of Pushkin. More and more young men take up the idea. The attraction of the club is that Pushkin's poems are learnt, Pushkin's life and career are studied, as are his habits of fighting. Before long, groups of young men sporting Pushkin's sideburns roam the streets, quoting the poet and wielding large sticks. They soon terrorise the whole town, spreading fear and intimidation. Their leader unites them through hate; anyone who does not love Pushkin is their enemy. The more aggressive the leader is, the more respect and admiration he receives from his followers. The words that are spoken are not important, so long as they are spoken loudly. A simple recipe for tyranny.

The film concludes with a scene which is both comical and terrifying: a Pushkin look-alike makes a speech from the balcony of a government building before the massed ranks of the Club's members, clutching blazing torches and screaming in frenzied delirium. Although the speaker could be a parody of any political tyrant – Hitler, Stalin, Mussolini or Mao Tse-Tung – that is not important here. Mamin underscores people's herd instinct and idol worship, refraining from providing a cure, but exploring the origins of such conduct: the stupidity of some, the self-centredness of others, the indifference of still others, and the conformism of everyone else. Generally speaking, it is the reluctance to think for oneself and to change one's life which prepare the ground for a tyrant. Both in *Sideburns* and in *To Kill the Dragon* the people are horrified that nothing has changed but nevertheless still pursue their own narrowly selfish interests, unwilling to change anything themselves. It is easier to shout oneself into a frenzy and wait for a leader to emerge who will assume responsibility for the future.

The Past of the Fatherland Reviewed

7. Yuri Mamin. *Window on Paris*. The Parisian artist enters street life in St Petersburg.

The cinema of the late 1980s is thus characterised by the investigation of people's paralysis and herd instinct; this is more often than not achieved through allegories with the world of history, politics or literature. In exploring the reasons for inactivity and paralysis, film-makers indirectly defend the lack of positive action.

It is difficult to find any positive hero in *Sideburns*, and it is therefore interesting to note that Mamin's next film, *Window on Paris*, made after the collapse of the Soviet Union, continues the director's interest in the problems of the present; yet it is more upbeat. Mamin notes with more than a tinge of sadness that only society's surface details change, but not the inner substance. The film's central character is a schoolteacher, Nikolai, whose school has recently become a business school, and thus the portraits of Party leaders that used to adorn its walls have been replaced with huge pictures of foreign banknotes. Nikolai tells the headmaster that, although the school now trains the builders of capitalism instead of the builders of socialism, the end product is still the same: a lout and a thief. If, in his previous film, Mamin portrayed the herd as a monolith, here he distinguishes separate types.

From the point of view of Russian classical literature, these are all 'little people', socially insignificant personalities. At the table of a communal apartment we find a former Party bigwig, a talented musician turned teacher, and a shifty workman previously employed in the manufacture of musical instruments. Despite the differences in their political views and social status, they feel no antagonism towards each other, they do not quarrel over politics, indeed, they are profoundly indifferent to who governs them, be they communists, capitalists or whoever. They only thing they share is the dream of a better life: that may be to buy vodka, to catch fish, or to share a sense of the 'wonder of the world' with the schoolchildren. The spectator does not sense Mamin's ironic attitude towards the wishes of his characters for a better life. The state has not been able to do anything for them, and each of them tries to do something for himself, relying on his education, intelligence and skills. It is a sort of updated, contemporary version of Gorky's play *The Lower Depths* [Na dne], written at the beginning of the twentieth century, and its typical and easily recognisable characters and situations give a Russian audience much uncomfortable and frightening food for thought. Once again we return to the image of the ship that cannot sail anywhere.

The film has its fair share of the fantastic, as a wardrobe in the communal apartment offers a 'window on Paris', though which the characters pass and emerge in the French capital. With one step they pass from a poor, ruined country into a prosperous and thriving society. The director concentrates on the reaction of each of the characters as they look out on to wealth. Only the fisherman is pleased, as he has more luck in the Seine than in the Moika.[3] The others are unimpressed, and unprepared for the experience. Nikolai is the only character who seriously investigates the avenue of staying in Paris for good to make a career as a musician. Yet his dream ends in fiasco, as he can make money only by performing without trousers in an orchestra of a sex bar. Given this choice, he turns the job offer down. This triumph of human dignity and self-respect lifts the film out of the mire of sordidness and lost hopes. A spiritual leader, all the children in the school are drawn to him, and follow him back to St Petersburg. Perhaps, if they make a joint effort, theirs is the ship that will sail into the future. Many of today's people are doomed to remain grounded.[4]

In Karen Shakhnazarov's film *Dreams* [Sny, 1993] the crowd or the herd arouses both hatred and sympathy. The plot is ludicrously simple, but gives ample opportunity for the play of fantasy and absurdist slapstick. The nineteenth-century Countess Prizorova dreams that she is living in the 1980s, and that she is no longer a countess, but washing plates in a filthy kitchen. Here she is subject to the unwelcome attention of the firm's accountant, the most important man in the place. Soon she begins to dream of her husband Count Dmitri Prizorov, not as a most respectable member of the Tsarist government, but as a Soviet pensioner whose poverty forces him to agree to anything that will earn him some money, from selling pornographic postcards to blackmail to male prostitution. In other words, the same person can follow different paths under different historical conditions. Over the years a man may lose his self-respect, he may be humiliated through poverty, he may become cynical, like 'Dima' Prizorov, a character who has a spiritual affinity with Mamin's characters.

The Past of the Fatherland Reviewed

The plot does not stop there, however: although Dima Prizorov dreams that he is a film director, he internally remains the same. The words of Count Prizorov to the Tsarist government prove prophetic. As he analyses his dreams, he realises they are a prophecy, and that the government must change course to avoid a catastrophe. His words are suffused with despair as he predicts the coming of an age of loutishness and spiritual vacuum. Dreams will become reality. The neglect of human rights, spiritual values and society's living standards leads to the emergence and dominance of the mob, which gets ever larger and devours everything in its path. The mob can be easily governed, as it is both aggressive and trusting. It is easier to establish mob rule than to do away with it, for in the latter instance the mob must become a community of individuals.[5]

The herd, the mob, or the crowd is also at the heart of Andrei Konchalovsky's film *Riaba la Poule* [Kurochka-Riaba, 1994], the sequel, after almost thirty years, to *Asya's Happiness* [Asino schast'e, 1967]. If the earlier film provided a lyrical, sun-drenched account of life in the countryside, Konchalovsky's sequel starkly shows the village community as downtrodden and demoralised. The villagers are an uncouth, drunken and resentful mob, existing on a level only slightly higher than beasts, with little capacity for thought or reflection. Even the collapse of the Soviet Union has changed nothing in their collective psyche, as they reject all that is new and continue to live as of old, without any change. When one of their number attempts to better his material position, and works day and night to do so, the other villagers protest against such 'capitalism' and parade portraits of those communists (the Politburo) they still believe to be their leaders. Attempts for self-betterment in this environment are thus doomed to failure. As in the films of Yuri Mamin, people may complain loudly about the government, drink vodka to excess, but they themselves do nothing to improve society.

Apart from the theme of the leadership of a mob, several films of the 1990s are significant in an analysis of the treatment of the Stalin era in post-Soviet cinema. Ivan Dykhovichny's *Moscow Parade* [Prorva, 1992] exposes the immorality hidden behind the myth of Stalinist culture. The film juxtaposes a fictional plot to documentary material in order to comment on the nature of high Stalinist culture: the disciplined parades, monumental buildings and muscle-controlled bodies are contrasted with the decadent lifestyle of the characters. The façade of the New State hides behind it decadent and amoral conduct: the heroine is first raped, and later she seduces a worker.

Sergei Livnev's *Hammer and Sickle* [Serp i molot, 1994] parodies and mocks the myth-making of Socialist Realism and, at the same time, constructs a new myth of the Stalinist past. The film is about a demand made by Stalin in 1936 that the country should have more soldiers; the female Evdokiya Kuznetsova becomes the male Evdokim Kuznetsov, who turns out to be a successful worker in the metro construction brigade, is awarded a medal, and matched with kolkhoz worker Liza Voronina. They literally become models for Vera Mukhina's famous statue of 'The Worker and the Peasant', and a model Soviet

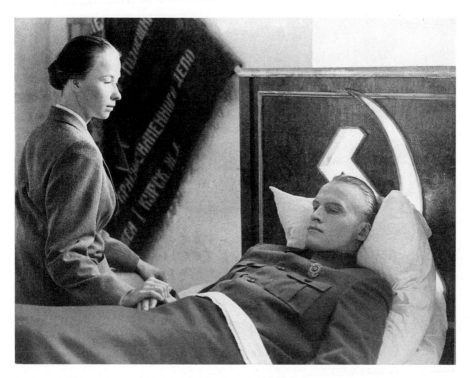

8. Sergei Livnev. *Hammer and Sickle*. Liza (Alla Kliuka) and Evdokim (Alexei Serebriakov).

family: they adopt a girl, Dolores, who has been orphaned during the Spanish Civil War. When Evdokim wants to break free from his 'model' existence, he challenges Stalin's control of his life. In a meeting with the leader he attacks him, and is shot. Paralysed and unable to speak, Evdokim is turned into a hero once more; he has supposedly saved Stalin's life and is exhibited as a museum piece.

Liza and Evdokim are artefacts, creations of a system, the model worker and peasant. Ideally, they will end like Evdokim in a museum, displayed to foreign visitors and pioneers as objects which will not change. Livnev creates a living monument with the paralysed Evdokim in a museum, resembling Lenin in the mausoleum, comfortably cushioned on a bed decorated with hammer and sickle, reduced to total passivity. An artefact, Evdokim is seemingly immortal, and even after a pioneer boy misfires a shot in the museum it is not clear whether he is dying or immortal. By making the statue come alive, Livnev freezes life in reality: 'History ... is known to be secondary, it is an occasion for an artefact, but not for cognition. It is not historical reality which is being reflected here, but a myth which has absorbed it.'[6] For Livnev, history is fragmented, a product of creative, artistic imagination in which the artefact man becomes a puppet in Stalin's hands, while the individual is destroyed.

The Past of the Fatherland Reviewed

9. Pavel Chukhrai. *The Thief.* Tolian (Vladimir Mashkov), Sania (Misha Filipchuk) and Katia (Ekaterina Rednikova).

Again, passivity and paralysis are explored; they provide the reason for the individual's incapacity to act in the present.

The theme of the individual becoming a willing agent of a tyranny features in Nikita Mikhalkov's celebrated *Burnt by the Sun* [Utomlennye solntsem, 1994], which shows the destruction of a loyal Soviet soldier, Sergei Kotov, in the purges of the 1930s. The rural idyll of the dacha with its Chekhovian atmosphere is juxtaposed to a second, parallel, political reality which interferes: the arrival of the tanks in the fields; the pioneers who march in honour of Stalin and who congratulate General Kotov; the gas attack evacuation practice; and the scenes at the construction site where a hot-air balloon is being built to raise Stalin's banner into the sky.

Equally obtrusive for Kotov is the arrival of Mitia, a childhood friend of Kotov's wife Marusia, who is now an NKVD officer with the remit to arrest Kotov. Mitia has accepted this job both for personal and political reasons: he plays different roles to win Marusia's and her daughter Nadia's heart, while all the time he is a calculating officer who cold-bloodedly prepares Kotov's arrest; he is a sad, lonely man who lost the meaning of his life ever since he was deprived of his love Marusia. Significantly Mitia has no parents, but lives with his tutor; to him, Stalin is a father-figure: when Stalin appears as an all-powerful pagan god, rising (on the banner attached to a balloon) as the sun is setting, it becomes clear that he is a father-surrogate to Mitia. The tyrant has assumed god-like status as his minions on earth carry out his orders in obeisance.

Finally, Pavel Chukhrai's *The Thief* [Vor, 1997] tells the story of the relationship between the boy Sania and the professional thief Tolian. The film is set in the early 1950s, when the cult of Stalin was at its height. Throughout the film images of Stalin recur: the tattoo on Tolian's chest, banners carried by performers at the circus, pictures adorning the walls of apartments Tolian is about to rob, toasts made to Stalin by people sitting at a table. The cult of the leader is linked to fatherlessness: Sania's father died in the war, and Tolian becomes a surrogate father in the same way as Stalin is a surrogate father for Tolian, for the Russian people. This is made explicit in the final episode of the film: the time now is the present, Russia is torn by civil war, possibly in Chechnia. Sania, aged forty-eight, is now a high-ranking military officer; the inference is clear: without the father-figure as leader, Russia is doomed. Chukhrai's film offers a worryingly pessimistic view of Russia's future desolation without authority, without the father's 'strong hand'. Yet at the same time mothers and their children are being evacuated in a protected car of the train: Sania will take them to safety, ensure their survival, and thus the future of the new generation.

Russian cinema has not become thoroughly debased through commercialisation or the lifting of censorship: 'Perhaps the problem Russian critics and film-makers must consider now concerns the possible displacement of Communist and Socialist Realist ideology with that of commercialism, with its trappings of the tyranny of the box office and the gratification of the producers. Fortunately, not everyone is taken in by the lure of the dollar.'[7] The traditional Russian themes of the individual and society, the 'little man', freedom and necessity, faith and the lack of it, remain, and are developed in line with the new conditions in Russia today. Directors in Russia are trying to overcome the dead legacy of the Stalinist past that proved to exist not only in political structures but in the very souls of the people. It is much easier to change a political system than to change the soul of a man who, from his earliest years has been paralysed by fear and the official doctrine that he is a nonentity, and that the collective is all. One wants to believe that real change is now taking place, the people are at last finding their feet and their voice, and believe that 'killing the dragon' is not just a possibility, but a necessity. One wishes to believe that the ship will, after all, set sail.

11. New Versions of Old Classics: Recent Cinematic Interpretations of Russian Literature

David Gillespie

Screen adaptations of works from literature have always been popular in cinema industries throughout the world, and some of the world's greatest films have been based on literary works (in particular, novels). In Russia, in the early years of cinema, on which the new Bolshevik government placed great store, the Formalist literary critic Boris Eikhenbaum (in 1926) realised the potential of literature to 'pass through' the screen, and cinema's consequent advantages over the theatre:

> It appears that literature can be adapted to the screen more easily than to the stage. Live theatre does not translate literature onto a different plane, for we remain in the sphere on which the whole theatrical system rests – the sphere of the spoken word. Literature is definitely diminished on the stage, being deprived of a whole series of its methods and potentialities (episodes, digressions, descriptions, details, parallelisms, and so forth) ... Literature into cinema is a phenomenon of quite a different order. It is neither staging nor illustration, but rather translation into film language.
>   This is precisely the point: that cinema is not simply a moving picture, but a special photographic language. This language, in all its 'naturalism', does not materialise literature as theatre does. What results, rather, is something analogous to a dream: a person approaches; now you can see only the eyes, now the hands – then everything disappears – another person – a window – a street, and so on. Music too enhances this impression, enveloping the film in an atmosphere of emotions stimulated by sound.[1]

Eikhenbaum thus identifies this relatively new art as a system of signs to be read and interpreted in pursuit of meaning, as in literary texts. The purpose here will also be served by analysing films as texts, with particular attention paid to narrative, plot and character.

In the art of cinematic adaptation, the director/screenwriter not only uses the raw material of the text as the basis of a film script, but also reworks it, and may adapt or change, however subtly or radically, the meaning of the original to suit the theme of the film. Morris Beja sets out the basic dilemma:

> If we may oversimplify for the sake of discussion, there are probably two basic approaches to the whole question of adaptation. The first approach asks that the integrity of the original work – the novel, say – be preserved, and therefore that it should not be tampered with and should in fact be uppermost in the adapter's mind. The second approach feels it proper and in fact necessary to adapt the original work freely, in order to create – in the different medium that is now being employed – a new, different work of art with its own integrity.[2]

In a recent study, Brian McFarlane takes the debate further. He examines the intertextuality at the heart of adaptation, and differentiates between 'transfer' and 'adaptation'. Himself adapting the Formalists' distinction between *fabula* (the basic story: what happens) and *siuzhet* (the narrative plot: how it is told), McFarlane demonstrates that a novel's essential story can be easily *transferred* to film, but the art of *adaptation* is in the film-makers' use of narrative and filmic devices with which to create an original work. Thus, the issue of a film's fidelity to the original text is not important; rather, what the director does with it is the main criterion for critical evaluation:

> Those elements of the novel which require *adaptation proper* may be loosely grouped as (in Barthes's term) *indices*, as the *signifiers of narrativity*, and as *the writing*, or, more comprehensively, as *enunciation*, to use the term now commonly employed in film theory. The film version of a novel may retain all the major cardinal functions of a novel, all its chief character functions, its most important psychological patterns, and yet, at both micro- and macro-levels of articulation, set up in the viewer acquainted with the novel quite different responses. The extent to which this is so can be determined by how far the film-maker has sought to create his own work in those areas where transfer is not possible. He can, of course, put his own stamp on the work by omitting or reordering those narrative elements which are transferrable or by inventing new ones of his own: my point is that, even if he has chosen to adhere to the novel in these respects, he can still make a film that offers a markedly different affective and/or intellectual experience.[3]

Russian cinema offers some good examples of how film-makers can adapt and 'reorder' literary works. Iosif Kheifits's *The Lady with the Lapdog* [Dama s sobachkoi, 1959] 'translates' Chekhov's drama with great fidelity (right down to the dialogue), and is distinguished by the excellent playing of the two leads (Iyia Savvina and Alexei Batalov). Furthermore, the gentle, lyrical pacing and evocative setting help vividly re-create Chekhov's sardonic picture of the complexities of relationships for a modern audience. Nevertheless, in certain background scenes the film serves up a depressing picture of the social ills (poverty, despair, moral corruption of the upper classes) of Tsarist Russia.

The Past of the Fatherland Reviewed

Kheifits's film, despite its closeness to Chekhov's text, thus conforms to Socialist Realist demands that the Tsarist past be shown critically, and that the old world be portrayed as ultimately doomed.

There are other, more mundane, reasons for the attraction of literature for film directors in post-Soviet Russia. In a time of rapid change and the destruction of old values, the classical literary tradition offers almost ready-made screenplays and familiar material. Furthermore, the literary heritage remains one of the few bastions of certainty and national identity amid chaos and disruption. Both writers and film-makers look into their own culture and history for absolutes in a destabilized world. Reinterpretations of literature, especially in the modern Russian context, also make a statement about contemporary mores or the socio-political environment. Even amid the new commercial realities of post-Soviet Russia, writers and directors still strongly feel the pull of civic-mindedness that has been a feature of Russian culture throughout its development.[4]

My purpose, then, is to examine the new aesthetic possibilities film-makers have exploited in the post-Soviet age, and the uses (albeit still civic-minded) they have found for them. Nowhere, it seems to me, is this more promising than in the cinematic treatment of pre-1917 Russian literature.[5] Recent directors have, as if taking their cue from McFarlane's thesis, taken the original text and changed it, in a variety of ways, to make it relevant for the modern age. To be sure, the original text becomes a cipher for an exploration of Russia's historical destiny. I intend to look in some detail at two recent Russian films in particular: Sergei Bodrov's *The Prisoner of the Mountains* [Kavkazskii plennik, 1996], based on the story of the same name by Lev Tolstoi, and Valeri Todorovsky's *Katia Izmailova* [Podmoskovnye vechera (Evenings Around Moscow), 1994], based on Nikolai Leskov's *Lady Macbeth of Mtsensk* [Ledi Makbet Mtsenskogo uezda]. These films have been chosen for two reasons: first, to illustrate the various bold and challenging ways in which directors have adapted their source material; second, to show how cinema is adept at responding to the new challenges of post-Soviet Russia more immediately, and perhaps with more effect, than literature. Both directors, in their differing ways, give the original text new meaning, and address the cultural and political issues of the age.

Just as in the 1990s there is in the West an obsession with transferring the English literary heritage to the big screen, there is at present something of a revival, if only in relative terms, in modern Russian cinema of screen interpretations of works from the classical literary past. This is somewhat surprising, given the near collapse of the Russian film industry since 1991.[6] Among films produced during the last two or three years are *The Little Demon* [Melkii bes, 1995], directed by Nikolai Dostal and based on the novel of the same name by Fedor Sologub, *The Fatal Eggs* [Rokovye iaitsa, 1995], directed by Sergei Lomkin and based on the satirical novella by Mikhail Bulgakov, and Sergei Gazarov's *The Government Inspector* [Revizor, 1996], based on the famous play by Nikolai

Gogol.[7] This latter film boasts an impressive cast, including Evgeni Mironov in the title role, with the internationally acclaimed Nikita Mikhalkov, Oleg Yankovsky and Marina Neelova, and offers a faithful rendering of the motifs, characters and themes of the original. It falls down, however, in its sheer lack of discipline and its inability, given the comic possibilities of Gogol's text, to be funny (apart from one or two cameos). However, it has a topical dimension: Gogol's acerbic satire on corruption and bribe-taking among government officials is not out of place in the chaotic and crime-ridden Russia of Boris Yeltsin. A word should be reserved here for *The Horses are Carrying Me Away* [Nesut menia koni, 1996], directed by Vladimir Motyl and based on Chekhov's novella 'The Duel'. Motyl transposes Chekhov's themes and characters to a modern, post-Soviet setting, with the emphasis on sex, sexual jealousy and betrayal, as if offering a statement on the moral corruption of the modern Russian intelligentsia that has sold its soul to commercialism. Motyl's film, though, is unrelievedly dull, and fails to engage.

Of course, it is not only in the last few years that Russian film-makers began experimenting, with varying degrees of originality and success, with literary texts. There were certain bold strokes during the so-called 'stagnation' years of Brezhnev's rule, where allegory was the dominant tool. In films directed by Nikita Mikhalkov, in particular, the fidelity to the literary original did not conceal a clear contemporary dimension. Both *Unfinished Piece for Mechanical Piano* [Neokonchennaia p'esa dlia mekhanicheskogo pianino, 1977], based on Chekhov's play *Platonov*, and *Several Days from the Life of Oblomov* [Neskol'ko dnei iz zhizni Oblomova, 1979], based on Ivan Goncharov's novel *Oblomov*, are ostensibly about the failed ideals of the Russian intelligentsia in the late nineteenth century. However, it is not difficult to see that the spiritual and moral impasse in which they find themselves can be directly related to the dead-end the intelligentsia inhabited in the late Brezhnev years. In *Unfinished Piece for Mechanical Piano*, all the characters are locked within themselves, unable to establish lasting bonds or relationships. At the same time they do not want to change anything in their world, a charge levelled by dissidents such as Andrei Amalrik and Alexander Solzhenitsyn at the Soviet intelligentsia of the late 1970s. Mikhalkov's interpretation of Oblomov is also something of a departure from the original text, as the character is not shown negatively but rather with sympathy, as a naïve childlike dreamer unable to adapt to the modern materialistic and cynical world. Again, the contemporary relevance would be evident to a discerning public.

Mikhalkov is just as well known in Russia as an actor, and one of his best-remembered roles is as the rake Paratov in *A Cruel Romance* [Zhestokii romans, 1984], directed by Eldar Riazanov and based on the play *Without a Dowry* by Alexander Ostrovsky. Mikhalkov brought to his role a modern interpretation not too dissimilar to his own publicly exhibited persona: an affluent, devil-may-care playboy with foreign friends, a taste for good living and fashionable

The Past of the Fatherland Reviewed

amorality. It is as a result of her infatuation with Paratov that the heroine Larisa dies, killed by her spurned lover and abandoned by those she thought of as her friends. A similar theme, about the destruction of feminine beauty and purity by male baseness and duplicity, is contained in the film *My Affectionate and Tender Beast* [Moi laskovyi i nezhnyi zver', 1978], directed by Emil Lotianu and starring Oleg Yankovsky. Based on the Chekhov novella 'Drama during the Hunt' [Drama na okhote], it became popular both because it touched on the 'eternal' Russian theme of beauty and its destruction, and also for its catchy theme tune, whistled and hummed by thousands of Russians even today. Another film that could be mentioned here is Gleb Panfilov's *Vassa* (1983), based on the play *Vassa Zheleznova* by Maxim Gorky. It is about a capitalist family faced with collapse, and the efforts of the matriarch to keep it together. Despite a realistic portrayal of family life at the turn of the century, and a powerful performance by Inna Churikova in the title role, the film, like the play, symbolises the inner corruption and eventual demise of capitalism in Russia in the early twentieth century. It thus conforms to the prevailing ideological demands of the Soviet era.

Nevertheless, these films appeared during what came to be called 'developed socialism', supposedly a half-way house between socialism and communism, when the state was encouraging an upbeat, self-confident and occasionally aggressive foreign and domestic policy. These films were addressing a Russian audience, however, with the clear message (a particularly Russian nineteenth-century one) that man was inwardly torn by doubt and failing to accomplish anything in life other than the destruction of that which he held dear. This reminder from Russia's literary past, or rather a continuing paradigm of beauty subverted and destroyed by evil, served to undermine the positivist ethos of the times.

Under the new freedoms of *glasnost*, directors were able to be bolder and show a gift for innovation in their films, and their treatment of classical Russian literature gave them new, censorship-free possibilities. Mikhail Shveitser's 1987 film of Tolstoi's novella *The Kreutzer Sonata* [Kreitserova sonata] offered a faithful rendering of the original plot, a harrowingly unflinching record of domestic violence in a loveless marriage, with careful attention to period detail. It was only the lifting of certain taboos that made Tolstoi's nineteenth-century frank treatment of sex, and a relatively honest discussion of homosexuality, possible within the film. It is also the first Soviet film, to my knowledge, to contain a spoken obscenity (also contained in the original text) meant to be plainly heard by the audience.

This brings me to *Katia Izmailova*. In Leskov's story of 1865, Katerina is the bored wife of a well-to-do merchant who is much older than she, and who often spends time away from home. She begins a passionate and uninhibited affair with Sergei, a steward on the estate. During one of her husband's absences her affair with Sergei is discovered by her father-in-law Boris Timofeevich,

New Versions of Old Classics

10. Valeri Todorovsky. *Katia Izmailova*. Sergei (Vladimir Mashkov) and Katerina
(Ingeborga Dapkunaite).

whom she then poisons. Katerina and Sergei then murder her husband on his
return. A further victim of their spiral of violence is the child Fedor, Boris
Timofeevich's nephew, who could benefit from the resulting inheritance. All
the while Leskov emphasises the unbridled passion and desire Katerina and
Sergei have for each other. Inevitably, they are caught by the police, and
sentenced to hard labour in Siberia. On the way to their place of exile, Sergei
begins an affair with another female convict, Sonia, and taunts and humiliates
Katerina in front of the other convicts. On a river crossing, Katerina seizes
Sonia and jumps overboard with her. Both of them perish in the icy water.
Leskov's novella is a bleak and uncompromising story of greed, lust and murder,
set in the materialistic world of the merchant class, but largely eschewing
social or political comment. In Roman Balayan's 1989 film of *Lady Macbeth of
Mtsensk*, a brutally faithful rendering of the original, the sex and eroticism of
Leskov's original are to the fore. Balayan shows us a rotten, debased world,
recognisably set in the Russian provinces of the nineteenth century, where the
two murderous protagonists care only for money and sex, and so are ultimately
doomed.

In Todorovsky's film, the action is brought forward to the present, and is set
in the 'new Russian' world of affluence, stylish clothes, fashionable furniture

The Past of the Fatherland Reviewed

and opulent interiors. Katerina is working as secretary to Irina Dmitrievna, a romantic novelist, and is married to Mitia, her son. She begins an affair with Sergei, a carpenter working in the house (with whom Irina Dmitrievna had also been having an affair), and, when the affair is discovered by her mother-in-law, she kills her. Mitia soon finds out about the affair, and is killed by Sergei. His body is buried in the forest. Katerina and Sergei then begin to put their own ending to Irina Dmitrievna's last novel, but it is rejected by the local publisher. Their relationship does not last, as the restless Sergei rekindles his interest in a local nurse, Sonia. Katerina gets her revenge by driving her car off a bridge with both her and Sonia inside.

There are thus several significant departures from the original nineteenth-century text, in particular surrounding the personality of Katia. The first obvious departure is that instead of a hated father-in-law, Katia kills her mother-in-law. In actual fact the killing is not the calculated murder by Leskov's cold-blooded heroine, but rather an impulsive, almost accidental act. Irina Dmitrievna is a writer-figure, and Katia seeks to assume her mantle and fame. Moreover, Katia and Sergei try to replace Irina Dmitrievna's original text with a happy ending, the same happy ending Katia would like to see in her relationship with Sergei. Life must thus imitate literature. However, the upbeat ending is rejected by the publisher; correspondingly, Katia's life will not end happily.

The second important departure is in Katia herself. In Todorovsky's film she is not the passionate, wilful *femme fatale* of Leskov's text. Rather, she is cold, aloof and calculating, and even her suicide is not caused by the impulse of the moment, but a preconceived and well-planned act. She tries to make her life conform to literary paradigms, dominated by the 'happy end' of conventional romance. Life-as-literature is the film's major theme, and it is significant that Sergei's initial seduction is conducted as Katia is typing up Irina Dmitrievna's text (as Katia says, 'I am not writing, I am retyping').

The third and most telling departure is in the figure of the police chief Romanov, absent in Leskov's text, to whom Katia confesses her crime. He dismisses her confession, saying he needs more evidence. Romanov is clearly based on Porfiri Petrovich, the investigator in Dostoevsky's *Crime and Punishment* to whom Raskolnikov eventually confesses. Not only does Todorovsky introduce this character into his plot, but then subverts it: in Dostoevsky's novel Porfiri Petrovich waits for Raskolnikov to confess, knowing him already to be guilty, yet in Todorovsky's film Romanov rejects her confession as inadequate. Katia's desire to become part of a literary tradition once more fails. Her aspiration to be a writer fails; the Dostoevskian baring of her soul is dismissed; finally, her own 'happy end' is destroyed by the discovery that her lover is fickle and shallow. Todorovsky's Katia is no Lady Macbeth, doomed by the strength of her own passion and ambition, but rather a modern, self-aware woman with intellectual and cultural aspirations who is destroyed by the reality of the world around her.

Todorovsky, then, has made a film that makes more than a nod to the nineteenth-century literary tradition. Todorovsky refers to this tradition and effectively subverts, then rewrites it. He has substantially revised and adapted the original text, in particular by adding some new elements, in order to give that text a relevance to the new Russia. The bones of Leskov's story are 'transferred', but what McFarlane terms the 'signifiers of narrativity' are adapted to create a new, radically different narrative. We are left with the impression that Russian literature of old, so often vaunted as an absolute value in itself, is seen as inadequate for the modern world, it can no longer guide or teach 'how to live'. Modern art forms, such as cinema, can frame and illuminate individual lives, but no longer have to offer solutions.[8] It is thus no accident that many of the film's conventions make direct reference to the cinema of America and France, arguably the leading cinematic nations in the world. Thus, the basic plot is a retread of Bob Rafelson's *The Postman Always Rings Twice* [USA, 1981] and the interment and disinterment of Mitia's body is reminiscent of Henri-Georges Clouzot's film *Les Diaboliques* [France, 1954]. The reference to *film noir* is not fortuitous, for with its mood-setting score, destructive emotions and gloomy settings, *Katia Izmailova* seems almost designed for a French audience (indeed, it is a Russian–French co-production).

'The Prisoner of the Caucasus' is the title of poems by both Alexander Pushkin and Mikhail Lermontov in the early nineteenth century, as well as a short story by Lev Tolstoi. In Pushkin's poem, a Russian nobleman serving in the Caucasus is captured by Circassians, and strikes up a relationship with a local girl. Pushkin's hero is full of admiration and respect for the dignity and strength of his captors. The girl falls in love with him, and helps him to escape. The epilogue contains Pushkin's diatribe against Russian conquest and imperialism. Lermontov's poem revisits Pushkin's, but ends tragically when the Russian is killed within sight of his own camp, and the girl is drowned in the Terek river. Lermontov is at pains to emphasise the grandeur and beauty of the mountains of the Caucasus, and his most famous work, the novel *A Hero of Our Time*, is also set amid a military campaign in the Caucasus.

Tolstoi's story concerns a Russian officer, Zhilin, who is serving with his unit in the Caucasus during the last century. He is captured by the Tartars as he attempts to leave his fort to return to mainland Russia. They keep him in a remote mountain village in order to extort a ransom for his release from his family. He is soon joined by a fellow officer, Kostylin, also being held hostage. They are both under the charge of Abdul-Murat, who has a young daughter Dina. They try to escape and are captured, after which their Tartar captors become more brutal and uncompromising. One old man in the village has lost seven of his sons fighting the Russians, and shot the eighth himself, after he had gone over to the Russian side. He wants Zhilin and Kostylin killed summarily. Zhilin, however, establishes a tenuous relationship with Dina, he makes her clay dolls, and she eventually helps him escape a second time, this time successfully.

The Past of the Fatherland Reviewed

Bodrov retains the plot and characters, but updates the setting to more recent times: the Chechen war.[9] There are, however, significant changes to the 'signifiers of narrativity' in Tolstoy's text. Zhilin and Kostylin are ambushed and captured by rebels while out on a routine patrol. Abdul-Marat wishes not to ransom his prisoners, but to exchange them for his son, who is a prisoner of the Russians in the local garrison town. During their first, unsuccessful, escape attempt, Kostylin kills two men. On their recapture Kostylin is executed by the rebels. Abdul-Murat's son is killed by the Russians as he tries to escape, but Abdul-Murat finally allows Zhilin to walk away in an act of mercy.[10] The final shot of the film obviously borrows from Coppola's anti-war *Apocalypse Now* [USA, 1979], as Russian helicopter gunships fly over Zhilin's head on their way to destroy the village he has just come from.

The Russian troops throughout the film are portrayed as brutal, occupying forces, who think nothing of shooting at the locals, and who trade their guns for vodka. Kostylin, as played by Oleg Menshikov, regards the locals as little more than cannon-fodder, vowing to return to the village in which he languishes at some future date to kill all the inhabitants. Only Zhilin, a raw conscript from a small village, treats his captors with respect and tries to understand them. Kostylin, the professional and cynical soldier, represents the Russia of aggressive imperialism and oppression; Zhilin represents the values of meekness, humility and respect for others.

Abdul-Murat's final act of mercy displays dignity, forgiveness and repentance. Here, too, Bodrov reworks Tolstoi's original, for whereas Tolstoi makes no effort to understand the Tartars or their culture, Bodrov shows in detail the rebels' culture, their world and their feeling of injustice.

The Prisoner of the Mountains is a film that attacks Russia's aggression towards the smaller nations and cultures that are contained within its borders, and is therefore not only about the Chechen war.[11] It is about war in general and the hatred it engenders, but it is even more than that. The reference to *Apocalypse Now*, another powerful statement about the devastation, both of the land and the spirit, caused by hatred and war, gives the film further depth. Moreover, Bodrov's film is fundamentally about intolerance, hate and the evil that bring about only suffering and the destruction of communities. It is also about Russia's search for identity in its post-imperial world, its attempt at self-definition through a perception of an alien culture, 'the other'.[12] Susan Layton has recently shown how the Russian literary treatment of the Caucasus in the nineteenth century helped construct Russia's own national identity:

> The literary Caucasus was largely the project of Russian men, whose psychological needs it so evidently served. However, both sexes within the romantic era's élite readership could enhance their national esteem by contemplating their internally diversified orient. Effeminate Georgia fed the conceit of Russia's European stature and superiority over Asia. But knowledge of Russia's own Asian roots defied permanent repression, especially when a French consul in

11. Sergei Bodrov. *The Prisoner of the Mountains*. Zhilin (Sergei Bodrov jr) and Kostylin (Oleg Menshikov).

> Tiflis or a visiting marquis in St. Petersburg was ever ready to castigate the tsars' 'rude and barbarous kingdom'. Under these conditions, Russians converted the Caucasian tribes into gratifying meanings about their own undeniable cultural and intellectual redardation *vis-à-vis* the West.[13]

As Russia, in the form of Zhilin, understands and respects 'the other', so can Russia adapt to a new, post-imperial role with its neighbours.

Bodrov's film updates Tolstoi's text, but also addresses the same question posed by all the writers of the nineteenth century who explored the Caucasus, 'the other', in a search for the 'true' Russia. Russia's search for identity through its relations with non-Russians is made startlingly new and topical, especially with its reliance on other, non-Russian, cultural reference-points. *The Prisoner of the Mountains* can thus be listed alongside such recent films as Yuri Mamin's *Window on Paris* [Okno v Parizh, 1993], and Petr Todorovsky's *Intergirl* [Inter-devochka, 1989], where the quest for 'Russianness' is juxtaposed with visions of Western lifestyles and mores.

Apart from its anti-war message, *The Prisoner of the Mountains* is also a deeply literary film. As if to remind us of its heritage, the title and author of the original work are scratched on a school blackboard in a scene featuring Zhilin's mother. After his execution, Kostylin 'reappears' to Zhilin. The motif of the

The Past of the Fatherland Reviewed

dead coming back to life to confront the living is common in Russian literature, and has been treated by such writers as Pushkin, Gogol and Odoevsky in the nineteenth century, and Bulgakov in this. With its intertextual game-playing and firm basis in literary tradition, *The Prisoner of the Mountains* demonstrates a high level of sophistication and maturity in contemporary cinema.

Both Todorovsky and Bodrov have taken their nineteenth-century literary texts, reshaped them, rethought them and reinvented them for the modern age. By way of contrast, Yuri Grymov's 1998 film of *MuMu*, based on the 1852 story by Ivan Turgenev, sets the narrative firmly within the milieu of nineteenth-century Russian serfdom, but adds modern motifs. Ostensibly the tale of Gerasim, a mute serf forced by his callous lady landowner to drown his beloved puppy (called Mu-mu, as it is the only oral sound Gerasim can produce), and thus an attack on the cruelties of serfdom, the film emphasises the sexual dissoluteness of the landed classes (masturbation, lesbianism and quirky cross-dressing). The director obviously wishes to merge the Russian literary heritage with the modern permissiveness so recently espoused by Russian directors. Yet despite the crudity and naturalism of the images (cucumbers, blood, sperm-like fluids slowly running down the wall, beheaded fish, lingering close-ups of raw meat), there is nothing fresh in the portrayal of the peasant masses as stupid and docile, and our knowledge of the iniquities of serfdom is not significantly enhanced.

These are undoubtedly traumatic times for Russian film-makers, given the collapse of state funding and the difficulties in getting projects off the ground. But change also throws up new challenges and new aesthetic possibilities. There are grounds for optimism: the quantity of films being made may have decreased, but the quality of some of those that are produced testifies to intelligence, boldness and wit. This, given that Russian film-making is only a few years out of the dark ages of totalitarian control, is remarkable in itself. Not only are directors prepared to rework and rethink the classical literary heritage, but they approach the original works in a fresh way that can both produce a new text and also occasion a radical rethink of the original. Furthermore, a rereading of the original can provide a direct relevance for the new post-Soviet age. Above all, these two films demonstrate that Russian film-makers, coming from a tradition that goes back as far as Eisenstein, can rely on aesthetic means in order to make a political point, and that there is a particularly Russian (both Soviet and post-Soviet) contribution to the art of cinematic adaptation.

Part IV

The Russian Idea for Contemporary Film-makers

12. Representation – Mimicry – Death: The Latest Films of Alexander Sokurov

Mikhail Iampolski

1

In 1995 Alexander Sokurov made *The Eastern Elegy* [Vostochnaia elegiia]. In 1996 he made two feature films: *Mother and Son* [Mat' i syn], and the short film *Robert. A Fortunate Life* [Rober. Schastlivaia zhizn']. The topic for this latter film had emerged from a project for a series of films about the Hermitage which was never completed. From the entire repertoire of world painting Sokurov chose the eighteenth-century French artist Hubert Robert.[1] The film begins with a direct reference to *The Eastern Elegy* in the frames shot in the No Theatre and contains echoes of *Mother and Son*. Although this commissioned film seems ephemeral, it is an important link in Sokurov's work in the mid-1990s; it is a kind of theoretical manifesto.

The desire to make a film about painting is justified in Sokurov's case by his continually growing interest in purely painterly issues, which comes to the forefront in *Whispering Pages* [Tikhie stranitsy, 1993], *The Stone* [Kamen', 1992], and *Mother and Son*. However, the choice of Robert is not trivial: Robert was a prolific landscape painter who specialised in painting ruins and imaginary architecture; as an artist he is of little general interest. Sokurov himself fully recognises the real standing of this master in the history of art and he characterises his place in cultural history as follows: 'How lucky he was! He was in tune with his time. He did not allow himself to take even one pace ahead, but proceeded, step by step, second by second.'

It is partly this convergence with his time that motivated the film-maker to entitle the film *A Fortunate Life*. I do not know to what extent Sokurov would apply such a description to his own career. To some extent, Robert is both Sokurov's fortunate antagonist and his fortunate double.

Why did he choose Robert?

Robert was neither the first nor the last painter of ruins. The first master of ruins was Giovanni Paolo Panini,[2] who was followed by his well-known pupil Giovanni-Niccolo Servandoni.[3] The most renowned painter of this group, Piranesi,[4] is undoubtedly of the greatest interest to us. During the twelve years Robert spent in Rome he worked with both Panini and Piranesi, who had one thing in common: a direct connection with the theatre and architecture. Servandoni was famous as a theatre designer, a follower of Bibiena, and also as an architect with whose name the first neo-classical monument in France is associated: the façade of the Saint-Sulpice Church in Paris. Piranesi was similarly trained as an architect and theatre designer.

This characteristic is essential for Sokurov, who connects the landscapes of Robert directly with the theatre, albeit with an exotic form: the No Theatre. Robert's landscapes are not really paintings at all; they are a theatrical representation of imagined constructions. They are not paintings in the sense that the canvas space is turned into a mere theatricalised surrogate for a three-dimensional space in which (and only in which) a phantom building exists. Admittedly, in the majority of cases this building is already a ruin when it appears on the canvas. In other words, at the moment when it is made real, it exists no longer as an ideal structure, but merely as the remnant of a vanished ideal.

Robert differed from Panini or Salvator Rosa in that his ruins were not merely an attribute of an ideal landscape but the dominant motif of his paintings. Robert's pictures were not so much landscapes with ruins as ruins in a landscape. The ruin literally jumps out of the canvas and into reality. Servandoni's emergence as a master of neo-classicist architecture reflects the literal transition of the ruin as a fragment of classical Roman construction into reality. Saint-Sulpice stands literally as a restoration in stone of what existed on the canvas as a mere theatrical attribute, a fragment of an ideal past.

It is this characteristic, the subsidiary role of the painterly dimension in relation to architecture, that brings the painting of ruins close to the art of cinema. Cinema space is also functional, and has meaning only when it embodies the location of all the action and the characters. Hence the suspicion which always surrounds any kind of cinematic pictorialism. The signifiers of cinematic space are 'transparent' (let us use this linguistic definition), they do not stop the spectator who is momentarily admitted to the objects and bodies arranged in this space. The same happens with the ruin in Robert: it is interesting only as long as it does not interfere with the self-representation of the object and the body, which are united in the architectural ruin.

Sokurov is aware of this characteristic of Robert's paintings but he plays upon it in a totally unexpected way. He departs radically from the standard model of filming paintings. In films about art, the painter's canvas is usually filmed in a way that creates the illusion of a penetration into the inner world of the canvas, that suggests its inhabitation from the inside. This characteristic was taken to almost absurd lengths by Akira Kurosawa in *Dreams* [Japan,

1990], where he literally penetrated the landscape of Van Gogh, transformed into a studio set. In the recent television series *Yo-Yo Ma Inspired by Bach*, a similar experiment was conducted with Piranesi's 'Carceri': the cellist was placed in a huge ruined dungeon copied from an engraving by Piranesi, which had been made three-dimensional with the help of computer graphics.

The penetration 'inside' the canvas, indicative of the subsidiary role of the painterly dimension in cinema, is usually based on a few simple principles. First, the camera is positioned at a perpendicular angle to the canvas, which is lit in such a way that the surface will not reflect and will thus be invisible. The painting is shot like a window, following the favoured model of linear perspective. Second, the frame or the edge of the canvas is never in the field of vision. The canvas is divided into fragments and significant details, which are linked to one another by the movement of the camera. A temporal dimension is thus imposed upon the canvas, and an intrusive narrativity turns the space of the painting into narrative space. As a result of such simple manipulations the painterly quality is moved into the shadow while the object itself acquires a self-sufficing significance.

Although Sokurov does not scorn such poetics, he places them in a completely different context. Robert's paintings are filmed inside the empty spaces of palace architecture, which no longer resemble museum space. Often, the pictures are not hung on the wall, not located on a surface, but are placed inside the architectural volume. Sokurov systematically films the pictures and the space surrounding them from a low angle, a device typical of Robert's painting itself; thus the viewer sees the impressive columns and the massive relief of the ceilings. Everything is designed in such a way that the camera does not lead the viewer inside the canvas, but instead leads the canvas out into the architectural space. In his own way, Sokurov is doing the same as Servandoni: the ruin seems to step outside the limits of the canvas into the surrounding volume and is restored to its ideal whole. Montage, camera movement, and the system of dissolves are structured so that they underline the unity of the columns both within the canvas and outside it, the movement of the architrave in the painting and that of the ceiling paintings in the three-dimensional palace. Moreover, Sokurov creates an amazing unity of tonality and colour between the architectural space and Robert's painting.

At a first glance, such an approach seems radically to contradict Robert's painterly quality, almost a shocking cinematographisation of the painting, which moves into the narrative space of cinema; but in reality, as is often the case with very radical experiments, Sokurov achieves the diametrically opposite effect. The representational space of Robert's paintings is not opened up, but closed; it becomes impenetrable, because Robert's paintings appear in Sokurov's film not as windows into the imagined world of an architectural Utopia, but as an object situated in space. Here it is, in front of us, with a heavy baroque frame, filmed from below with a wide-angle lens so that the edges of the canvas taper upwards, and merge visually with the columns of the museum architecture. Sokurov often films the paintings from a strange side angle that distorts the image and, above all, makes the shining surface of the canvas clearly visible.

In other words, Sokurov's 'architecturalisation' of painterly motifs goes so far that the picture, as a physical object, becomes a sort of architectural structure. In extremis, the picture itself is seen as a ruin. The nostalgic contemplation of the ruin inside Robert's paintings becomes partly equivalent to the contemplation of Robert's pictures today. Both refer to an irretrievably past age, and remind one of a lost classical harmony.

Sokurov plays upon the possibilities of entering the painterly space of Robert's canvases with the help of the strategy discussed above; at the same time he plays upon the complete closed structure of Robert's world. In one of Robert's landscapes he finds the figure of an artist, who is sitting on the ground with his back to a large architectural fragment, while drawing in his sketchbook the ruin of a magnificent colonnade. This probable self-portrait of Robert features several times in the film. The spectator may take the position of Robert's double, not in front of the ruin, but in front of Robert's picture which acts as a substitute for the ruin.

What does it mean: to contemplate a ruin? And why does this contemplation afford the viewer such pleasure – or good 'fortune', if we are to use a word which figures in the film's title.

A ruin is a strange object. On the one hand it seems to have no inner life; this is clearly visible in Robert's paintings, too. One's gaze passes straight through a ruin. Exposure and transparency are the particular qualities of a ruin. On the other hand, a ruin is a riddle, an allusion to something irretrievably lost, and hence incomprehensible, inscrutable. In Philippe Hamon's words: 'Representing the presence of an absence, embodying something virtually depleted of meaning, the ruin functions as a sort of negative punctuation of space, as an "objective riddle".'[5] Rilke also wrote about 'a secret through and through, on every spot, so that there is no need to hide it'.[6] This thought struck him in Karnak in Egypt with its endless colonnade. Something similar happens to the ruin which has its secret turned inside out.

The secret in question here is the secret of time.

Alois Riegl noted that some buildings bear in them what he calls the 'intentional commemorative value', in other words, they lay claim to eternity and independence from time.[7] In one way or another, the majority of man's creations form a challenge to time, which is expressed in smooth ideal surfaces, in the geometry of form, and so on. That is why architecture is so often incompatible with nature. In a ruin nature takes its revenge, writing the movement of time on to human creation and returning it to the forms of nature. Georg Simmel wrote: 'The natural process has coated the creation of man with a patina and covered its original surface, hiding it completely.'[8] The fascination of the ruin stems from the disintegration of artificial human form which returns to the architectural structure its harmonious unity with nature, a unity that it did not possess originally.

The work of time is expressed in the erosion of the surface, of the 'skin' which covers it.[9] The skin bearing the imprint of time, decay and death – this has occupied Sokurov for a long time. The skin becomes of particular significance after *The Second Circle* [Krug vtoroi, 1990] in which the contemplation of 'dead' texture, among others the skin of a dead man, occupies a central place. But in *Robert* the notion of skin is transferred from an object – the body inside the narrative space – on to the surface of the painter's canvas. Sokurov unexpectedly moves towards the layers of paint and shows them with stark magnification and from an angle which discloses a bumpy and completely unfigurative relief. The surface of the painting then emerges from an acute angle, covered with cracks and flutes. Off-screen the voice of the director explains: 'The body of Robert's painting. This is its skin, its living layer of skin. This body breathes and frequently falls ill.'

Thus the painting finally turns into a ruin, an object of self-representation. Sokurov invites us to see what, in effect, is not a matter of the viewer's perception. In doing so, he creates a highly significant opposition between the visible and the body, between appearance and essence. In this opposition the painted ruin with its harmonious aura belongs to the sphere of appearance, making invisible and shielding the 'body of the painting', its 'living layer of skin'.

Illness, time and disintegration as discovered by Sokurov on the surface of the canvas remind us that the cinematic image has no surface. The emulsion of the film cannot be regarded as the surface of the image. First, any scratches on it relate to the particular print, but do not affect the original. Second, they are projected on to the screen together with the photographic image and therefore are not separable from it in the same way that a layer of paint is separable from the space of its representation. The screen, after all, does not belong to the film, and bears no permanent traces of time.

Since cinema cannot normally reproduce the opposition 'appearance/body' which is so important for the film about Robert, Sokurov systematically gives meaning to this opposition in his films, beginning with *The Stone*, which is constructed as though the image had the surface of a painting. The imitation of surface in *The Stone* relies upon two main components: first, the heightened texture of the image, its systematic 'veiling' which creates the effect that many frames appear as though shot through a slightly clouded glass, i.e. they have an autonomous surface. Second, the strange angular displacement, the distortion of the image, imitating the view of the surface from an oblique angle. This unusual deformation is particularly striking because it introduces the same anamorphic effect as, for example, in Holbein's 'The Ambassadors'. In Holbein the anamorphosis of the skull may be deciphered by looking at the painting from an angle. But in real life we cannot look at a body from an angle and cannot imagine this body as anamorphic. Sokurov, however, works with the reality in front of the camera as though it were painted!

2

The analogy to be drawn between painting and a ruin is, of course, far from a complete one. The main difference lies in the fact that the traces of time are visible on the 'skin' of the ruin and act as a special object for contemplation. The same traces are invisible on the body of a picture, or at least they are not intended for contemplation. The surface of a painting and the surface of a ruin also differ in function.

The problems Sokurov scrutinises remind one of the long-standing discussion in American art criticism which began with Michael Fried's article 'Art and Objecthood' (1967). Fried, following Clement Greenberg, expressed the view that Modernist painting on the whole is oriented towards optical illusion while minimalism, which was popular at the time of publication of Fried's article (Fried calls it 'literalism') evidently rejects optical illusion for the sake of a direct presence of the object: 'objecthood'. Fried determined this 'objecthood' as a 'new theatricality':

> the literalist espousal of objecthood amounts to nothing other than a plea for a new genre of theater, and theater is now the negation of art. Literalist sensibility is theatrical because, to begin with, it is concerned with the actual circumstances in which the beholder encounters literalist work. Morris makes this explicit. Whereas in previous art 'what is to be had from the work is located strictly within [it]', the experience of literalist art is of an object in a *situation* – one that, virtually by definition, *includes the beholder*.[10]

Objecthood presupposes an emphasis on the material, on texture, on the 'skin' of the object, making its physical presence tactile and tangible. The object turns from an optical illusion into a theatrical property.

It is curious that Sokurov, who is unlikely to be familiar with Fried's theories, introduces theatre into his film about Robert: Japanese No Theatre, which he interprets from the outset as an 'optical' space, closed for the spectator, in which bodies and objects have no objecthood à la Fried. Sokurov even comments: 'The actors appear out of the mist and are weightless.' Through a fade-in, mist fuses the stage of Japanese theatre with the narrative space of Robert's paintings; neither is accessible to the spectator. Yet the museum colonnade in which the paintings are located unexpectedly acquires an almost theatrical quality, so that the actual painting in the frame is transformed into a theatrical object.

Fried thinks in categories of incompatible oppositions: either art and optic-ality, or object and theatricality. The sphere of objecthood is, above all, sculpture. For Fried, a painting cannot fully become an object, even when it possesses volume, as in Ronald Davis's work. Fried explains why objecthood is not fully achievable by painting: 'the fundamental difference between paintings and objects is that a painting is so to speak *all* surface, *nothing but* surface, whereas no ordinary object, however thin or flat can be described in those terms'.[11]

A painting has no physical thickness, no three-dimensionality, even when its surface is covered with a quasi-sculpted layer of paint. In an article about Larry Poons, Fried discusses his so-called elephant-skin pictures, where the surface feels sculpted rather than painted. Nevertheless, in Fried's view the colour and pigment which compose this relief enter into a battle with the texture and do not allow the picture to become exclusively an object.

Fried's views and the discussion on minimalism cast light on those aspects of Sokurov's work which go beyond film aesthetics and enter the sphere of visual arts.

In Sokurov's film Robert's paintings are only externally distant from Larry Poons's experiments with his 'elephant-skin' pictures. The paradox is that these pictures are objects in that their layers of paint are affected by traces of disease, death, disintegration, which are also the bearers of objecthood. It is obvious that only an object, and not an optical illusion, can be subject to disintegration and dying; only an object exists in a world vested with temporality (which is quite integral to theatre). But this 'skin' of the painting is always ready to disappear from the spectator's field of vision, in which optical illusion reigns. For Robert, the ruin dominates paradoxically in that world of illusion in which there is no time, no disintegration, no death; yet the ruin expresses disintegration, death, decay and temporality in its very essence.

The relationship between the physical, mortal objecthood of the painting as an object and the illusory ruin as a motif in painting constitutes the main problem for Sokurov. On a superficial level this problem may be expressed thus: the objecthood and decay of the ruin-painting must vanish in order to give an extra-temporal representation of the decay and objecthood of the ruin within the optical space of the picture. Cinema can facilitate the transition from objecthood to illusion by means of some specific representational strategies: camera angles, the distance and proximity of the camera and so on.

The difference between Sokurov and Fried lies in the fact that Sokurov does not oppose the objective to the optical as a radical, insoluble dichotomy. The ruin in optical space figures as the *self-representation* of the decay of the painting as an object. There is no inner clash between colour and relief, no inner conflict as in Fried. Sokurov thinks as if the relief vanished while representing its objecthood in the colour.

The situation is complicated by the fact that both ruins are linked by the theme of death. Death in the layer of paint is a slow development of disintegration, it is a process. Death in the painted ruin can only be represented, since the ruin no longer depends on the course of time and has successfully and definitively escaped from death.

The Russian Idea for Contemporary Film-makers

Robert. A Fortunate Life belongs to a number of films that Sokurov has made about death. This theme runs through many films, from his first – *The Lonely Voice of Man* [Odinokii golos cheloveka, 1978–87] where, incidentally, a ruin figures, to *Maria* [1978–88]. But as a focal point of film aesthetics the theme emerges after *The Second Circle*, which expresses the most hopeless and tragic view of the world for Sokurov. In subsequent films the theme remains constant, but is focused more distinctively on the opposition between death and its representation that is so characteristic of *Robert*; gradually, it appears in less hopeless tones. In *Mother and Son* the mother's slow death is set against the background of an extraordinarily beautiful image, reaching a peak of genuine cinematic pictorialism. This beauty, as far as I am aware, has provoked the most varied reactions from spectators and has been interpreted as a manifestation of aestheticism. In my view, it is possible to understand the meaning of this beauty in *Mother and Son* with the help of *Robert*, which provides a commentary on the feature film.

How does death in Sokurov destroy objecthood and turn it into representation? In order to explain this it is best to use an unusual example. In his classical essay on mimicry, Roger Caillois expressly discusses the strange mimetic transformation of a living insect into dead matter. He describes widely known cases of mimicry of insects posing as dead leaves, dry branches and so on; however, this does not end with the external similarity between the living and the dead organism. While engaging in mimicry, the insect merges with its environment, becomes invisible, dissolves in space. Caillois describes mimicry in terms of psychasthenia, a weakening of the ego and blurring of the borderlines between organism and environment; this he calls 'temptation by space'.

Mimicry is a state that alleviates the incompatibility of Fried's opposition between object and illusion, theatre and painting. Adorno wrote about the 'aversion to mimicry' as a reason for the emancipation of music and its approximation to a 'quasi-linguistic logic'. He interpreted Wagnerian theatricality as a 'regression to mimicry', i.e. as regression from the quasi-logical to the spatial-representational.[12] Caillois asserted that

> space is indissolubly perceived and represented. From this standpoint, it is a double dihedral changing at every moment in size and position: a *dihedral of action* whose horizontal plane is formed by the ground and the vertical plane by the man himself who walks and who, by the fact, carries the dihedral along with him; and a *dihedral of representation* determined by the same horizontal plane as the previous one (but represented and not perceived) intersected vertically at the distance where the object appears.[13]

The necessity of these two dihedrals is explained by the fact that they allow the blending of perceived and represented space. Psychasthenia weakens the ego, the subject no longer feels itself in space as something separate from it, it no longer feels the place in which it is inscribed, and seemingly moves into the space of the representation. Such, according to Caillois, is the mechanism of mimicry. Rosalind Krauss sums up the essence of the procedure thus: 'the distant object is no longer perceived in a tactile immediacy of the "toehold", but now, hovering on the horizon of experience, it can only, Caillois insists, be grasped as representation'.[14]

The psychasthenic dissolution in the representational layer occurs as a result of the 'subject's' loss of autonomy, of a clear understanding of its place as something separate from the environment. Of course, Caillois writes about insects, to which the term 'subject' can hardly be applied. I think, however, that his understanding of mimicry can be transferred from the world of insects to an object like the ruin. The ruin 'behaves' amazingly like a psychasthenic or an insect engaging in mimicry. I have already mentioned that an integral architectural structure does not usually merge with nature, but is separated from it. The ruin gradually returns to that environment to which the integral structure was opposed. It loses its autonomy, but at the same time gains some additional nostalgic, 'aesthetic' dimension, defining its distance and gradual transition into the representational.

It is of particular importance to note that this transition into the representational mode is connected with death. Death, inscribing itself on to the building, destroying its depth, turning it into 'skin all over', facilitates the transition of the ruin into the representational, and its loss of its 'place' in the *here-and-now*. Death engenders the aesthetic, it is an immediate condition of its emergence. While the object is alive it cannot transgress the boundary separating it from the surrounding space; it cannot become a dot of colour among other dots of colour.

Sokurov calls Robert's life a fortunate one, because his small double on the canvas for ever contemplates the ruin in that other world in which there is no death, but only its aesthetic representation. This representation cannot be understood merely as a false vision; it is a manifestation of the non-representable in the world of representation, of the directly tactile in the world of vision.

Sokurov introduces the painting on which the painter himself is shown in front of a ruin with a quotation from Dostoevsky, which stands as a kind of epigraph to the entire film:

Without noticing how it came about, I found myself in another land; everything was the same as in our country, but it all seemed to be radiant with triumph finally attained. Tall, beautiful trees stood in all the splendour of their blossom, and their countless leaves – I am sure of it – greeted me with their soft, endearing rustling, as if whispering words of love. At last I saw the people of this happy land. These people clung to me and caressed me. Every one of them was eager to soothe me. They did not question me about anything, but somehow they seemed to know everything already.

This 'other land' exists beyond life, its inhabitants live outside time, which

12a. Alexander Sokurov. *Mother and Son*. Mother (Gudrun Geier).

12b. Alexander Sokurov. *Mother and Son*. Landscape.

does not permit absolute knowledge. The people of this 'happy' land 'know everything already'. And the world of this happy, timeless knowledge is above all a beautiful, aesthetic world. It is the world of aesthetic eternity into which mortal reality turns.

In *Mother and Son* the tension between the textured, the tangible and the painterly reaches its limit. This tension had already featured in *Save and Protect* [Spasi i sokhrani, 1989] and, above all, in *The Stone*. But here the fantastic pictorial quality of the landscape is linked directly with the death of the mother whom the son carries into the space of nature. The film is literally the story of death as a transition from the corporal to the visual, as a growth of an aesthetic illusion from the process of dying. This illusion exists in the world outside time, it is immortal, it is simultaneously the illusion of immortality and therefore this film – despite its inner tragedy – is more optimistic overall than *The Second Circle*, with which it is linked by its subject matter.

The final part of *Mother and Son* is devoted to the eventual entry of the hero into the painterly landscape. The entire episode is built upon a principle established in *The Stone*: the deformation of landscape, treated as though it were condensed and stretched upwards. In addition, Sokurov also plays upon the relief of the landscape: the slopes of an abyss, of a hill, distorting space and allowing it to be 'shot from an angle'. The space appears as if filmed obliquely, just as the director filmed Robert's paintings obliquely. From this space 'perceived obliquely' he moves to the plane of representational illusion, when the hero becomes almost a dot of colour in a colourful pattern woven from light and shade. In this transition the haze of floating clouds plays an essential role, creating the sensation of some kind of transparent *surface* on the landscape. Sokurov's camera also captures a field of grass bending in waves under the strong wind; the texture here is rendered as a skin of transformations and transitions.

At the very end of the film, as in *Robert*, the image of death appears: the dead texture of the mother's hand which the son holds, discovering in his young and healthy body the invisible work of death: the furrows and deformations on an unnaturally extended neck. The body here undoubtedly resembles a ruin in Robert's painting.

3

The idea of death as dematerialisation is thousands of years old. The innovation of Sokurov lies in his reading of this dematerialisation as a transition to the representational, to visual illusion.

The Eastern Elegy is also devoted to the space of death. This film appears from the very beginning like a dream about the island of the dead; this, however, is not taken from European tradition (the Celts, Böcklin), but is a free stylisation of an archaic Japanese world mystically emerging from the mist. The narrator

The Russian Idea for Contemporary Film-makers

(Sokurov himself) appears at the beginning of the film as a silhouette against the background of the sea, on whose smooth surface the shape of an island appears through the mist. 'An island has emerged from the sea. And here am I on the island.'

Entering the space of death is a central motif of the film. And this process of entering is built along the model of the psychasthenic loss of the *here-and-now*. Sokurov's comments often address this theme: 'Where am I? In paradise? But then why am I so sad?' Or: 'What a strange dream. I don't remember where I come from. Where is my homeland? I don't remember.' Or: 'Is this my house or not?'

In *The Eastern Elegy* this entry into the other world has several particular features. Narrator Sokurov is shown exclusively as a dark silhouette. This silhouette, filmed against the light, turns into a shadow on the fine paper screen of a traditional Japanese house. The transition of the silhouette into a shadow is of great importance: it establishes the barely noticeable transformation of the silhouette of a three-dimensional body into a flat projection on to the screen. This is indeed the transition into the 'representational' which is shown simultaneously as a transition into the sphere of death and eternity, and as a transition from the three-dimensional world to a flat surface, a plane: 'The shadow forestalls ... The door is weightless like a sheet of paper.'

The souls of the dead, by contrast, have no silhouettes, their faces are out of focus, but are somewhat blurred and scarcely distinguishable spots which appear as if from the mist. One of the souls emerges almost imperceptibly in the dark corner of an empty room and talks about the mist, which is dispersing, allowing people to recognise one another. This reference to mist in the narrative of a figure who is almost conjured up from the mist reminds one of the duplication of the ruin in the film about Robert. The soul says: 'As is the custom, the one you long for and love emerges from the mist.'

The silhouette, the shadow and the misty spot are all interconnected as different stages of the transition from the world of objecthood to the optical world. This transition is presented as a gradual blurring of line and contour, the gradual dissolution of the body into an illusion. The mimetic disappearance is also linked with the collapse of the body's autonomy and, accordingly, of the contour.

It is obvious that in *The Eastern Elegy* Sokurov goes farther than in any of his other films in his negation of line. A large part of the image is out of focus, filmed through a cloudy haze or edited as a frame projected twice through the mist. In his negation of line Sokurov joins a respected tradition that begins with Leonardo, who recommended the use of chiaroscuro for the modelling of the body, avoiding clear outlines and replacing them by 'smoky boundaries'. Leonardo explained the impossibility of clear contours by the fact that 'the boundaries of these bodies are demarcated by their surfaces and the boundaries of surfaces are lines, which are not part of the extension of that surface nor of the air, in which such surfaces are clothed. Hence that which is not part of anything is invisible, as is proved in geometry.'[15]

Yet for Sokurov the most important device to blur contours derives from Vermeer of Delft, whom Salvador Dali called 'the artist of death'. Scholars have long remarked upon a strange peculiarity of Vermeer's painting: in the places where he needs to underline the contour, he completely destroys the detailed depiction of the background. Here, for example, in 'The Lacemaker' the threads which the girl holds in her left hand are drawn as fine lines behind which the vaguely outlined hand immersed in the shade completely disappears. Art historians have explained this peculiarity as the result of the use of a badly focused camera obscura. But, as Daniel Arasse has shown, Vermeer artificially reproduces the effect of a bad camera obscura. He fixes not what the eye perceives in nature, but what is visible in the camera, which produces a transition from objecthood to opticality.

In reality, destroying the differentiation of the background, he renders the background as background, that is, as a potential, undifferentiated totality of all possible figures. And in doing so, according to Arasse, he 'makes the background flow into the figure'.[16] As a result, this interaction, this interpenetration of background and figure, creates the effect of the emergence of the figure from the background, its gradual appearance from an undifferentiated potential. This is how Arasse defines the principle of Vermeer's painting:

> his pictures do not allow resolution by the viewer. The term resolution here must be understood in two senses, optical and logical: the painting resists both visual and conceptual resolution. It inserts a screen to preclude discriminated vision; not can it be resolved on the level of its contents. It does not permit elucidation, nor transformation into something other than a surface of colors present and representing something. The double barrier to 'resolution' assures Vermeer's painting its effect of presence 'between the seen and the unseen', to cite Vasari [...], the fiction of living.[17]

Of course, Sokurov's system does not copy that of Vermeer. In Vermeer the effect of presence and abundance is connected with a strange combination of resolution and diffuseness. In Sokurov this balance is destroyed in favour of imprecision. But nevertheless, the blocking of a clear vision in both artists serves to achieve the effect of emergence. The phrase already cited ('As is the custom, the one you long for and love emerges from the mist') must be understood in terms of *emergence*, the slow *appearance* from the undifferentiated. The difference between the system in *The Eastern Elegy* and in Vermeer lies in the fact that this emergence is never achieved through contour. The figure never emerges quite fully, as though it were moving all the time from non-existence towards presence; it is this *movement* towards presence which makes the *fixation* of meaning impossible.

In Sokurov this movement towards presence takes a paradoxical form,

The Russian Idea for Contemporary Film-makers

because it is connected with death and non-existence. The undefined bodies of those who have died, or rather the physical manifestations of their souls, emerge from the mist. The movement towards presence here can be linked to death, because it is a movement towards representation, transcending temporality.

Jean-Luc Nancy has demonstrated that *existence* is connected with *Being* as with *possible* existence. 'But', he remarks, 'the relation to the possible is that of (in)decision.'[18] Indecision always distinguishes the relation to the possible, which has not been realised. Nancy therefore points to the necessity of 'the decision of existence', which he connects to thought, and eventually to meaning.

For Sokurov the movement towards presence occurs paradoxically beyond the decision of existence. It remains in the sphere of the possible, which can never become real, and can never become existence in time: it is a movement towards presence in the sphere of death. Hence the insurmountable imprecision of the relationship between Sokurov's souls and the sphere of the possible. On a most obvious level this imprecision is expressed in the blurred contours, the indefinite outlines, but also in the diffuseness of the meaning.

We are accustomed to think of the sphere of representation as a sphere of meaning and relatively clear signs. The transition to the representational is usually understood as a transition to the area of the thinkable, the formulated and the imaginable. Sokurov's eternity, however, is devoid of such an optimistic precision. The representational here is the sphere of the potential, the sphere of Being.

In an essay about Abbas Kiarostami's film *And Life Goes On* [Iran, 1991], Nancy tried to analyse the film image not as projection or representation, but as 'the world beyond' (*le dehors du monde*), in which life goes on. Nancy considers the beginning of Kiarostami's film as emblematic: it deals with the consequences of an earthquake: 'The film begins slowly, it gradually discovers or rediscovers the possibility of the image which will initially […] consist of close-ups of ruins, lorries, abandoned objects, excavators, of dust and fragments of rock piled up on the road.'[19] Life gradually emerges from this chaos, which is its inverse side. For Nancy, this movement, this endless *glissement* of life in the film runs parallel to the imprecision of meaning, which he designates as 'signlessness'.

The image emerges from the ruins, from the chaos of death as the inverse side of life itself, and not its representation. In Sokurov something similar may be discovered, but in different terms. In *The Eastern Elegy* the representational quality itself is immersed in *glissement* and imprecision. The image (representation) appears really life-like, emerging from death as from the ruins.

4

What is the connection between the undefined body of death in *The Eastern Elegy* and the ruin in Robert's painting, which slips away from time and enters the sphere of the eternal and never-changing? They are connected by the undefined concept of resemblance.

Resemblance is one of the permanent motifs in Sokurov's work, clearly present already in *Anaesthesia Dolorosa* [Skorbnoe beschuvstvie, 1983–87]. Usually it takes the form either of a game of masks, or the use of models (smaller copies), as, for example, in *The Days of the Eclipse* [Dni zatmeniia, 1988] or *Save and Protect*. In *The Stone*, a turning-point in Sokurov's career, resemblance becomes one of the main themes of the film.[20] The dead Chekhov, as though coming alive again and returning after death to his house, gradually discovers in himself a resemblance with his own photos, that is with his own representation. In *The Stone* the motif of representational mimicry is conveyed most powerfully. But already in *The Second Circle* there is an episode that establishes an uncanny resemblance between the face of the dead father and that of the living son. In order to make this resemblance clearly discernible, the dead mask of the father is juxtaposed not with the cinematic image of the son's face, but with his hologram, i.e. with an immobile representation. Sokurov proceeds from the notion that resemblance can be realised and discovered only in the sphere of the image. Resemblance also relates to the sphere of 'thought', and therefore that of meanings.

Resemblance, however, is achieved by Sokurov not so much on the basis of the deadening within immobility, but rather by means of transformation of the form which arises as a consequence of death.

Space in cinema usually is described as existing before material objects like the space of the theatrical stage. Objects merely come to fill this space. The space is autonomous and not at all connected with the objects. In *The Eastern Elegy* there is no autonomous space; space emerges from some plastic 'khora' together with the bodies. 'Resemblance' is connected with the emerging space itself; it develops as the space of representation gradually takes shape.

In *Save and Protect* Emma Bovary is duplicated by a mask, which is an image of Emma, already touched by death. The mask is made from the face of the actress who plays Emma, and is an almost exact copy. Almost, but not quite. The mask has rougher, more deformed and immobile facial features. Death is not only the end of mobility, of *glissement* (to use Nancy's expression), but also a deformation. Death inscribes itself on to the face of the living as the efface-ment of fine nuances, the coarsening of features. A mask is always a rougher copy and is therefore associated with death: it is the mask of death. The coarsening features, the effacement of fine details, of nuances of individuality are also well revealed in the ruin, which destroys clear and filigree contours. The ruin, like the 'mask of death', is always characterised by a figurative, 'morphological exuberance', i.e. by a surplus of matter, a 'thumping out' of figuration, characteristic of 'any spot, any material chaos'.[21]

This 'morphological exuberance' ensures the *resemblance*, and it allows two forms to lose clarity of contour and to enter into a relationship of formal

The Russian Idea for Contemporary Film-makers

equivalence. Resemblance emanates from the ruin as does life, which is always richer and more excessive than any form. In *The Stone* Chekhov initially looks like a mask, from which 'resemblance' gradually emerges. The stone is partly a sign of that material, morphological exuberance that hides the form within itself.

The diffusion in space of the butterfly engaged in mimicry is as much an appearance of death as the dispersal of form. But even the transition of the picture (as an object that disintegrates) into representation, into the image of the ruin in *Robert*, is possible only because of morphological hypertrophy: the layer of paint which seems to have no material volume suddenly rears, cracks, deepens. Morphological expansion allows the painterly layer to discover the *resemblance* with the ruin.

Resemblance lies at the basis of ideas, of what Sokurov defines as 'fortunate life'. Robert himself survived at the time of the French Revolution because of an act of 'resemblance': a man with a similar surname was executed instead of him. Resemblance and death are inseparable.

In *The Eastern Elegy* 'morphological exuberance' is expressed in the blurredness of contours. The figures in the film emerge both as a potential, which has not yet decided to exist, and as figures, in which the potential for resemblance grows. The misty faces of the souls of the dead are juxtaposed in the film with insects (including the butterfly), and with ancient stone sculptures. These sculptures are anthropomorphic figures, marked by time and deprived of fine plastic working. They are half-figures, half-stones. I think that these rough statues in Sokurov carry some indefinite, 'swelling' 'resemblance'. They are like the souls of the dead in their lack of clarity and the 'morphological exuberance' of their features. In some respects they resemble the colossi, the rough stone statues which replaced the bodies of the dead in ancient Greece.[22]

Giorgio Agamben believes that the colossi were a material embodiment of 'that part of the person that is consecrated to death and that, insofar as it occupies the threshold between the two worlds, must be separated from the normal context of the living'.[23] Funerals, or the destruction of the sculpted double, were thus necessary actions to liberate man from the phantom of this intermediate life between two worlds. The intermediate, which has not yet 'decided to exist', distances itself due to 'resemblance' into the limbo of representation, the sphere of the image. It acquires 'resemblance' and enters the sphere of mimicry, where everything is 'resemblance' because of this distancing.

In Robert's painting, where the artist himself is represented with a sheet of paper in front of a ruin, a trebling of representation takes place: Robert's picture is itself represented as a ruin; the ruin is shown on the canvas; but this ruin composed by Robert is in turn fixed on the sheet of paper by Robert's double. It is true that the viewer does not see this third copy. The picture shows the transfer of the ruin into the sphere of representation as an eternal, never-ending process, symbolised by the whiteness of the paper. At the same time, the eternal – the ruin in the painting – never completes its transition into image. This paradoxical status of eternity – as something halted in the realisation of its potential – reflects the essence of Sokurov's film art of recent years. It is best expressed in the allegory of the ruin, in which death always appears as a halted mimetic transition into the imprecision of the surrounding space.

Despite all its idiosyncrasies, Sokurov's method forms part of a particular cultural tradition: the tradition of the dissemination of the aesthetic into the non-aesthetic spheres. The aestheticisation of the non-aesthetic is characteristic of classical Russian culture, but also of European Romanticism. In 1995 Sokurov defined the task of culture in this way: 'Only culture, only spirituality are capable of reconciling man with his inevitable departure into another world; and of preparing him to cross that boundary, as far as possible in an elevated spiritual and mental state. All my films are about that. I have no other song to sing.'[24] Art plays the role of religion, with which it is traditionally associated, but extends into the political sphere as, for example, in the documentary about the war in Tadzhikistan *Voices of the Soul* [Dukhovnye golosa].

The 'aesthetic' takes particular forms in Sokurov's work. It is generally beyond classical beauty, since it continually challenges form. The mimetic dissolution of the object in the space of representation simultaneously leads to the object's loss of form. In this sense, the ruin is an ideal object, since it becomes 'aesthetic' because of the loss of clarity of form. Aestheticisation in Sokurov is accompanied by a crisis of representativeness. Form is replaced by a constant process of growth and collapse.

This interpretation of space, this consistent rejection of classical Cartesian representation (which places everything in relation to the point of view of linear perspective that coincides with the point of location of the subject), is typical of Sokurov. Cartesian space is built on the opposition of subject and object. But mimetism, described by Caillois, above all casts doubt upon the autonomy of the subject, which dissolves in the space of representation.

Sokurov's space is a place for *glissement* and non-distinction between subject and object, thought and the external world. In this sense, Sokurov's aesthetic is close to the practice of European Romanticism, which also completely aestheticises the world and at the same time experiences the most acute crisis of representativeness.[25]

This position ultimately bears witness to the artist's unwillingness to be judged by the laws of art. His works are always situated, as it were, outside the sphere of *form*, and therefore outside the sphere of art. But they speak also of an unwillingness to be judged by the laws of politics, ethics or religion. The fruits of the artist's work are too openly aesthetic for such a judgement. This situation of the existence of a culture 'in limbo', considered by Kierkegaard in *Either/Or*, forms the dramatic essence of Sokurov's position in contemporary cinema.

13. The Meaning of Death: Kira Muratova's Cinema of the Absurd

Graham Roberts

> Tuzenbakh: 'Meaning? ... Look out there, it's snowing.
> What's the meaning of that?'
>
> Anton Chekhov, *The Three Sisters*, 1900

> Clov: 'I love order. It's my dream. A world where all would be silent and
> each thing in its last place, under the last dust.'
>
> Samuel Beckett, *Endgame*, 1958

Kira Muratova is without doubt one of Russia's most important and influential film directors alive today.[1] Since the release of her previously banned films in the late 1980s, she has increasingly attracted critical attention, both in Russia and in the West. At home and abroad, most scholars maintain that she is primarily interested in moral, social or spiritual issues.[2] The director herself, on the other hand, has described her early work as 'provincial melodrama',[3] and has gone so far as to characterise one recent picture, *Enthusiasms* [Uvlechen'ia, 1993], as 'superficial'.[4] Critical readings of Muratova's work to date – including the director's own pronouncements – raise more questions than they answer, however. Among the most important issues are the following: is there a common thread running through her apparently disparate work? Is she interested primarily in moral and social problems? What are the aesthetic principles underpinning her films? And what is her place in the context of Russian and European culture?

The aim of the present article is to go at least some way towards answering these questions, by analysing the key thematic and aesthetic aspects of Muratova's four most recent films, namely *Asthenic Syndrome* [Astenicheskii sindrom, 1991], *The Sentimental Policeman* [Chuvstvitel'nyi militsioner, 1992], *Enthusiasms*, and *Three Stories* [Tri istorii, 1997].[5] What these apparently disparate works have in common is, as I hope to show, a sense of the Absurd, the realisation that there are no longer any certainties, that human existence is chaotic and alienating, that all human effort is ultimately rendered meaningless by the inevitability of death, and that there is no possibility of transcendence.[6]

Asthenic Syndrome – apocalypse now

Nothing in Muratova's previous output, however stylistically innovative and ideologically heterodox, quite compares to *Asthenic Syndrome*. This, Muratova's last film before the break-up of the Soviet Union, has been described by one Soviet film critic as 'probably the most interesting and most profoundly sincere' film of Gorbachev's cultural thaw.[7] While there are those who would take issue with that particular judgement, there can be little doubt that *Asthenic Syndrome* paints a very bleak picture of the Soviet Union at the end of the 1980s, as a society on the brink of almost total political, social and moral anarchy.[8]

Asthenic Syndrome begins as a monochrome picture which focuses upon a woman called Natasha.[9] When her husband dies, Natasha is overcome with grief and suffers a breakdown. After the funeral, she wanders around town hurling abuse at everyone she meets. Unable to carry on, she resigns from her job as a doctor at the hospital, and subsequently sleeps with a drunk who propositions her, before suddenly kicking him out of bed. The end of this film, which lasts thirty-eight minutes, is not the end of *Asthenic Syndrome*, however. Muratova's film, now in colour, shows a Soviet film-house, where the audience have just been watching the same film about Natasha as the one we have just seen. One member of the audience (which collectively leaves, in obvious incomprehension at what they have just witnessed) is Nikolai, who becomes the main focus of the rest of the film.[10] Nikolai is in fact a highly ineffectual teacher of English who is regularly abused by his pupils (one of whom even gets into a fight with him during a class). He presents a stark contrast to Natasha, since he is permanently listless and constantly falling asleep as a consequence of the 'asthenic syndrome' from which he suffers (the first time we see him, at the end of the 'Natasha' film, he is already asleep).[11] This second, much longer, section of *Asthenic Syndrome* ends with Nikolai alone, abandoned by everyone he knows, asleep on the floor of an empty train as it rumbles through the metro.

Here and throughout the film, the viewer is presented with an almost apocalyptic sense of 'terminal' decline, both on a personal and on a social level. Images of moral breakdown abound, and include foul language, sexual promiscuity and violence. In one scene, Nikolai collapses on the floor of an underground station only to be ignored by scores of his fellow passengers, who simply walk past him. Humans are just as indifferent towards animals, as is suggested by one of the film's most harrowing scenes, which features images of stray dogs about to be put down.

In the chaotic and valueless society which Muratova depicts in *Asthenic*

Syndrome, there are now no words, no signs, no narratives which might be able to impose any order, any certainty, any Truth. Indeed, this society itself is presented by the director as an unstructured, centreless mass of disconnected, fragmentary, already-quoted signs and discourses, whose proliferation virtually obliterates any 'plot' in the conventional, teleological sense. At one moment during the early part of the 'Natasha' film, for example, the frame becomes filled with photographs – and particularly photographs of Natasha's husband – over which the camera lingers for an inordinate length of time. In a similar vein, the 'Nikolai' film contains countless snatched images of words and narratives which, since they are decontextualised, inevitably take on a different meaning. These include: the stream-of-consciousness monologue which Nikolai delivers while alone in a classroom and surrounded by countless busts of Lenin; the propaganda concerning the free and comprehensive nature of the Soviet education system, which Nikolai's pupils recite off by heart both in English and in Russian; and the 'Marseillaise' and the 'Internationale' which Nikolai's colleagues hum in the staffroom. Most curious of all are the stories/speeches articulated (all at once) by three patients at the mental institution in which Nikolai finds himself towards the end of the film: one talks about having a snake inside his body,[12] another talks as if delivering a lecture to young drug addicts, while a third explains the importance of choosing appropriate colours when painting.

All these different discourses (to which one might add a woman's 'masculine' swearing, 'Fuck your mother' [*eb tvoiu mat'*] in the penultimate scene) play a crucial role in evoking a fragmentary, centreless and directionless world, a place where all truths, all ideologies are relative, and there are no longer any absolute certainties. One is left at the end of *Asthenic Syndrome* with the overwhelming impression that, to paraphrase another master of the End, Samuel Beckett, we must go on speaking, even though we have nothing more to say.[13]

Asthenic Syndrome does not just tell us, however, that the late USSR is close to anarchy. It also reminds us, time and again, that life is rendered meaningless and absurd by the inevitability of death. This is the universal truth at the heart of the film. Death is most conspicuous in the opening scenes at the cemetery, and in the burial of Natasha's husband (whose corpse we are shown as it lies in an open coffin). This is then augmented by the countless photographs of those buried at the cemetery, which fill the screen for a time, and the photographs of Natasha's husband, which she contemplates when she gets back to her flat. The idea of death is also suggested at the very end of the film, with the image of Nikolai alone and spread-eagled on the floor of the railway carriage as it hurtles through the underground system. Although only sleeping he nevertheless lies in cruciform position. In this way he unwittingly becomes a Christ figure – but this is a Christ who offers no salvation, not even transcendence, simply the prospect of eternal semi-existence neither alive nor dead.

The myths of redemption peddled by Dostoevsky and Tolstoi (to whom three old women refer in the opening shot) are revealed for what they are – lies.[14] The world inhabited by Natasha and Nikolai is truly Absurd in the sense in which Eugène Ionesco described it in 1957: 'Absurd is that which is devoid of purpose ... Cut off from his religious, metaphysical, and transcendental roots, man is lost; all his actions become senseless, absurd, useless.'[15]

The Sentimental Policeman – law and disorder

By comparison with *Asthenic Syndrome*, the plot of *The Sentimental Policeman*, a French–Ukrainian co-production which appeared in 1992, is limpidity itself. Tolia Kiriliuk, a policeman, discovers a baby girl lying in a cabbage patch.[16] He has her christened Natasha before taking her to an orphanage. He and his wife Klara (herself an orphan) eventually decide to adopt the girl. They are prevented from doing so, however, by the staff at the orphanage, who hand her over instead to a woman named Elena Zakharova (the doctor who initially examined Natasha when Tolia found her). Determined to adopt Natasha, Tolia and Klara take their case to court, only to lose out to Zakharova, who is told she can keep the child. As the two of them walk along the street after the court hearing, Tolia muses on the nature of love, and Klara tells her husband that she is pregnant.

In a number of ways this film echoes *Asthenic Syndrome*.[17] Most important, perhaps, is the theme of social disorder. This is first evoked early in the film, when, as Tolia walks home after finding Natasha, he stumbles across a group of men who are hurling abuse at each other while out walking their dogs. In the next scene, which takes place in the police station, two policemen laugh uncontrollably while discussing the gruesome details of a murder. As in the earlier film, here too we are shown humankind's cruelty to animals. In one particular scene, Muratova's camera suddenly and unexpectedly focuses on a television screen, on which we see images of stray dogs and cats being rounded up by the city pound.

These themes undoubtedly provide a link with *Asthenic Syndrome*. In many ways, however, *The Sentimental Policeman* represents a significant transition from its predecessor. There is less reference to contemporary social and political realia, for example. Another important difference is that the comic tone is much more sustained in *The Sentimental Policeman*. This is especially true of the courtroom sequence towards the end of the film. The judge gets Tolia's name wrong, and then appears to lose all interest in the proceedings, until he is reminded of what is going on by his deeply embarrassed deputy, who apologises for him. When Tolia is called to the stand, he simply gets up, walks to the other side of the room, returns to his seat and sits down again. Before the judge retires to consider his verdict, he asks Tolia disarmingly: 'Why don't you simply have a child of your own? It's so simple and so nice.' (It is shortly after this scene that Klara announces that she is expecting a baby.) To cap it all, Muratova even treats us to something of a *deus ex machina*, as if parodying the contrived plots of canonical Soviet cinema: out of the blue Zakharova's adopted son turns up, thereby confirming her credentials as a worthy adoptive mother. While undoubtedly constituting a satirical sketch on some of the worst foibles of the Soviet legal system[18] (although released in 1992, the film was shot in 1991), this entire scene also contributes significantly to the comic ambience which in turn underpins the Absurd in this film.

The Absurd in *The Sentimental Policeman* goes much deeper than courtroom farce, however. Muratova creates a sense of the Absurd by means of two closely related themes. The first is human solitude and alienation (the individual is cut off from other individuals). The second concerns the arbitrary nature of chance and fate (the individual is cut off from the world).[19] A clear indication of how alienated people are from each other is given by the difficulties they experience when communicating. Whereas in *Asthenic Syndrome* Muratova presents us with a plethora of *decontextualised* discourses, all struggling for supremacy, in this, her next film, discourse is as it were *disconnected*.[20] In one early scene a man turns up at the police station, explains to Tolia that his mother won't let him back into the house after 11 p.m., and pleads to be allowed to sleep in one of the police cells. Despite the fact that this man repeats his request several times over, and in a truly pathetic tone of voice, Tolia remains so indifferent that he does not even answer. Tolia and Klara themselves constitute an interesting illustration of the problems of communication. The way they are shown getting up every morning (in their sparsely furnished, brightly-lit flat), mechanically doing the same things at the same time, makes them appear especially close. Yet they spend so little time actually talking to each other. When Tolia does speak to Klara, he reveals that he doesn't even know the colour of her eyes. There is something highly unnatural about the way these two people communicate; no wonder Klara becomes exasperated at one point and shouts at her husband for never arguing with her! Tolia and Klara are not alone in experiencing problems communicating. When the doctor is unexpectedly reunited with her adopted son, she tells him, 'When you were small you used to say you liked our cat because it let you stroke it', whereupon he corrects her: he used to say he liked their cat 'because it looked like a tiger cub'. If some people are poor listeners, others have great difficulty expressing themselves in language. The old nurse who announces to Tolia and Klara that Natasha has already been adopted has trouble pronouncing the word meaning 'has been adopted'. She reads the word in a variety of morphological forms ('usynovliaema', 'usynovli*o*na', 'usynov-liaetsia', 'usynovlen*a*'), even though she is ostensibly reading from a book (she also uses the verb reserved for adopting a male child, instead of the word 'udocherit'', which means 'to adopt a daughter', and which would thus have been appropriate here).

At other times in this film, language becomes mechanical, depersonalised.

The first time we see this occurs during the dog-owners' dispute. One after the other, the residents who poke their heads out of their windows say exactly the same thing: 'Take those dogs away, they're preventing me from sleeping.' In a later scene, when Tolia returns to the orphanage in an effort to see Natasha again, he is confronted by two nurses who both tell him, using identical language and in virtually synchronised speech, that he cannot come in because one of the boys has scarlet fever and a quarantine has been imposed.

Elsewhere, characters recite whole monologues which by their length (if not their subject matter) are inappropriate to the context in which they are delivered. When Tolia and Klara confront the nurse who was on duty the day that Natasha was (purportedly) handed over to Zakharova, the nurse responds by telling a story. Her tale – which lasts more than five minutes – describes a forest, situated next to a cemetery, which she visited first as a child, and then as a young woman, and in particular the difficulty which the snowdrops that grow there have of breaking through the dead leaves and snow and blooming in the open air. While her story is not entirely irrelevant to the situation, since she compares the force with which a snowdrop pushes out from under the snow to the energy with which a child leaves its mother's womb, she can hardly be said to have answered Tolia's question as to why Natasha has been given away.

As this last example illustrates, language in *The Sentimental Policeman* serves not to bring individuals closer together, but rather to underscore the unbridgeable gulf that exists between them. If people are isolated from each other, they are also profoundly alienated from the world in which they live, a world whose workings remain a complete mystery to them. Prompted by his 'chance' find of Natasha (he calls this a meeting [*vstrecha*] rather than a find), Tolia engages one morning in the following dialogue with his wife:

Tolia: Do you remember how we met for the first time?
Klara: On the dance floor?
Tolia: That wasn't the first time, but the second. That meeting was prearranged. What about the first time we met? How did we meet?
Klara: In the student hostel.
Tolia: I didn't say where, I said how?
Klara: What do you mean, how?
Tolia: Was it prearranged? Did we know about it?
Klara: It was chance.
Tolia: So we might not have met then?
Klara: No, that's not possible.
Tolia: But you just said it was chance.
Klara: It was chance.
Tolia: So then we might not have met at all?
Klara: No, that's not possible.
Tolia: But it was pure chance that we met?
Klara: It was chance.

The Russian Idea for Contemporary Film-makers

Tolia: So we mightn't have met at all?
Klara: No, that's not possible.
Tolia: But it was chance that we met?
Klara: It was chance.
Tolia: But we mightn't have met at all?
Klara: That's not possible.
Tolia: Bu-u-ut we met by chance?
Klara: By chance. You might have popped into the student hostel on another occasion.
Tolia: I never went there either before or after we met.
Klara: I ...

As well as demonstrating humankind's inability to comprehend the workings of chance (let alone articulate it in language), this brief exchange also serves as a further reminder of the problems humans have in communicating, even with those closest to them. The important points to note here are: first, Klara fails to understand Tolia's question (she does not even look at him during the entire exchange); second, their respective tones of voice indicate that while Tolia feels great anxiety at the implications of his question, Klara feels nothing but indifference; third, the repetition of words and phrases reinforces Tolia's sense of desperation; and fourth, the conversation comes to an abrupt end, without a solution to the problem being reached.

For Tolia, the real significance of the notion of fate is that it means that people can be held responsible for their actions. As he says to another man (another policeman!) who claims (rather like Klara) that it was pure chance that he found Natasha: 'So according to that way of thinking all children are born by chance, and everything is the product of chance, and nobody is responsible for anything and nobody is guilty of anything and we have no obligations and consequently none of this holds the slightest interest for me and life is boring, and it's as if I were nobody at all.' This short speech encapsulates the existential dilemma that weighs so heavily on Tolia's shoulders once he has found Natasha – a dilemma which goes right to the heart of the Absurd; if there is no order, then there is no meaning, and our lives have no significance, we are nobody.

Ultimately, however, Muratova's film fails to answer Tolia's question. Despite Tolia's insistence that his meeting with Natasha was preordained (and he certainly appears to have *known* he was going to find her, laying his ear to the ground as if trying to pick up her crying), we are left unsure whether our lives are ruled by fate or blind chance, order or chaos. This is the significance of the judge's verdict, since it shows that whatever he may believe, Tolia was *not* fated to bring up Natasha. Indeed, the judge functions primarily as a foil to Tolia's belief in fate (and thereby in an ultimate meaning to life). As he says to Tolia at one point during the hearing: 'I like listening to you. At least it takes my mind off the various unpleasant, undesirable, *absurd* [*nelepykh*] and incomprehensible details of life' (my emphasis). From this perspective, *The Sentimental Policeman* is about one man's struggle against the Absurdity (or perhaps the absurd*ities*) of life. Natasha, then, might be said to embody Tolia's refusal to accept that life is absurd, meaningless.[21] So does the fact that he and Klara lose Natasha make this refusal a futile gesture? The fact that they are soon to have a baby of their own suggests not. It also makes *The Sentimental Policeman* the least pessimistic of all Muratova's films discussed here.[22] Unlike *Asthenic Syndrome* it begins and ends with birth, rather than death (life, however fragile, also triumphs over death in the nurse's monologue). Death rears its head once again, however, in Muratova's next film, *Enthusiasms*. It does so, moreover, in the most unexpected ways.

Enthusiasms – a race against time

Whereas *Asthenic Syndrome* generated a great deal of critical admiration for Muratova, *The Sentimental Policeman* was met largely with indifference. *Enthusiasms*, on the other hand, mostly caused bewilderment. Given the subject matter of this film (the world of horse racing), and the virtually total absence of any story line (even when compared to the earlier film), such a reaction is hardly surprising. At an international film festival where *Enthusiasms* was shown in 1994, Muratova urged viewers to take the film at face value, adding that any attempt to analyse it would be a waste of time.[23] The 'action' (for want of a better word) takes place between the gardens of a hospital, a hippodrome and a circus. Among the characters who participate in the film are a nurse, Lilia, who has a habit of telling stories (played by Renata Litvinova, who wrote much of the script), her female companion, a circus performer who spends much of the film in a ballerina's tutu, and trainers and jockeys (including one jockey who has recently had a bad accident, and is now wheelchair-bound, with most of his body in plaster). As *Asthenic Syndrome*, *Enthusiasms* contains fragments of a number of different 'plots'. The injured jockey longs to get back on a horse, for example, while there is a love affair between the circus performer and another of the jockeys. The film contains a number of scenes of horse racing and training, with jockeys chatting among themselves, trainers shouting abuse or encouragement at jockeys, and trainers arguing with each other. For most of the film Muratova invites us either to listen to the nurse's stories (she has a particularly captivating voice) or simply to admire the grace and poise of the racehorses (whether at full gallop or resting in their stables). The horses' beauty is matched by the splendour of the film's score, which contains quotations from numerous works by Beethoven (without the incongruity prevalent at the start of *Asthenic Syndrome*, with Mozart as the backing to a scene where workmen torment a cat).

Muratova has said of *Enthusiasms* that 'this is a superficial film. [...] it is a film about the surface of things. But it is a very deep film about the surface.'[24] Yet this is precisely what makes the film worth analysing. The first thing to

The Russian Idea for Contemporary Film-makers

13. Kira Muratova. *Enthusiasms.*

remark is that *Enthusiasms* seems so different from Muratova's preceding two films. The rural, not to say bucolic ambience of *Enthusiasms* is in direct contrast to the oppressively urban setting of *Asthenic Syndrome* and *The Sentimental Policeman*. References to contemporary social and political reality, so abundant in the earlier films (albeit less so in *The Sentimental Policeman*), are conspicuous by their absence in *Enthusiasms*. In contrast to the nervous conditions from which Natasha, Nikolai, Tolia and Klara all suffer (in varying degrees), the characters in *Enthusiasms* display a remarkable *joie de vivre* (in truth, it should be noted that very little happens which might threaten their physical and psychological well-being). Gone too is the embedded structure of *Asthenic Syndrome* with its film-within-a-film.

In many ways, however, *Enthusiasms* is a continuation and intensification of the themes, aesthetic devices and other features to be found both in *Asthenic Syndrome* and in *The Sentimental Policeman*. For example, each of these films contains scenes involving characters who are episodic but nevertheless significant. In all three films, characters repeat phrases or snatches of dialogue for no apparent reason. Each film contains visual incongruity: in *Asthenic Syndrome* the camera lingers an inordinate length of time on a plastic shopping bag with a woman's face on it; *The Sentimental Policeman* opens with a shot of a policeman performing what resembles a ballet in a cabbage patch; while at one moment in *Enthusiasms*, the nurse appears standing against the mountains and wearing a medieval knight's helmet. At times in *Enthusiasms*, this visual incongruity verges on the surreal.[25] The image of the ballerina walking around a stable dressed in nothing but a tutu is a good example of this.

Another feature which connects all three pictures is the fact that characters are prone to telling impromptu stories which have no apparent connection to the rest of the film. We have already seen how, in *Asthenic Syndrome*, Nikolai lands himself in the ward of a mental hospital, surrounded by unidentified patients who spend their time reciting monologues. In *The Sentimental Policeman* extended monologues are delivered by the farmer on whose land Natasha is found, and by a woman in the courtroom, as well as by the nurse in the orphanage. In *Enthusiasms*, it is another nurse who delights in the telling of seemingly 'irrelevant' stories. At one moment, for example, she delivers a monologue about the 'peak of beauty', explaining how each human being always experiences a time in their life when they are at their most beautiful, but that this moment can only ever be transitory. As she puts it: 'Some people are given minutes, others just instants, while with others beauty can seem to last for months. All the time beauty is at its peak. And then it disappears somewhere. Others have a beautiful face for years. How can I explain it? But beauty always rushes towards the finale, towards its own self-destruction.'[26] She recalls an acquaintance, one Sasha Milashevsky, to whom this happened, before mentioning another friend who phoned her from somewhere in the East to warn her to beware 'beautiful, dangerous situations', and then concludes by quoting the song, 'Diamonds are a Girl's Best Friend'. Another monologue which the nurse recites concerns the fate of a former friend of hers, a certain Rita Goethe. When Rita died, she informs us, the pathologist responsible for examining her body threw a cigarette end into her stomach before sewing her up again.[27] In an even more bizarre twist, she concludes by revealing how she and her friend wanted to buy Rita a white burial dress, but instead purchased a red carp.

What these monologues suggest (and this is what more than anything else connects *Enthusiasms* with *Asthenic Syndrome*) is that death and its inevitability makes life an absurdity, a joke as sick as the pathologist's gesture, as senseless as the purchase of a red carp for a funeral. It is no coincidence that the theme of death is introduced after barely five minutes, when the nurse, in her first appearance, describes the physical details of autopsies in the hospital morgue. As if fully cognisant of death and its existential ramifications, the characters of *Enthusiasms* try persistently – passionately, even – to give life meaning, to fill in the void of existence. Ultimately, however, their 'enthusiasms' [*uvlechen'ia*] are nothing more than 'diversions' or 'distractions' [*razvlechen'ia*] – efforts to evade the Absurd, as futile as any attempt to stay beautiful for ever.[28] As in *Asthenic Syndrome*, to attempt to escape from the human condition is highly dangerous, as the jockey temporarily paralysed by plaster has found to his cost.

Throughout *Enthusiasms*, incidences of incongruity and irrelevance reinforce this sense of the absurdity of life. There are instances of visual incongruity, some of which have already been mentioned. To these one might add the

The Russian Idea for Contemporary Film-makers

'photographs' of centaurs (mythical creatures who possessed a man's head, trunk and arms, and a horse's body and legs) that are produced at various moments throughout the film by one of the peripheral characters, a photographer. There is also aural incongruity: at one point, the nurse walks through a field, but we hear the sound of bombs dropping and weapons firing, as if she were in the middle of a battlefield. There is, finally, incongruity between what a character says or wants, and what they do. When the nurse and the ballerina visit a stable, they are asked to leave. The nurse says, 'I want to go away, I shall go away', but she stays. This is an excellent example of the divorce between will and psyche so prevalent in Absurdist fiction, where the split within the individual implies the absence of a stable identity, and reinforces the divorce between the individual and the world (a divorce already keenly felt by the central characters of Muratova's two preceding films).[29] Ultimately, everything is futile; 'Everything's the same, whether you live or die', as one character laments. Attempting hopelessly to give meaning to our stubbornly meaningless lives, we resemble those stable hands who try so long and hard to get the horses to go into the stalls at the start of the race, with varying degrees of success. Or again, we are like the cats and dogs who are shown in the film being trained to run endlessly and aimlessly around a circus ring. As another character puts it, the point is not the race, but rather to 'keep on moving'.

Enthusiasms is indeed, as Muratova herself put it, a 'deep film about the surface of things'. On the surface, it appears to be a film about the fulfilment of desires.[30] When read 'against the grain', however, and particularly when placed alongside *Asthenic Syndrome* and *The Sentimental Policeman*, it emerges as a deceptively disturbing and sinister picture about that archetypally Absurdist dilemma – the meaninglessness of life, the inevitability of death, and the impossibility of transcendence (since all we have is the 'surface' of things). All these characters are engaged in a struggle with their own mortality, a race against time – hence the rows of clocks that the camera shows us just before the start of one of the races. It is a race which they cannot hope to win, however; indeed, the nurse's monologues function primarily as ironic commentaries on the other characters' enthusiasms, underscoring their futility.

Three Stories – a few short films about killing

Muratova's characters employ a range of strategies in order to escape the Absurd. In *Asthenic Syndrome* they tell stories, in *The Sentimental Policeman* they go looking for babies in cabbage patches, while in *Enthusiasms* they ride horses. In *Three Stories*, on the other hand, they kill other people. To summarise the plot(s) of *Three Stories* is a good deal easier than with *Enthusiasms*.[31] As its title suggests, the film is structured as a trilogy of apparently independent scenarios, which take place in different locations and involve different characters. In the first film, entitled 'Boiler House No. 6' ['Kotel'naia No. 6'], a man named

Evgeni (Zhenia), played by Sergei Makovetsky, kills a young female neighbour after an argument over a bar of soap. Muratova shows him taking the body to an old acquaintance who works as a stoker in a boiler house at the zoo, whom he asks to burn the body. The stoker, however, refuses, and this story ends with him desperately afraid that he will be unable to keep his friend's terrible secret. This film lasts just over 22 minutes. The second 'volet' of this triptych, entitled 'Ophelia' ['Ofelia'] is more than twice as long (just over 54 minutes). The eponymous heroine, who calls herself Ophelia in honour of Polonius's daughter from Shakespeare's *Hamlet*, works as a medical secretary at a maternity hospital (this story is written by Renata Litvinova, who played the nurse in *Enthusiasms*, and who stars as the secretary here). Adopted as a child (a detail which echoes the plot of *The Sentimental Policeman*), she bears a grudge against women who impose a similar fate on their offspring by giving them away. She kills one woman, Tania, after she gives up her child for adoption, before tracking down an older woman who may have been her own mother and murdering her too. In between the two murders she sleeps with a doctor who works with her at the hospital. After the allegro of the first story and the scherzo of the second, the tale which closes Muratova's film feels more like an adagio. In this story, entitled 'Death and the Maiden' ['Devochka i smert''], a young girl kills the old man (Oleg Tabakov) who is looking after her while her mother is at work by putting rat poison in the water which he drinks.

Each of the stories is autonomous, performed in a particular 'key': first incongruity and superfluousness, second theatricality, and third power and violence. Let us begin by looking at the first story. The incongruity of the boiler house itself (hardly the first thing which comes to mind when one thinks of a zoo) is reinforced by the figure of the stoker, a small, squat man named Gennadi who looks oriental, wears a 'Rambo' T-shirt, speaks with a strong Ukrainian accent and spends more time declaiming the poetry he writes than stoking the boiler (he is played by the same actor, Leonid Kushnir, who played the role of the incongruous-looking judge in *The Sentimental Policeman*). The contrast between Gennadi's pretentiously grandiose verse, an amalgam of Romantic, Futurist and Symbolist clichés, and the prosaic nature of his physical surroundings (the boiler house) is particularly marked (a similar contrast occurs when Gennadi discovers the young woman's corpse, to which he responds, 'How horrible ... I'm a poet'). Zhenia also appears out of place, not just in the boiler house where he insists on wearing his hat, coat and scarf despite the heat, but outside in the zoo, lugging around the wardrobe containing the dead woman's body.[32] It should be added that the immediate reason why Zhenia slit his neighbour's throat – an argument over a bar of soap – is perhaps the most incongruous feature of all.[33]

The theme of incongruity is reinforced when about one-third of the way through the story a man steps suddenly into the boiler house from another room. This, as Gennadi explains, is one of his relatives, a male prostitute

14a. Kira Muratova. *Three Stories*. Ophelia (Renata Litvnova).

14b. Kira Muratova. *Three Stories*. Zhenia (Sergei Makovetski) in 'Boiler House No. 6'.

named Veniamin who owes him money; he lives in the shower room adjacent to the boiler house, and uses it as a brothel.[34] Fat, bald, camp and quite grotesque, he reappears from time to time dressed in nothing but a leather thong, a long coat and laurel leaves on his head, and sings operatic arias. These scenes are so bizarre as to create the same kind of 'surrealist' ambience found at times in *Enthusiasms* and indeed earlier works by Muratova.[35]

The whole plot of the second story, 'Ophelia', is built on and around the kind of incongruities which abound in 'Boiler House No. 6'. For example, there is the fact that a murderous woman lands a job in a maternity ward, and the narrative juxtaposition of acts of potential life-giving (sex) and actual life-taking (murder). In a similar vein, there is also the ironic distinction between Shakespeare's Ophelia, a pure, innocent maiden who suffers death by drowning (her fate is mentioned several times in the film), and Muratova's anti-heroine of the same name, who is anything but innocent, and who actually kills someone by pushing her off a pier.

The key to this, the film's second story, is not so much incongruity, however, as a self-conscious, profoundly anti-realist theatricality. This aesthetic is established right from the opening shot, with its artificially geometrical *mise-en-scène*. Ophelia, or Ofa as she is called, is seen standing on a stairway in the hospital, in pristine white uniform. She puts her mask on and turns to walk up the stairs, just as a crowd of medics, each wearing identical white uniforms, walk past her down the stairs, each taking their masks off. The anti-realist atmosphere is maintained in the next scene, in which Ofa goes to one of the wards to see Tania, to check that she has not decided to give her new-born baby up for adoption. The bizarre feel of this scene comes partly from Ofa's habit of repeating what she says ('Tania, Tania, Tania, Tanechka', or 'ne molchi, ne molchi', for example), and partly from Tania's reaction (she is silent throughout and adopts the air of a simpleton in a manner reminiscent of a circus clown). The next four scenes all depict dialogues between Ofa and the doctor (Ivan Okhlobystin) who is in love with her, and each of them is shot as a highly theatrical and self-conscious tableau. At first we see them in a corridor, then at the top of the stairs in front of a picture of the madonna and child (!), then by a wall covered with pictures of medical instruments, and finally by another wall on which hang anatomical representations of the human head. Their behaviour is stylised throughout: *he* smokes a pipe in an affected way rather like Sherlock Holmes and speaks in an artificially high tone of voice, almost in verse; *she* on the other hand continues her habit of repeating certain phrases ('siuda idut, idut siuda'), and plays the stereotypical role of a cold, unfeeling woman as she tells him in measured, almost recited tones: '[She:] I came to see you. [He:] Well? [She:] I've seen you. Now I'm off. Let go of me, doctor.'

This self-conscious, anti-realist aesthetic, which is present more or less throughout 'Ophelia', is enhanced by the story's intertextuality. Most obvious are the references to Ofa's namesake from Shakespeare's *Hamlet*. When Ofa

The Russian Idea for Contemporary Film-makers

finally confronts her 'mother', for instance, she finds her reading about Ophelia, whom she describes as her favourite literary character. There are also allusions to other films and film genres. For example, the film's constant connections between sex and death (Ofa kills Tania with a stocking, crouching over her body in a sexually suggestive manner, and then goes to have sex with the doctor) puts one in mind of the work of Spanish director Pedro Almodovar (at one moment Muratova shows us Tania crouching down and urinating, in what may be a visual reference to a specific scene from Almodovar's *Tie Me Up! Tie Me Down!* [Atame, Spain, 1990]). When Ofa first goes to see the woman who might be her mother, her mackintosh and thick red lipstick, and her adroit use of her pocket mirror to catch a glimpse of the woman's face through the window, all combine to give her an aura of a *film noir* heroine.[36] Alongside these intertextual allusions, the 'Ophelia' story also contains embedded within it actual representations of visual art.[37] The room where Ofa and the doctor sleep together is in fact a studio which belongs to an artist friend of the doctor's. At the beginning of the scene which takes place here the spectator is shown first a close-up of Ofa's finger as she traces the swirls on a marble plinth, and then a whole series of paintings, most of which are either abstract art, naïve art or folk art.[38]

The dominant mode of 'Ophelia', then, is an anti-realist theatricality, characterised by much textual and intertextual play. On its own, of course, such an aesthetic does not suffice to make *Three Stories* an 'Absurdist' film. Rather it functions to underline the divorce between Muratova's filmic text and the world to which it purports to refer. As such, it buttresses the film's Absurdist theme of human alienation, both from the world and from other humans (a theme which is now treated in a much darker manner than in *The Sentimental Policeman*). Examples of such alienation abound in 'Ophelia' (and indeed throughout *Three Stories*). Abandoned as a child, Ofa herself hates all people, men, women and children, and likes only animals. A strikingly succinct image of human loneliness, of the human inability to communicate, comes when an old woman, whom Ofa walks past while pursuing her second murder victim down to the pier, is heard to shout up to her even older mother from the street below, 'Why do you never pick up the phone when I call?' – to which her mother replies, 'Why do you never phone me?' There is, in fact, a link between this theme and the film's visual aesthetic; the camera never adopts the visual perspective of a character, thereby reinforcing the spectator's impression of alienation.

This sense of human alienation and isolation is present throughout the third story, entitled 'Death and the Maiden'. This story contains only two characters, and the action hardly ever shifts from the one location, namely the veranda of the old man's house. The old man's isolation is accentuated, moreover, by his immobility (he is paralysed and wheelchair-bound). At the end of the film, as if to emphasise his imprisonment, the little girl walks out from the veranda into the garden beyond the house, leaving her guardian dead in his chair. The fact that the camera observes the girl *from within the house* means that the viewer shares the old man's sense of isolation and imprisonment. Until his death, the old man talks all the time, but either people hang up on him (as in the first telephone call where he diagnoses a patient as suffering from hysteria and recommends that they be put in a home), or he is forced himself to hang up on them (he has to curtail the final conversation, during which he tells a friend that old people need special love, when the poison starts to take effect). He spends most of the time talking to the girl, but he can hardly be said to communicate with her in any genuine sense. How can he when, as he puts it himself, it is impossible to know what she is thinking: 'It would be interesting to know what you're thinking about, what's going on in your head.'

In this profoundly alienating world, human relations are motivated by the desire to manipulate and control other people. The theme of power, and specifically the power to kill, is immediately flagged as a theme in the extended opening shot, in which the old man's cat plays with a chicken's carcass. The old man himself tries to control the girl's every movement, as witnessed by the frequency with which he uses the word *nel'zia* ('it is forbidden') while speaking to her.[39] Power is also the significance of the game of chess, which the old man says rather incredibly at one stage that he is going to try to teach the little girl. Chess is perhaps the ultimate power game, since the object is to capture, or 'kill' the king (the English phrase 'checkmate', and indeed the Russian word for chess, 'shakhmaty', both derive from the Persian expression meaning 'the king is dead'). Significantly, it is just at that moment when he is explaining to her the power which the queen enjoys over all the other figures that the girl capriciously sends all the chess pieces flying off the board, as if she wants absolute power for herself (her gesture can also be interpreted, of course, as a refusal to live by anybody else's rules but her own).

Ultimately, all the main features of *Three Stories* which have been discussed here – the visual and aural incongruity, the anti-realist theatricality, the play of irrelevance, the emphasis on the individual's isolation from the world and alienation from every other individual – reinforce the sense of the Absurd. The 'absurdity' of existence derives from the absence of any certainties (is the old woman *really* Ofa's mother?), the meaninglessness of life, the inevitability of death, the impossibility of transcendence, and the divorce between humankind and the world. Death is never far away; as the old man in the third story puts it, reminiscing about his ancestors, 'people generally die'. This renders our existence as individuals meaningless, while at the same time giving it universal significance (this is one of the central paradoxes of the Absurd). Either we realise this truth, and thereby live a hell on earth (hence the significance of the image of the boiler house), or we remain in the dark, rather like the two blind cripples who stumble their way along the pier at the very end of 'Ophelia'.

The Russian Idea for Contemporary Film-makers

Muratova and the Absurd

Muratova's vision in the four films under discussion here is profoundly Absurd: life is chaotic and meaningless, there is nothing that we mortals can do to avoid death, and nothing which might afford us transcendence to a higher realm. All we can do is try to distract ourselves from this 'absurd' truth, by means of whatever 'enthusiasm' we choose, be it telling stories, adopting lost children, riding horses, painting pictures, or even making films. Ultimately, however, there is no escape. Ophelia is right when she explains to her 'mother' shortly before she kills her that 'nothing depends on us' [*nichego ne zavisit ot nas*], not because our lives are ordered by Fate (as she and Tolia believe), but rather because there is little if anything we as humans can do to bring order to the chaos that is human existence.

Of course, the Absurd is articulated with varying degrees of intensity, and explored from a different angle, in each of these films. In *Asthenic Syndrome*, for example, the focus is very much on the social and moral chaos of the late Soviet era. *The Sentimental Policeman*, on the other hand, is the least pessimistic of the four, Tolia and Klara forming an island of hope for the future, especially now that she is pregnant. With *Enthusiasms*, contemporary social problems are conspicuous by their absence, Muratova instead treating the viewer to a truly spectacular visual and aural experience. Finally, *Three Stories* is the director's most intimate and most sinister work (it also signals a change in her attitude towards domestic animals, who are now just as aggressive as humans). Despite their differences, however, these films are united by their director's vision of the Absurd. In this respect they belong to a well-established Russian tradition which has its roots in Gogol's Petersburg Tales, and Dostoevsky's Ivan Karamazov, whose dictum, 'if there is no God, then everything is allowed', is especially appropriate to Muratova's most recent picture.

Should we fall into abject despair at Muratova's vision of the Absurd? Despite everything, there is a residual humanism in all Muratova's work (not just those films discussed here). All we can do, it would seem, is help each other through this world, even if this amounts to nothing more than the blind leading the blind (rather like the two cripples on the pier). Little seems to have changed in the century separating Chekhov's *The Three Sisters* [1900] and Muratova's *Three Stories*; as Russia plunges further into post-Soviet chaos and we in the West wallow in postmodern angst, we can just hear Chekhov's Olga softly lamenting, 'If only we knew, if only we knew.'

14. Dmitri Astrakhan: Popular Cinema for a Time of Uncertainty

Julian Graffy

Dmitri Astrakhan, who was born in 1957, graduated from the Leningrad State Institute for Theatre, Music and Cinema in 1982 and began work as a theatrical director. He was artistic director of the Sverdlovsk Young People's Theatre from 1981 to 1987, and in 1987–90 he directed at the Bolshoi Drama Theatre and other Leningrad theatres, and abroad. From 1991 to 1995 he was artistic director of the N. Akimov Comedy Theatre in St Petersburg. He has directed over thirty plays.

Though he made a film for television in 1987, Astrakhan's cinematic career began in the early 1990s, and he has so far made six feature films. Unlike the majority of his director contemporaries who made their reputations during the 1990s, he spurns 'auteur' cinema in favour of catering to popular taste.[1] He sprang to prominence with his 1995 film *Everything will be OK* [Vse budet khorosho], which took as its title a colloquial phrase which commentators on Astrakhan's work have seized upon as a clue to the understanding of all his films. The plot of an Astrakhan film first establishes the identity and values of a community, a family or other group, and then brings them to a point of crisis in which they are required to make a choice. The phrase 'Everything will be OK' (which, of course, is ritually invoked when things are presently not OK) is evocative of the determination to survive adversity that distinguishes all Astrakhan's characters.

1

Astrakhan's first feature film, *Get Thee Hence!* [Izydi!], was made in 1991, a year of uncertainty and reassessment, both in Soviet cinema and throughout society, a year that ended with the demise of the Soviet Union. The urge to address hitherto impossible subjects in late Soviet cinema included a turning to Jewish themes in a number of other films of the period. Some of these were set in the

162

The Russian Idea for Contemporary Film-makers

past, such as Alenikov's *The Carter and the King* [Bindiuzhnik i korol', 1989], taken from the work of Isaak Babel, or Gorovets's *Ladies' Tailor* [Damskii portnoi, 1990], set in Kiev during the Second World War. Others were set in the present, some of them involving an outsider's entry into a previously hidden Jewish world, notably Valeri Todorovsky's *Love* [Liubov', 1991] and Pavel Lungin's *Luna Park* [1992].[2]

Get Thee Hence! is set before the Russian Revolution and draws upon the work of Sholom Aleichem, Isaak Babel and Alexander Kuprin. A village trader, Motl Rabinovich, is given permission to open a dairy in town. He dreams of eventually moving to St Petersburg and becoming a millionaire. Back in the village he and his wife are visited by a crowd of noisy Jewish relatives. His daughter Beilka elopes with Petka, the son of a Christian neighbour, is baptised into the Orthodox Church (and therefore changes her name), and marries him. Petka and Beilka also dream of life in St Petersburg. When the couple return home, both sets of parents accept the marriage despite their initial shock. Thus the village's Jews and Christians become relatives. But a pogrom breaks out in the town and the village's Christian population are encouraged to attack Motl's house. The family prepares to flee but, when their house is already burning, Motl turns back, walking towards his attackers wielding an axe.

In this film, Astrakhan sets up a model that will remain of crucial importance to him throughout the decade. At the centre of his world are a home and a family, their rituals, their meals, their celebrations, often including a marriage feast, all observed with attentive sympathy. Here is an idyll of personal security in the certainty of a community. Yet this idyll is under threat. Most obviously the threat comes from outside, in the form of pogrom, a motif advertised at the very start in a mysterious scene of a funeral which seems to turn into a Jewish exodus (a scene which is then regularly repeated and becomes comprehensible only at the end of the film). The sense of omen is adumbrated in other scenes, of the killing of a gypsy horse-thief and of burning buildings. More enigmatically, the idyll is undermined from within, in temptation by a dream of leaving, a seduction that affects both Motl and his daughter, and that has its cultural roots in the biblical story of Adam and Eve's dissatisfaction with their paradisaical state.

In the end, however, the threatened paradise is defended, both by the characters and by the stance of Astrakhan himself. Motl is tall, generous, confident, popular and speaks good Russian, a figure strikingly at odds with the traditional topos of the Jew as victim, as seen, for example, in Alexander Askoldov's film *The Commissar* [Komissar] (based on a story by Vasili Grossman) which, though made in the 1960s, was released only in 1988 in the middle of the new concern with Jewish themes. Motl's return to try to defend his house and its values suggests a renunciation of his attempt to escape from the weight of history, and a recognition that the happiness he sought at a distance in time and space may turn out to be unattainable. In this sense *Get Thee Hence!* is close to Todorovsky's contemporary *Love*, for in both films the hero is shocked to find those he loves harassed into exodus (into emigration to Israel in the case of *Love*) and moved through pity to resist their attackers. The contemporary reverberations of the film are also apparent in the anachronistic calmness with which Motl and his family react to Beilka's marrying a gentile.[3]

Thus, despite its historical setting, *Get Thee Hence!* speaks directly to the time in which it was made. A stable environment is visited by sudden upheaval, which involves making a number of choices, specifically between staying in the familiar but unchallenging present or leaving for a world that contains both opportunity and uncertainty. Though this new world is enticing, it has to battle against a feeling of identity with the world being left behind, particularly when that world comes under threat. But the final reassertion of old values itself involves a change, an increase in the self-awareness and the resourcefulness of the hero. Though Astrakhan's next three films abandon the Jewish world and are set in the present, the model established in *Get Thee Hence!*, a model of a cinema for a time of uncertainty, continues to apply.

2

You are My Only One [Ty u menia odna, 1993] is set in St Petersburg in the post-Soviet present, with a number of flashbacks into the Brezhnevite past. It tells the story of a forty-year-old engineer, Evgeni Timoshin, his doctor wife Natasha and their teenage daughter Olia. Timoshin's place of work is going to be swallowed up in one of the American–Russian 'joint ventures' that were so fashionable at the time, and he knows he is in danger of losing his job. It transpires that the American side of the new company is run by an old friend of his, Alexei Kolyvanov, who had emigrated in the 1970s, taking with him his sister Ania, at the time a schoolgirl with a hopeless crush on Timoshin. It is Ania who returns to St Petersburg to conduct negotiations. She is still besotted with Timoshin and offers him a glamorous new life working for the company and studying in Los Angeles.

As in *Get Thee Hence!*, the centre of gravity of *You are My Only One* is the family home, but here the expansive southern village is replaced by a cramped, decrepit flat in St Petersburg with all its concomitant social and personal tensions, observed in shockingly familiar detail.[4] All the aspirations of Timoshin and Natasha have been thwarted by post-Soviet economic and social chaos, and their life is a succession of social and psychological humiliations, large and small. Timoshin, the well-educated engineer, has had to take on a second, nocturnal job, taking delivery of dairy products and guarding them in a refrigerated van. Their young upstairs neighbour ruins their peace with amplified rock music. Even their sexual life is hampered by the arrangements of their flat and their fear that their sleeping daughter will awake. Natasha's job, which involves her in giving advice about 'erogenous zones' to a sexually frustrated

The Russian Idea for Contemporary Film-makers

15. Dmitri Astrakhan. *You are My Only One*. Evgeni Timoshin (Alexander Zbruev) and Natasha (Marina Neelova).

but distinctly bemused middle-aged couple symbolically extends the humiliation of attempting to adapt to the new 'free' mores to all of post-Soviet society.

In this impossible situation the Timoshins seek refuge in dreams of distance. The film is framed with monochrome class pictures from their schooldays and is regularly punctuated by nostalgic recollection of their teenage years and of their joyous wedding. For them, at least, the years of Brezhnevite stagnation are now remembered as a time of youthful hope, encapsulated in their meeting at a teenage party to the sound of Beatles' music (the record is still prominently visible in the present flat), in the exuberance with which their friends hijack their dull Soviet wedding ceremony, and above all in the use as the film's musical backbone of the song 'You are My Only One' ('Ty u menia odna') by the bard Yuri Vizbor, for the music of the bards, of Vysotsky, Galich, Okudzhava and others, was one of the key sources of spiritual vitality in this period, a signature of its incorrigible hopes.

Distance in time is paralleled by distance in space. As in *Get Thee Hence!*, the characters are tested by a dream of leaving. But this time the promised land is not St Petersburg (where they already are), but the key dream destination of the twentieth-century consciousness, America. Thus America and the American model enter Astrakhan's mythology. America, like the past, is present from the very start of the film; all the main characters either emigrate (as do the

Kolyvanovs) or dream of emigration. Since the only traditional way out except for Jews has been by marriage, Natasha encourages Olia's friendship with a boy whose father may be about to leave, offering a variant of the 'marrying out' model set in *Get Thee Hence!*[5] That this America is a mythical Russian expression of the hope of a better life is demonstrated both by the fact that America is represented in the film predominantly by émigré Russians, and also by the explicitly conventional expectations Natasha has of life in California (where else?). Her list of desiderata, 'a flat, a car, a dacha [sic], furniture and an aeroplane', a list which evokes a positively erotic enthusiasm in the Timoshins, is later touchingly downgraded to 'a limousine, a villa and a bra'.[6]

The mutual fascination of America and Russia, extending from the pole of attraction to the pole of competitive distrust, has spanned the twentieth century, and thus, specifically, the history of Russian cinema. Famously, pre-Revolutionary Russian films disdained the 'happy end' of American cinema and had to be re-shot (with happy endings) for export. Immediately after the Revolution, however, Lev Kuleshov looked to the American model of entertainment cinema and tried to apply it to the Bolshevik context.[7] Ideological competition with America provoked a special genre in Soviet film in which an American hero or heroine comes to the Soviet Union and embraces its values, finding both ideological understanding and personal happiness. Particularly germane to *You are My Only One* is Grigori Aleksandrov's 1936 musical *The Circus* [Tsirk], in which Liubov Orlova plays Marion Dixon, an American circus artiste who finds love and happiness in Moscow. Marion is vainly lusted after by her sinister German manager, von Kneischitz, who attempts to suborn her with dresses and furs and with the following words (spoken in English): 'Mary! I love you. Let us go away from here! ... To California! To the ocean! To the sun! There you will forget Moscow!' Marion angrily rejects his offer, as, eventually, and more resignedly, Timoshin turns down the very similarly expressed offer of the lovelorn Ania.

In fact, throughout the late Soviet period, this model of a Westerner's journey to Soviet enlightenment had been socially unpicked in various ways, concretely by an increase in Soviet emigration to America, Europe and Israel, and later by the return of the émigrés, both physically, on visits, and in the return of their art. In the late 1980s the émigré and his views on all subjects, both Western and Russian, became a short-lived object of fascination to Russian society.[8] In cinema this return became a stock subject for 1990s films.[9]

You are My Only One concludes, however, with an explicit rejection by the hero Timoshin of the seductive American dream. His final encounter with Ania takes place outdoors early on a snowy morning and is shot to look like a classical Russian duel. At this point Timoshin finds the spirit to tell Ania that 'I don't need all that ... I don't love you, do you understand that or not?', provoking her to rush off in her absurdly extravagant furs and attempt to throw herself from a high window before returning, calmer, to tell him: 'Everything will be fine! Farewell! (Proshchaite!)'. This word, 'proshchaite' is itself symbolic in the culture of the period, for one of the anthems of the time is the song 'The Last Letter' by the group Nautilus Pompilius, on their album *Prince of Silence* [Kniaz' tishiny, 1989], which contains the words 'Your washed-out jeans / have become too small for me./ They taught us for so long / to love your forbidden fruit', and has as its refrain 'Good-bye Amerika / where I have never been / Good-bye forever', later repeated as 'where I shall never be'.[10] Thus, crucially, both song and film suggest, if only tentatively, a sobering of the late and post-Soviet consciousness, an awareness that the (Russian) America of their aspirations will remain, for most of them, an illusion, the stuff of fairytale.[11]

In this context the end of the film represents a reassertion of Russian values, the values of naturalness, vital energy and melodramatic sentimental excess[12] – it is noticeable that Ania, even as a child, is displayed as a repressed, non-participant watcher, a motif that is echoed both in the KGB man who spies from the stairs on her brother and his fiancée, and later in her own bodyguard who takes up the same position outside Timoshin's flat. Thus, though Timoshin had spoken with bitter irony early on in the film when, provoked by Natasha's bitter complaints and crushed by Ania's initial failure to acknowledge him, he had insisted that life in their awful flat 'suited' him (*udobno*), by the end it is clear that on a profound psychological level his words are true.

Astrakhan's films are always centrally about men, and the film's analysis of maleness is part of its general reassertion of (idealised) Russianness. At the beginning of the film the young Timoshin is seen winning a boxing bout against a stronger opponent after being given words of rhetorical Soviet encouragement by his coach, and thus winning the admiration of both Natasha and Ania. Later, in his post-Soviet weakness, his male energy seems to be stripped away from him. He is bullied and manipulated by his wife. He protests ineffectively against his noisy neighbours. On two occasions, first by Natasha before the arrival of the American delegation, and later by Ania in an expensive hard currency store, he is dressed by a woman. The emasculating force of this action is crudely brought to our attention by his pivotal meeting, outside Ania's hotel, with a grotesque double, a transsexual prostitute, also there to visit his 'buyer'.[13] On his return after this sobering encounter, Timoshin finds the resources, like the hero of *Get Thee Hence!*, to defend his home: he stops the infuriating music by the simple expedient of beating up his awful neighbour and his guests.[14]

The film concludes with a quintessential Astrakhan scene, a *plein air* Russian meal. Timoshin's birthday is celebrated in a feast organised by his errant father (earlier glimpsed passionately bemoaning the demise of Soviet power), the father's beggar lady friend and their cronies, who perform an impromptu rendering of the title song 'You are My Only One'.[15] The broad inclusiveness of the Russian spirit leads them to invite assorted street people, but also the neighbour, with whom Timoshin is reconciled, and Ania's minder, who has come, symbolically, to return Timoshin's passport after Ania's abrupt return to America. Thus the fairytale of escape has been replaced by another persistent and flattering Russian myth, the myth of endurance and survival. But it is notable that *You are My Only One* rejects an unequivocally happy ending. Instead, when Timoshin calls out, 'Natasha! You are my only one!', she does not seem to hear, and a shot of his inscrutable face is followed by a final still of them as seven-year-old schoolchildren, implying that if he has rejected the dream of spatial distance, the nostalgic pull of the past remains strong.

3

Everything will be OK, Astrakhan's most famous film and one of the biggest box office hits of its year, revisits several of the concerns of *You are My Only One*, but with a greatly increased number of leading characters and a much more densely detailed plot. Kolia Orlov, who has a job at a metal works in a nondescript provincial town, is seen off to army service by Olia Tuzova, whose father, Semen, lives with Kolia's mother, Katia, in the factory's hostel. Olia writes to him giving news of all the hostel's other inhabitants, including the Samsonov family, whose life is made miserable by the father Andrei's drinking, Sergei Karelov, who has abandoned his girlfriend Vera to go off to become a pop star, and wheelchair-bound grandad Volodia. Upon Kolia's return he and Olia decide to get married. Katia sees on television that Konstantin Smirnov, who had been her first love, has become a new Russian millionaire and is about to open a 'Russian Disneyland' in their town. He returns with his son, Petia, a mathematical genius who has studied at Princeton and won the Nobel prize for mathematics at the age of twenty. Smirnov insists on funding Kolia and Olia's wedding, but must first have talks with Ahira, a visiting Japanese millionaire businessman. Petia and Olia are attracted to each other. Grandad Volodia receives a letter from his long-lost wife, Natasha.

Next day, Petia visits Olia and flirts with her. Smirnov invites the Orlovs and the Tuzovs to a grand party for the launch of his Disneyland project. Olia and Petia are drawn further together. Kolia fights Petia, and later, after a row with Olia, he tries to kill himself, but they are reconciled. Karelov returns for Vera as he had promised. That night, while Semen and Kolia are drunk, Konstantin Smirnov sleeps with Katia Orlova and Petia Smirnov with Olia, but next morning both women renounce their great loves. That day the Samsonovs visit the ballet. The director calls the police when Samsonov sits his son, Petka, in Ahira's box, but Ahira intervenes in the ensuing fight on Samsonov's side.

Olia and Kolia are married and return to the hostel for the celebrations. Grandad Volodia hooks his wheelchair to a passing lorry and is driven off to be reunited with his wife. Konstantin Smirnov tells his son that Olia loves him and that he must go and take her from Kolia. He briefly joins the wedding party, but prepares to leave without her. At this point Kolia intervenes and

The Russian Idea for Contemporary Film-makers

16. Dmitri Astrakhan. *Everything will be OK*. Konstantin Smirnov (Alexander Zbruev)
and Olia (Olga Ponizova).

packs the lovelorn pair off together, insisting that he will survive, that 'everything will be OK'.

The main setting of *Everything will be OK* is the hostel of the local metal
works, the shared home of most of the film's protagonists. Here they are all
thrown together in hectic community and all their cares, hopes and secrets are
common currency. The stable family of conventional Soviet art has taken a
buffeting. Katia Orlova has long since discarded her husband and lives,
raucously, with Semen Tuzov; grandad Volodia's wife, Natasha, has disappeared;
Karelov has seemingly abandoned Vera. Life in the hostel is also marked by
bouts of legendary Russian drinking, both solitary and communal: by Samsonov,
by Tuzov and his 'folk orchestra', by Kolia and his young friends.[16] Astrakhan
has no illusions about the mundane post-Soviet world. Despite their genuine
sense of community – every event is the excuse for a shared, convivial meal –
they all sheepishly find reasons not to drive grandad Volodia to his rediscovered
wife. And yet the precision and sympathy of the social observation portrays,
in Natalia Sirivlia's words, 'the typical day to day life (*byt*) of ordinary Soviet
[sic] people with a plus sign'.[17]

The abundance of the fabled new Russians erupts into this parched world
with the return of Konstantin Smirnov. Olia had already begun to make
adjustments to the new order, by studying English and 'marketing', but Smirnov,
'one of our country's biggest entrepreneurs', is its quintessence. The mixing of

the codes of the old and the new Russia is humorously encapsulated when a man staying in the hostel on a business trip (*komandirovka*) sees Smirnov's bodyguard's gun and immediately concludes that he has stumbled upon the mafia. Smirnov puts on a magnificent party with fireworks, typical of the ostentation of the new Russia. It is there that Petia further betrays his feelings by making Olia the 'queen of the party', rather than Masha Saveleva, the recently crowned 'Miss Television' (as has been fixed in advance by Smirnov's oleaginous master of ceremonies).[18] It is notable, however, that Smirnov, as well as bringing the bracing future to the town and the hostel, also brings nostalgia for a distant, blissful past, for he enters Katia's room (and the film) by the window, just as he had done twenty years before when he was Katia's 'first love'.[19]

Yet again, the film's plot turns upon a seductive dream of leaving. Here too, marriage is seen as an escape route. Katia's fury at her son for deciding to marry Olia is mainly motivated by her realisation that in doing so he will lose the chance of marrying a 'town girl' and moving out into an urban flat. But the true dream destination is, of course, abroad, encapsulated in the advertising poster of a tropical sunset with the legend 'The astringent taste of another life' that recurs throughout the film. The film's 'foreigners' are uniformly represented as active and successful, both the Japanese, Ahira, and his delegation, which includes a hypnotist healer, and the 'Americans', Smirnov, with his Disneyland, and Petia, the precocious Nobel laureate who has studied at Princeton.

The sense of their power and his weakness is made clear in the encounters between Kolia and the Smirnovs. First, when he visits the hotel room (like the visiting Ania in *You are My Only One*, Smirnov no longer has a Russian 'home', but lives in the best hotel in town) in search of a job, his indecision leads Smirnov to ask him rhetorically, 'Do you want anything?' and, 'Do you have a dream?', before concluding that Kolia is incorrigible. The humiliation of Kolia continues when he is outboxed by the physically weaker Petia, for though Kolia has been strong enough to win his army bouts, Petia has, gallingly, been trained by Smirnov's bodyguard, Uncle Vova, who has previously been a world boxing champion.[20] The subdivision of the world into winners and losers is made explicit at the end of the film when Smirnov tells Petia to go and claim Olia – the world, he insists, is divided into 'the strong and the weak', 'those who can turn their fate and those who go with the current'.

The crudity of Smirnov's subdivision hints at a crucial aspect of Astrakhan's method. This is a film which deals openly in myth and archetype, openly but also knowingly, using them for its own ends. Olia's gushing letter to Kolia with its talk of army friendships that last a lifetime is set against the reality of fights and bullying. When little Petka Samsonov goes to the ballet he finds that it is the world of 'fairytale', but in fact several of the characters in the film are consciously imagined in fairytale roles. Smirnov, appearing through the window, is a Prince Charming for Katia, and a fairy godfather for the young couple,

The Russian Idea for Contemporary Film-makers

whose every possible desire he anticipates. Ahira, complete with Samurai sword, is an Eastern wizard, flying in, as tradition requires, from distant lands. Olia herself is a (very practical and worldly) Cinderella,[21] and Petia, insipidly handsome, her own Prince Charming (they even have a scene in which she tries on clothes until she finds something that 'fits'). Sergei Karelov is a Dick Whittington figure, who goes to the capital and makes his fortune.[22] Combined with this use of archetype is a frank dealing in absurdity, from the twenty-year-old Nobel prize winner to the unbelievably solicitous and well-mannered OMON police officer who apologises to Samsonov and his family for the behaviour of his 'idiot' men, recalling the famous (and famously mocked) boast of Mayakovsky, 'My police force looks after me.'[23]

The film also contains miraculous cures: Samsonov is instantaneously weaned from his inveterate drinking, grandad Volodia and his wife 'take up their bed and walk', indeed dance. Grandad himself represents the stereotype of 'love to the grave', and his determination to take his own measures to be reunited with his wife is signposted by the longing gazes he casts at his climbing gear. Thus Astrakhan continually and unapologetically, in Viktor Shklovsky's words, 'lays bare the devices' of his film.[24] It is perhaps this knowingness (which recalls the poetics of 1930s Soviet musicals) that has disorientated Russian critics, several of whom have been moved to apoplexy by *Everything will be OK*, though there are others who seem more attuned to his purposes, notably Evgeni Margolit, who astutely suggests that the film 'restores audience cinema and gives the viewer back his dignity' after all the excess and despair of recent years.[25] For any reading of the film that suggests its makers harbour a genuine illusion that 'Everything will be OK', or support an uncritical acceptance of the New Russian, Americanophile recipe for a happy life, must be discarded. Konstantin Smirnov, the multi-millionaire, remains lonely and unfulfilled. Olia and Petia, who get their American dream, are the least interesting, least engaging characters in the film. This is partly because of the blandness of their youthful prettiness and of their acting. It is also because of the thinness and conventionality of their imagined America. The most extensive 'American' scene in the film is a charmless and vulgar encounter between them, in which Olia demands 'a black limousine, a white limousine, and a villa … in California',[26] all of which Petia already has, which develops into a witlessly imagined musical soirée with 'Mr President' and culminates in a ridiculous and otiose (Russian) concern for their crying baby. It is also fundamentally important that they are given this dreary bliss only after both showing that they are prepared to renounce it – Olia when she leaves Petia and returns to Kolia, afraid that 'he'll die without me' (she is deluding herself), and Petia at the end when, told to 'decide his own fate' by his father, he does so in the opposite way from what his father had intended, by sacrificing Olia to Kolia (his offer is not taken up).

These figures should be contrasted with those who stay, notably Kolia, Katia and Tuzov, who are drawn much more fully and are not figures out of a happy fairytale. Thus, once again, Astrakhan's greatest sympathy (like that of his audience) lies explicitly with the excluded mass who will *not* taste the astringent new life. The conservative, healing vision of the film involves the re-establishment and defence of old values for a time of crisis.

Katia Orlova is offered a fairytale escape that combines a rediscovery of a lost past love with departure (in Smirnov's words and another Astrakhan litany) 'To the Canary Islands, Tahiti, the moon ... I can do it.' Though her emotions are clearly touched, she knows that the past cannot be recaptured, replying: 'It's too late for me, Kostia. Where would I go? And anyway, I don't deserve the Canary Islands, I don't deserve you.'[27] This notion of being 'undeserving' (belied for the viewer both by the plot and by Irina Mazurkevich's luminous performance) is also very Russian (and very un-American), and links with a central Russian myth, and a central Astrakhan concern, that of the capacity for heroic renunciation, for the sacrifice of personal happiness. Thus Katia too undergoes a parting with illusions, her own 'Good-Bye Amerika'; at the end of the film she is scarcely prepared even to go there on a visit, threatening to tear up her ticket.

The myth of heroic self-sacrifice is connected with a myth of resourceful self-help, and here again, as in his earlier films, Astrakhan's eye is trained mainly on the male characters. The women in the film are defined by their relationships with their men. Vera waits, true and confident, for Karelov's return. Masha Saveleva, Miss Television, sets her cap first at the rock star Karelov, then at the mathematical genius Petia Samsonov, before finally settling for the Japanese millionaire Ahira.[28]

And all of these men, young and old, 'do it their way', make their own happiness. Free of illusions that the hostel's sentimental reaction to his wife's letter will actually be translated into practical help, grandad Volodia makes alternative plans, hooking his wheelchair to a passing lorry and hitching a lift, after confiding only in the boy Petka Samsonov.[29] Petka's father, Andrei, may be helped to stop drinking by the miraculous intervention of Ahira's hypnotist healer (itself a knowing nod in the direction of the post-Soviet vogue for healers à la Kashpirovsky), but this is only because his (Russian folk hero's) bravery in taking on and defeating the massed ranks of the OMON police has impressed the samurai in Ahira. And Sergei Karelov, initially taunted by Vera for his cult of Elvis Presley, becomes a great rock star exactly as he had promised, and returns exactly one year later (another folkloric motif) to reclaim her. He had promised to return in a white Mercedes; in fact, he returns with three. Thus again the Russians trump the Americans, for these cars, won by his own effort, spectacularly outclass not only the red Zhiguli given to Kolia by Smirnov, which drives up minutes before, but even the 'black limousine, white limousine' of Olia's Californian dream.

Semen Tuzov is yet another character who stays, and (in the manner of the popular anecdotes of the Khrushchev and Brezhnev periods) wins a victory

The Russian Idea for Contemporary Film-makers

over his American rival, both in the area of love, where despite the odds Katia remains with him rather than the considerably more dashing Smirnov, and in the area of music. Astrakhan uses music extensively as a bearer of meaning in all his films, but never more effectively than in *Everything will be OK*. American music is represented here by the aria 'Summer Time' from Gershwin's *Porgy and Bess*, which comes to be associated particularly with Petia and Olia, who pick it out on the piano in their first scene together and take it up again at their 'parting'. But the second line of this song, 'And the living is easy', stresses its inappropriateness for the contemporary experience of the Russian mass audience.[30] Tuzov offers, in response, his 'Orchestra of Folk Instruments', its members oiled by secret supplies of vodka. A poster describing him as a 'virtuoso balalaika player' is prominently displayed throughout the film. In ironic counterpoint to the dreams of foreign travel (and to the film's other poster with its 'astringent taste of another life'), it announces his 'Concerts in Kremenchug (a Ukrainian town midway between Kiev and Dnepropetrovsk) and its suburbs'. Yet, as Tuzov recalls in drunken effusion after Smirnov's party, his music had moved 'the great Russian composer Dmitrii Shostakovich' (a star of considerably greater luminosity than Gershwin) to tears, and to the asseveration that 'there are only two of us, you and I'. The vitality and primacy of Russian popular music is further underlined by the use of Karelov's rock music and of the popular ballad 'You Stand Alone by the Parapet' ('Ty stoish' odna u parapeta'), which is initially associated with Katia and Smirnov's youthful love, but which is played for her at the end by Tuzov. The Russian musical victory is cemented by a virtuoso open-air performance of 'Summer Time' by Tuzov and female balalaika and accordion players at the open-air wedding feast at the end of the film.

It should also be noted that these stoical Russian endurers are also rewarded with a trip abroad, but one accepted in the most mundane way. Ahira offers the Samsonovs an all-expenses-paid trip to Japan. Smirnov replies, 'If we have time, we'll drop by'. (A group photo of them with Ahira and Miss Television is later proof that they managed to do so.) Vera travels the world with Karelov, and actually tires of it, but carries on because 'Serezha's job' gives them no choice. At the end of the film Tuzov is preparing to visit his daughter in the USA. Thus glamorous and seemingly inaccessible foreign travel is rendered banal.

Only one character, Kolia, ends the film completely cut off from contact with the dazzling West.[31] That he is the film's central character is indicated in many ways. He is the first character seen at the beginning of the film, when he arrives at the metal works, and the last at the end, when he leaves it after work and utters the film's final words, 'Everything will be OK'. In the initial scene he is given a prophetic double, an old man who exultantly proclaims that after forty years at the plant he is retiring, only to die of a heart attack. The conventionality of Kolia's desires is immediately signposted: he wants to marry

Olia and have a family. In his simplicity, he is initially impressed and seduced by Smirnov's largesse, but his profound sense that all this is not for him is repeatedly indicated. When he first sees Petia the Nobel laureate he tells Olia, 'That's who you ought to be marrying'. Of course, when he first realises he is losing Olia he is assailed by jealousy – he tries to beat up Petia, but fate conspires against him, leading to his desperate complaint, 'He's a scholar, he's rich and I'm just a working man', and to Olia's retort, 'Paratrooper! You can't even give someone a beating. Is there anything you can do?', with its scarcely concealed sexual taunt. But soon, in a plot development which yet again should be seen less in the context of psychological realism than in that of sustaining Russian myth, he finds himself capable of renunciation, a renunciation symbolised both by his words 'I don't need all this' and by his insistence on being married in his own army uniform rather than in the expensive suit bought for him by Smirnov.[32] He returns all Smirnov's gifts, for as Ahira has sagely told Samsonov, 'Money doesn't bring happiness if it is not earned'. Later, when a repentant Olia tells him that she 'cannot' do as he insists, he replies, almost savagely, 'Well I can!' The seriousness with which he is tested is shown by his final 'jealousy fantasy' of Petia and Olia being thrown out of Princeton and the USA and reduced to begging on the streets (for a typically 'Russian' reason of taking to the bottle). But this weakness, too, is overcome, and the end of the film reveals the moral force that sustains him, a quintessential Russian alternative idyll of work in the factory, marriage 'to someone', and, on his days off, 'a fishing trip or gathering mushrooms'.[33] Kolia is, therefore, a traditional Russian hero, symbolised by his surname, Orlov ('eagle'), but also through the physical type of the actor, Anatoli Zhuravlev (effectively contrasted with the slightness of Mark Goronok who plays Petia), which recalls the simple heroic workers, capable both of heroic labour and of the heroic sacrifice of any personal agenda, in classical Soviet cinema. The film's final image is of Kolia striding purposefully down the road from the factory into the arduous Russian future.

4

In *Everything will be OK* Smirnov asks Katia, 'Do you want to go to the moon?' This rhetorical flourish is given material expression in Astrakhan's other film of 1995, *The Fourth Planet* [Chetvertaia planeta], based upon Ray Bradbury's *Martian Chronicles*, in which Colonel Sergei Beliaev heads a Russo-American mission to Mars, the fourth planet of the solar system.[34] He and his fellow spacemen, the Russian Igor Mikhailov and the American Sam Styron, discover that Mars is 'also' a provincial Soviet town of the Brezhnev years, the very town in which Beliaev grew up. The Martians have made use of their 'thought fields' to trick them back into their own past and their unfulfilled desires. All three of the spacemen have meetings with those who have been dear to them,

The Russian Idea for Contemporary Film-makers

but the story centres on Beliaev's encounter with his 'one and only love', Tania, who was murdered by a drunk that very day, twenty years ago. Beliaev manages to intervene and alter the past, saving Tania's life. But the cost to him of this achievement is to stay for ever in the Martian past, never returning to earth.

The Fourth Planet is a brilliantly orchestrated variation on themes already familiar from Astrakhan's earlier films. From an unsatisfactory present (which is here almost invisible), through the device of space travel which turns into time travel, Astrakhan and his heroes make a journey into the Soviet past.[35] Zarechensk, the provincial Soviet town of this *recherche du temps perdu* is lovingly observed and full of achingly familiar period markers. The courtyard (*dvor*) of Beliaev's childhood is inhabited by a persuasive company of old men wearing their war medals, nosy children, crones, feeble drunks and Soviet blonde beauties. Soviet banners bear all the usual Brezhnevite slogans, with the humorous addition of '$e=mc^2$' and 'Long Live the Theory of Relativity'. The music is a familiar mix of 'Besame mucho',[36] Italian pop, Russian ballads, and the cosmonaut song 'And Apple Trees Will Bloom on Mars'.[37] The triumphantly observed centrepiece of this nostalgic re-evocation is an extended scene in the Wave (*Volna*) restaurant, with its Soviet champagne and bowls of fruit, its band and its dancing, its shabby head waiter and even its suddenly erupting violence. For Beliaev, for Astrakhan and for his audience this is the epitome of communality, and the emotional power of family is also evoked through the reuniting of the other two cosmonauts with dead relations, Sam, the American, with his beloved grandfather, Orlov with his mother, who has made her arduous way from her collective farm, the 'Path to Communism'.

The tale of a trip to space in which the hero's desire and the power of his memory materialise his true love inevitably suggests the relationship of Kris Kelvin and Hari in Tarkovsky's *Solaris* [Soliaris, 1972], but Astrakhan is patently not interested in the philosophical abstractions which preoccupied Tarkovsky and his source writer, Stanislaw Lem.[38]

Space exploration was a fundamental constituent of Soviet propaganda in the Khrushchev and Brezhnev years, centring on the figure of Yuri Gagarin (Beliaev is mockingly called Gagarin in *The Fourth Planet*). But Khrushchev's grandiose plans were also mercilessly mocked in Elem Klimov's film *Welcome*, where listless young pioneers dutifully sing 'the song Gagarin sang in space' and a botched experiment in telepathy results in a dog called Cosmos cocking its leg.[39] An ironical approach to the whole Soviet space project was also recently expressed in Viktor Pelevin's 1992 novel *Omon Ra*, one of the most popular pieces of Russian fiction of recent years, and there are echoes of Pelevin's story here, in the scene where an army officer seeks recruits to become cosmonauts. Most recently the cosmonaut in Vladimir Mashkov's big popular hit of 1997, *The Sympathy Seeker* [Sirota kazanskaia, 1997], turns out to be a fraud.[40]

The most important link to be drawn, though, is a with a film from the very beginning of Soviet cinema, another time of major social upheaval in the wake of political earthquake, Yakov Protazanov's *Aelita* [1924], also set partly on Mars. If Beliaev and Tania are not doubles of Kelvin and Hari, they are just as distant from Protazanov's cerebral engineer Los and the imperious Aelita, 'queen of Mars'. Both Los and Beliaev are driven to Mars by a sense of erotic frustration, but the outcomes of their journeys are radically opposed to each other. Protazanov forces his engineer to renounce his illusions and return to earth, to acceptance of the mundane problems and mundane joys of contemporary life, which is also the stance taken by Astrakhan in his first three films. Here, by contrast, Astrakhan examines the implications of the alternative scenario, and allows his spaceman to remain in hermetic bliss.

The Fourth Planet is, in its own terms, a perfect film, engaging and witty, suffused by tender nostalgia. Its treatment of the simple man's search for happiness deals in the most overtly mythological and archetypal terms.[41] Tania tells Beliaev that she loves him, and 'everything else is unimportant'. Their constancy, expressed in a 'recognition scene' that directly echoes that between Katia Orlova and Konstantin Smirnov in *Everything will be OK*,[42] is here given a wish fulfilment reward which suggests that you have only to believe and you will be able to revisit and correct your past, complete your uncompleted agendas. Thus the weedy young Beliaev, who cannot do gymnastics or fight his rival for Tania's love, is avenged by the manly spaceman Beliaev who (like Samsonov in *Everything will be OK*) defeats an entire gang with aplomb.

Its very perfection hints that with *The Fourth Planet* Astrakhan has exhausted a creative vein, just as the glory of space exploration can be restored only by the melancholy of nostalgia. The American theme, though present, is also no longer significant – Sam Styron (the first *real* American to play an important part in Astrakhan's films) is neither the good guy nor the bad guy, and is notable mainly for the wry pleasure afforded to audiences by his Russian accent. The bliss of Beliaev and Tania at the end is a dead end, bought at the cost of sacrificing the vitality and unpredictability of life on earth, and arrestingly recalling the end of Mikhail Bulgakov's novel *The Master and Margarita*, in which the exhausted hero and heroine are likewise transported through space to a life of blissful oblivion, dream and, by implication, death.

5

These films are made by the same team: the scripts are all by Oleg Danilov, the photography is by Yuri Vorontsov, the design by Sergei Kokovkin and Maria Petrova, the new music, working in partnership with the popular songs of the Beatles, Vizbor and Gershwin, is always by Alexander Pantykin, who has also provided memorable music for several of the films of Vladimir Khotinenko. Astrakhan also uses his experience as a theatrical director to deploy his own group of repertory actors.[43] Like American cinema, popular Russian cinema has always known the audience appeal of familiar actors, and one of the great incidental pleasures of Astrakhan's films is seeing the same people popping up again and again in roles that are often variations upon themselves. Zbruev and Goronok, the hero past and present in *You are My Only One* become father and son in *Everything will be OK*. We can commiserate with Anatoli Zhuravlev, the boxer who loses the girl in both *Everything will be OK* and *The Fourth Planet*. Irina Mazurkevich graduates from a bit part in *You are My Only One* to a leading role in *Everything will be OK*, while other actors, notably Valentin Bukin and Viktor Gogolev, play a variety of secondary parts.

All these connections lead us to look at the films as a kind of single text, offering ever more abstract and theoretical variations on an archetypal pattern, culminating in the hints of metatextuality in *The Fourth Planet*.[44] Astrakhanland[45] is the domain of a male fairytale, combining love and bravery, in which a myth of leaving gives way to another myth, of heroism and stoic survival, in which the hero remains in or returns to his home and attempts to defend it from attack. These healing 'myths for an age of uncertainty' recall the fairytale cinema of another arduous time, the myths of achievement in the 1930s musicals of Grigori Aleksandrov, but, just as in 1930s popular cinema, the fairytales are treated with a knowingness by both makers and audiences, whose credulousness is always tempered by distance and irony.

6

Astrakhan's recent career has developed in a number of new directions. In 1996 he made a feature film *From Hell to Hell* [Iz ada v ad] for the Belarus film studios. It tells the story of a Polish Jewish couple from their marriage in 1938, through imprisonment in concentration camps and entrusting their daughter to a Polish couple, to the husband's escape to join the Russians fighting the Nazis, the wife's liberation, the refusal of the Polish couple to surrender the child and the death of the husband in a pogrom in the Polish town of Kielce in 1946. Astrakhan had dealt with similar subject matter in *Get Thee Hence!*, which also told of an idyll destroyed by a pogrom and ended with an exodus, though the tone of this film is infinitely darker. Here is another variant on the Astrakhan formula of a hero, initially unaware of the extent of the threat to his home and its values, or, as in this case, aware but tragically unable to resist, somehow finding the resources to fight to defend it. This time the hero is tested by events that are scarcely imaginable and the struggle ends in tragedy. The scenes of Jewish happiness and Jewish music-making are brief and suffused with a sense of doom. The literary sources of *Get Thee Hence!* in Babel and Sholom Aleichem that found space for joy and optimism are replaced, in Astrakhan's first film to be based predominantly on historical events, by a certainty that, for all the characters' courage, there can be no happy outcome for anyone. In its seriousness the film is Astrakhan's most ambitious yet; but though he achieves passages of an almost unbearable poignancy, *From Hell to Hell* is also marked by insufficiency of imagination – there are too many stock characters and too many formulaic speeches – and by uncertainties of tone, in the hints of the grand guignol of horror film. Though Danilov, Vorontsov and Pantykin were all again involved, three of the four leading actors had not worked for Astrakhan before. The desperate horror of his subject matter requires a delicacy that is sometimes beyond him and *From Hell to Hell* must be described as a bold but not wholly successful attempt by Astrakhan to extend his range.

Astrakhan then turned to television and made a ten-part serial *Waiting Room* [Zal ozhidaniia] for the main Russian channel ORT (Russian Public Television).[46] He followed this with a 'psychological thriller' *A Contract with Death* [Kontrakt so smert'iu, 1998], commissioned by the television station TV6 and shot in thirty-seven days. It tells of the invention by the brilliant professor Ignatovsky of a surgical procedure that enables any organ of the body to be transplanted from any donor to any beneficiary. A ruthless politician, Andrei Stepanov, already a member of the State Duma, but preparing a presidential bid with mysterious backers, is determined to use the professor's invention to capture public support by the promise of mass transplant surgery to deserving upright citizens from 'the dregs of society', drunks and criminals, the homeless and the mentally ill. They set up a 'Society of Mercy and Health' and take 'donors' from the streets to their 'sanatorium', but their dastardly plan is discovered and thwarted by the probity of the donors themselves and the professor's belated realisation of the extent of Stepanov's evil ambition. The film ends, however, on an admonitory note, as a TV talk show vote finds the Russian public overwhelmingly in favour of the scheme.

Astrakhan has said à propos of this film that 'You can make a comedy about serious matters',[47] but though the subject here is theoretically of fundamental importance, it is also unoriginal. It was treated with infinitely greater elegance and subtlety in Mikhail Bulgakov's 1925 fable *The Heart of a Dog*, already filmed in Russia.[48] The alliance of mad scientist and power-crazed politician in possession of a secret procedure that will give them infinite power has also fuelled countless films and innumerable television series broadcast on drab Saturday nights around the world. Astrakhan's scriptwriter, as ever, is Oleg Danilov, and he finds room for a recognisable hero in the figure of Anton, who is first employed to round up victims, but eventually, awakened by love, moves into the sanatorium himself and leads the defence of the place he has made his home. But there are scarcely any other Astrakhan signatures. He deploys almost none of his usual repertory actors. Though the cinematography is again by Yuri Vorontsov, *Contract with Death* is also Astrakhan's visually dullest film, its settings almost confined to the indistinguishable rooms of the sanatorium and to murky night scenes in its grounds. Though there are one or two jibes at the venality of Russian television and at the murky king-makers of post-Soviet politics, the film is overlong and the plotting utterly predictable. In short, Astrakhan has made his most anonymous and pedestrian film to date, a film that could have been made by anyone.

At the end of a decade of prolific activity, Astrakhan would seem to stand at a cross-roads. The brilliant intuition that produced a succession of compelling and amusing dramas that spoke directly to popular taste seems temporarily to have deserted him. But Astrakhan, who has said, 'All I think about is telling an engaging story', will no doubt surprise his audiences again.[49]

Appendix 1
Directors and Their Films

ABDRASHITOV, Vadim, b.1945. *The Word in Defence*, 1976; *Fox Hunter*, 1980; *The Parade of Planets*, 1984; *Plumbum*, 1986; *The Servant*, 1988; *Play for a Passenger*, 1995; *The Time of the Dancer*, 1997.

ALENIKOV, Vladimir, b.1948, lives in the USA. *The Carter and the King*, 1989.

ALIMPIEV, Igor, b.1955. *The Shell*, 1990; *A Physiology of Russian Life*, 1994.

ARANOVICH, Semen, 1934–94. Made mainly documentaries and films for television. *Dog's Year*, 1993.

ASTRAKHAN, Dmitri, b.1957. Directed for theatres in Sverdlovsk and Leningrad (1981–95). *Get Thee Hence!*, 1991; *You are My Only One*, 1993; *The Fourth Planet*, 1995; *Everything will be OK*, 1995; *From Hell to Hell*, 1996; *A Contract with Death*, 1998.

BAISAK, Gennadi, b.1944. *Play for Millions*, 1992; *Agape*, 1996.

BALABANOV, Alexei, b.1959. *Happy Days*, 1991; *The Castle*, 1994; *Trofim* (short film in the almanac *Arrival of a Train*), 1995; *Brother*, 1997; *Of Freaks and Men*, 1998.

BALAYAN, Roman, b.1941. Educated in Armenia; since 1970 director of the Dovzhenko Kiev Film Studio. *Dream Flights*, 1982; *Lady Macbeth of Mtsensk*, 1989; *First Love*, 1995; *Two Moons, Three Suns*, 1998.

BASHIROV, Alexander, b.1955. Debut with *The Iron Heel of Oligarchy*, 1998.

BEKMAMBETOV, Timur, b.1961, and KAIUMOV, Gennadi, b.1958. *Peshawar Waltz*, 1994.

BOBROVA, Lidia, b.1952. *Oh, You Geese*, 1991; *In That Land*, 1997.

BODROV, Sergei, b.1948. *Freedom is Paradise*, 1989; *I Wanted to See Angels*, 1992; *The Prisoner of the Mountains*, 1996 (UK release 1998); working on a new film, *The Kiss of a Bear*, lives in Los Angeles.

BORTKO, Vladimir, b.1946. *Heart of a Dog*, 1988; *Afghan Breakdown*, 1991; *The Circus Has Burnt Down, and all the Clowns Have Run Away ...* , 1998.

CHIKOV, Valeri, b.1950. *Russian Roulette*, 1990; *Stop Playing the Fool*, 1997.

CHUKHRAI, Pavel, b.1946. Son of Grigori Chukhrai. *The Thief*, 1997 (Oscar nomination).

DANELIYA, Georgi, b.1930. *Autumn Marathon*, 1979; *Passport*, 1990; *Heads or Tails*, 1995.

Appendix 1

DOSTAL, Nikolai, b.1948. *The Paradise-Cloud*, 1991; *The Little Giant of Great Sex*, 1992; *Little Demon*, 1995; *Cops and Thieves*, 1997.

DYKHOVICHNY, Ivan, b.1947. Actor at the Taganka Theatre; graduated from VGIK in 1983; *Moscow Parade*, 1992; *Music for December*, 1994; working on a script with Vladimir Sorokin: *The Kopeck.*

EVSTIGNEEV, Denis, b.1961. Debut with *Limits – Outsiders on a Contract*, 1993.

FILATOV, Leonid, b.1946. Actor at the Taganka Theatre. *Children of a Bitch*, 1991.

FOMIN, Oleg, b.1962. Actor. Debut as director with *The Cutter*, 1997.

GAIDAI, Leonid, b.1923. Director of many popular comedies of the 1960s. *Good Weather on Deribasov Street*, 1992.

GAZAROV, Sergei, b.1958. Actor and director. *The Government Inspector*, 1996.

GERMAN, Alexei, b.1938. *Road Checks*, 1971; *Twenty Days without War*, 1976; *My Friend Ivan Lapshin*, 1984; *Khrustalev, the Car!*, 1998.

GOROVETS, Leonid, b.1950. *Ladies' Tailor*, 1990.

GRAMMATIKOV, Vladimir, b.1942. Director of numerous children's films; *Little Princess*, 1997. Since October 1998 head of the Gorky Studio, Moscow.

GRYMOV, Yuri, b.1965. Clip-maker since 1988. *MuMu*, 1998.

I, Andrei, b.1959. *Scientific Section of Pilots*, 1996.

IBRAGIMBEKOV, Murad, b.1965. *The Waltz of the Golden Calves*, 1993; *A Man for a Young Woman*, 1996.

KAIDANOVSKY, Alexander, 1946–95. Actor and director. *The Kerosene Seller's Wife*, 1988.

KEOSAYAN, Tigran, b.1966. *Katka and Schizo*, 1992; *Poor Sasha*, 1997.

KHAMDAMOV, Rustam, b.1944. Hindered in his work for twenty years by the Soviet authorities; *Anna Karamazoff*, 1991, filmed as a French–Russian co-production starring Jeanne Moreau, withheld from distribution by the French producer.

KHOTINENKO, Vladimir, b.1952. *Mirror for a Hero*, 1987; *Sleeping Car*, 1989; *Patriotic Comedy*, 1992; *Makarov*, 1993; *The Muslim*, 1995; *Road* (almanac *Arrival of a Train*), 1995.

KHVAN, Alexander, b.1957. *Diuba-Diuba*, 1992; *Wedding March* (almanac *Arrival of a Train*), 1995; *Good Trash, Bad Trash*, 1998.

KONCHALOVSKY (MIKHALKOV-KONCHALOVSKY), Andrei, b.1937. Lives in the USA. *Asya's Happiness*, 1967; *A Nest of Gentlefolk*, 1969; *Uncle Vanya*, 1971; *Siberiade*, 1979; *Riaba la Poule*, 1994; *Odyssey*, 1997 (American TV).

KOVALOV, Oleg, b.1950. Film historian. *The Garden of Scorpio*, 1991; *Island of the Dead*, 1992; *Concert for a Rat*, 1995; *Sergei Eisenstein*, 1995; *Mexican Phantasies*, 1998 (a reworking of Eisenstein's lost Mexican film).

KRASNOPOLSKY, Vladimir, b.1933, and USKOV, Valeri, b.1933. Made a number of films for television. *The Thief Woman*, 1995; *Ermak*, 1989–96.

KRISHTOFOVICH, Viacheslav, b.1947. *Adam's Rib*, 1990; *Dead Man's Friend*, 1997.

LEBEDEV, Nikolai, b.1966. Debut with *The Snake Spring*, 1997.

LIVNEV, Sergei, b.1964. Scriptwriter for Soloviev's *Assa*, 1988; *Kiks*, 1991; *Hammer and Sickle*, 1994; from 1995 to 1998 head of the Gorky Studio, Moscow.

LOMKIN, Sergei, b.1956. *Fatal Eggs*, 1995.

LOPUSHANSKY, Konstantin, b.1947. *Letters from a Dead Man*, 1985; *A Museum Visitor*, 1989; *Russian Symphony*, 1994.

LUNGIN, Pavel, b.1949. *Taxi Blues*, 1990; *Luna Park*, 1992; *Line of Life*, 1996. Works in France, currently making a film about the Soviet poet Mayakovsky.

MAKAROV, Ilya, b.1963. Debut with *The Body will be Committed to the Earth and the Senior Warrant Officer will Sing*, 1998.

MAMIN, Yuri, b.1946. *The Fountain*, 1988; *Sideburns*, 1990; *Window on Paris*, 1993; *Kiss the Bride*, 1998.

MASHKOV, Vladimir, b.1963. Actor, making his directorial debut with *The Sympathy Seeker*, 1997.

MELNIKOV, Vitali, b.1928. *Tsar Aleksei*, 1997.

MENSHOV, Vladimir, b.1939. *Moscow Does Not Believe in Tears*, 1980; *Shirli-Myrli*, 1995.

MESKHIEV, Dmitri, b.1963. *Gambrinus*, 1990; *Cynics*, 1991; *Over Dark Waters*, 1993; *Exercise No. 5* (almanac *Arrival of a Train*), 1995; *The Bomb* (video), 1997; *The American Bet*, 1998.

MIKHALKOV, Nikita, b.1945. *A Slave of Love*, 1975; *Unfinished Piece for Mechanical Piano*, 1977; *Several Days From the Life of Oblomov*, 1979; *Dark Eyes*, 1987; *Urga*, 1991; *Burnt by the Sun*, 1994; *The Barber of Siberia* starring Richard Harris, Oleg Menshikov and Julia Ormond, 1998.

MOTYL, Vladimir, b.1927. *The White Sun of the Desert*, 1970, one of the classics of Soviet cinema; *The Horses are Carrying Me Away*, 1996.

MURATOVA, Kira, b.1934. Works in Odessa. *Brief Encounters*, 1967; *Long Farewells*, 1971; *Among Grey Stones*, 1983; *A Change of Fate*, 1987; *Asthenic Syndrome*, 1991; *The Sentimental Policeman*, 1992; *Enthusiasms*, 1993; *Three Stories*, 1997.

NOVAK, Vilen, b.1939. Works in Odessa. *Wild Love*, 1993; *Princess on Beans*, 1997.

OGORODNIKOV, Valeri, b.1951. *The Burglar*, 1986; *Prishvin's Paper Eyes*, 1989.

OVCHAROV, Sergei, b.1955. *A Fantastic Story*, 1983; *Lefty*, 1986; *It*, 1989; *Drum Roll*, 1993.

PANFILOV, Gleb, b.1934. *The Beginning*, 1970; *The Theme*, 1979; *Valentina*, 1981; *Vassa*, 1983; *The Mother*, 1989; *The Crowned Family*, 1998 (about the last tsar, starring Alexander Galibin and Linda Bellingham).

PEZHEMSKY, Maxim, b.1963. *Comrade Chkalov's Crossing of the North Pole*, 1990; *The Prisoners of Fortune*, 1993; *Out of this World*, 1997.

PIANKOVA, Natalia, b.1958. *Happy New Year, Moscow*, 1993. *Strange Time*, 1997.

PICHUL, Vasili, b.1961. *Little Vera*, 1988; *Dark Nights in Sochi*, 1989; *Dreams of an Idiot*, 1993.

PROSHKIN, Alexander, b.1939. *Cold Summer of 1953*, 1988; *See Paris and Die*, 1992; *The Black Veil*, 1995.

Appendix 1

RIAZANOV, Eldar, b.1927. Since *Carnival Night*, 1956, the leading director of light comedies in Russia; his films include *The Irony of Fate*, 1975; *Station for Two*, 1982; *Dear Elena Sergeevna*, 1988; *Promised Heavens*, 1991; *Hello, Fools!*, 1996. Currently working on *The Fat Man and the Thin Woman*, a lyrical comedy set in a dietary clinic.

ROGOZHKIN, Alexander, b.1949. *Chekist*, 1991; *Life with an Idiot*, 1993; *Peculiarities of the National Hunt*, 1995; *Block-Post*, 1998.

SAKHAROV, Alexei, 1934–1999. *Lady-Peasant*, 1995.

SELIANOV, Sergei, b.1955. *Angel's Day*, 1988; *All Souls' Day*, 1990; *The Time for Sadness Has Not Yet Come*, 1995; *The Russian Idea*, 1995. Head of STW Studio, St Petersburg.

SERGEEV, Viktor, b.1938. Since 1997 head of Lenfilm. *Schizophrenia*, 1997.

SHAKHNAZAROV, Karen, b.1952. Since 1998 director of Mosfilm. *We Play in a Jazz Band*, 1983; *Winter Night in Gagry*, 1985; *The Messenger Boy*, 1986; *The Tsar's Murderer*, 1991; *Dreams*, 1993; *The American Daughter*, 1995; *The Day of the Full Moon*, 1997.

SHENGELAYA, Georgi, b.1960. *The Money-Changers*, 1992; *Drive on!*, 1995; *The Classic*, 1998.

SNEZHKIN, Sergei, b.1954. *Emergency on a Regional Scale*, 1989; *Non Returnee*, 1991; *Flowers of Marigold*, 1998.

SOKUROV, Alexander, b.1951. *Lonely Voice of a Man*, 1978–87; *Maria*, 1978–88; *Sorrowful Indifference (Anaesthesia Dolorosa)*, 1983–87; *The Days of the Eclipse*, 1988; *Save and Protect*, 1989; *The Second Circle*, 1990; *The Stone*, 1992; *Whispering Pages*, 1993; *The Eastern Elegy*, 1995; *Mother and Son*, 1997.

SOLOVIEV, Sergei, b.1946. *A Hundred Days after Childhood*, 1974; *Assa*, 1988; *Black Rose is a Symbol of Sorrow* ... , 1989. From 1989 until 1997 chairman of the Union of Film-makers.

SUKACHEV, Garik, b.1959. Musician with the rock group 'Brigade S'. Debut as a director with *Middle-Age Crisis*, 1997.

SUKHOCHEV, Alexander, b.1956. *A Principled and Compassionate Look*, 1995.

SUKHOREBRY, Vladimir, b.1946. *The Raving*, 1994–96.

SURIKOVA, Alla, b.1940. *A Man from the Boulevard des Capucines*, 1987; *Moscow Holidays*, 1995; *Monday Children*, 1998.

TODOROVSKY, Petr, b.1925. *The Field Romance*, 1983; *Intergirl*, 1989; *Encore, Another Encore!*, 1992; *What a Wonderful Game*, 1995; *Menage à trois*, 1998 (remake of Room's *Bed and Sofa [Third Meshchanskaya]*, 1927).

TODOROVSKY, Valeri, b.1962. *Love*, 1991; *Katia Izmailova*, 1994; *The Land of the Deaf*, 1997.

TOT, Tomas, b.1966. *Children of Iron Gods*, 1993.

UCHITEL, Alexei, b.1951. *Giselle's Mania*, 1995.

URSULIAK, Sergei, b.1958. *Russian Ragtime*, 1993; *Summer Folk*, 1995; *Composition for Victory Day*, 1998.

VINOKUROV, Sergei, b.1963. *Vampire*, 1997.

YUFIT, Evgeni, b.1961. Works with V. Maslov. *Papa, Santa Claus is Dead*, 1991; *The Wooden Room*, 1995; *Silver Heads*, 1998.

Appendix 2
'Nika' and 'Kinotavr' Awards

Nika Awards, 1987–97

	Film	Director	Screenplay	Actor	Actress
1987	*Repentance* Tengiz Abuladze	Tengiz Abuladze (*Repentance*)	Tengiz Abuladze, Nana Dzhanelidze, Revaz Kveselava (*Repentance*)	Avtandil Makharadze (*Repentance*)	Nina Ruslanova (*Tomorrow was War*)
1988	*Cold Summer of 53* Alexander Proshkin	Andrei Konchalovsky (*Asya's Happiness*)	Yuri Klepikov (*Asya's Happiness*)	Rolan Bykov (*The Commissar*)	Natalia Negoda (*Little Vera*)
1989	*Ashik-Kerib* Sergo Paradzhanov	David Abashidze, Sergo Paradzhanov (*Ashik-Kerib*)	Alexander Mindadze (*The Servant*)	Oleg Borisov (*The Servant*)	Elena Yakovleva (*Intergirl*)
1990	*Asthenic Syndrome* Kira Muratova	Stanislav Govorukhin (Documentary: *We Cannot Live Like This*)	Stanislav Govorukhin (*We Cannot ...*)	Innokenti Smoktunovsky (*The Ladies' Tailor*)	Natalia Gundareva (*A Dog's Feast*)
1991	*The Promised Heavens* Eldar Riazanov	Eldar Riazanov (*The Promised Heavens*)	Revaz Gagriabidze, Georgi Daneliya, Arkadi Khait (*Passport*)	Oleg Yankovsky (*The Tsar's Murderer*, *Passport*)	Inna Churikova (*Adam's Rib*)

1992	*Encore, Another Encore!* Petr Todorovsky	Nikita Mikhalkov (*Urga*)	Teimuraz Babluani (Georgia) (*Sun of the Sleepless*)	Elguzha Burduli (*Sun ...*)	Tatiana Vasilieva (*See Paris and Die*)
1993	*Makarov* Vladimir Khotinenko	Tomash Tot (*Children of Iron Gods*)	Petr Lutsik, Alexei Samoriadov (*Children ...*)	Sergei Makovetsky (*Makarov*)	Marina Neelova (*You are My Only One*)
1994	*Enthusiasms* Kira Muratova	Kira Muratova (*Enthusiasms*)	Irakli Kvirikadze, Petr Lutsik, Alexei Samoriadov (*Limits*)	Evgeni Mironov (*Limits*)	Ingeborga Dapkunaite (*Katia Izmailova*)
1995	*Peculiarities of the National Hunt* Alexander Rogozhkin	Alexander Rogozhkin (*Peculiarities ...*)	Valeri Zalotukha (*The Muslim*)	Alexei Buldakov (*Peculiarities ...*)	Nina Usatova (*The Muslim*)
1996	*Prisoner of the Mountains* Sergei Bodrov	Sergei Bodrov (*Prisoner ...*)	Arif Aliev, Sergei Bodrov, Boris Giller (*Prisoner ...*)	Oleg Menshikov, Sergei Bodrov jr (*Prisoner ...*)	Elena Safonova (*The President and his Woman*)
1997	*The Thief* Pavel Chukhrai	Pavel Chukhrai (*The Thief*)	Alexander Mindadze (*Time of the Dancer*)	Vladimir Mashkov (*The Thief*)	Ekaterina Rednikova (*The Thief*)

Kinotavr – Open Russian Festival (held annually in Sochi)

	Grand Prix	Best Actor	Best Actress
1990 (Podolsk)	*Revenge* E. Shinarbaev		
1991	*The Children of a Bitch* Leonid Filatov	V. Ilyin (*Children of a Bitch*)	
1992	*The Sun of the Sleepless* T. Babluani (Georgia)	Evgeni Mironov (*Love*)	Tatiana Dogileva (*The Afghan Breakdown*)
1993	*Encore, Another Encore!* Petr Todorovsky	Alexander Zbruev (*You are My Only One*)	Tatiana Vasilieva (*See Paris and Die*)
1994	*Little Angel, Bring Happiness* Usman Saparov (Turkmenia)	Igor Skliar (*The Year of the Dog*) Vladimir Mashkov (*Limits*)	Inna Churikova (*Casanova's Cloak*)
1995	*Peculiarities of the National Hunt* Alexander Rogozhkin	Alexander Baluev (*The Muslim*)	Nina Usatova (*The Muslim*)
1996	*The Prisoner of the Mountains* Sergei Bodrov	Oleg Menshikov, Sergei Bodrov jr (*The Prisoner …*)	Natalia Koliakanova (*A Principled and Compassionate Look*)
1997	*The Brother* Alexei Balabanov	Sergei Bodrov jr (*The Brother*)	Alla Kliuka (*From Hell to Hell*)
1998	*The Time of the Dancer* Vadim Abdrashitov	Alexander Zbruev (*The Sympathy Seeker*)	Zinaida Sharko (*Composition for Victory Day, The Circus Burnt …*)

Notes

1. Introduction

1. Daniil Dondurei, 'Artistic Culture', in D. Shalin (ed.), *Russian Culture at the Crossroads* (Boulder, CO and Oxford, 1996), pp. 259–78. Dondurei describes ways of money-laundering, see pp. 268–9.

2. Miroslava Segida in 'Segida-Info', *Iskusstvo kino* 4 (1996), p. 76 (for film production 1918–95).

3. The Federal Law on Cinema ('O gosudarstvennoi podderzhke kinematografii') was passed by the Duma on 17 July 1996, ratified by the Council of the Federation on 7 August 1996, and signed by the President on 22 August 1996.

4. See Anna Lawton, *Kinoglasnost* (Cambridge, 1992), pp. 53–4. The speeches of the Congress were published in *Iskusstvo kino* 10 (1986), pp. 4–125.

5. My summary for Kovalov's text is adapted from *Seans* 12 (1996), p. 79.

6. See Dondurei, 'Artistic Culture', p. 275.

2. The Russian Idea

Translated by Natasha Synessios, annotated by Birgit Beumers. This article was first published in *Seans* 12 (1996), pp. 76–82, and is published here with kind permission of the author.

1. Kitezh is a mythical city sunken in the lake 'Svetlyi Iar'; only the believer can see it under the surface of the water.

2. Mikhail Sholokhov, *Quiet Flows the Don* (1928–40); Il'f and Petrov, *The Golden Calf* (1931).

3. A *lubok* is a print made from a wood-cut, which is often hand-coloured; it is part of primitive folk art.

4. Epigraph to *The Brothers Karamazov* from John 12.24.

5. Mikhail Chekhov, 'Sovetskim fil'movym rabotnikam po povodu "Ioanna Groznogo" S. M. Eizenshteina' (31 May 1945), in *Literaturnoe nasledie*, 2 vols (Moscow, 1986), vol. 2, pp. 164–76.

6. Naum Kleiman, director of the Museum of Cinema, Moscow, and film-maker Sergei Yutkevich edited a photo-film of *Bezhin Meadow* with the film material that had survived.

7. Slogan or myth of the 1930s to make people accept low pay, long working hours and bad housing.

8. Grigori Aleksandrov (1903–83) was an actor, then assistant to Eisenstein. In the 1930s he began making musical comedies, which were highly successful with audiences

at the time: *Jolly Fellows* [Veselye rebiata, 1934]; *The Circus* [Tsirk, 1936]; *Volga-Volga*, 1938; and *The Radiant Path* [Svetlyi put', 1940].

9. The 'Black Hundred' or 'chernosotentsy' were monarchist groups used to combat the revolutionary movement of 1905–7.

10. Alexander Rzheshevsky wrote the script for *Bezhin Meadow* and *A Simple Case*.

11. Demian Bedny (1883–1945), writer and poet, ardent supporter of Socialist Realism.

3. No Glory, No Majesty, or Honour

Research for this article was supported in part by a grant from the International Research and Exchanges Board (IREX), with funds provided by the National Endowment for the Humanities and the US Department of State. Neither of these organisations is responsible for the views expressed.

1. Vladimir Solov'ev, 'Russkaia ideia' (transl. from French by G. A. Rachinskii), in *Sobranie sochinenii*, 14 vols (Brussels, 1969), vol. 11, pp. 91–117 (p. 89). Tim McDaniel, *The Agony of the Russian Idea* (Princeton, 1996), p. 24.

2. Solov'ev, 'Russkaia ideia', p. 101; Nicolas Berdyaev, *The Russian Idea* (transl. by R. M. French), (Boston, 1962), pp. 198, 253.

3. Berdyaev, *The Russian Idea*, p. 8.

4. Ibid., pp. 3, 5.

5. Vucinich in Ibid., p. xx.

6. Berdyaev, *The Russian Idea*, p. 3.

7. Ibid., pp. 7–8.

8. See G. P. Fedotov (ed.), *A Treasury of Russian Spirituality* (New York, 1948), p. 31; Paul Bushkovitch, *Religion and Society in Russia: The Sixteenth and Seventeenth Centuries* (New York and Oxford, 1992), p. 12.

9. Scholars disagree on whether Kurbsky actually was: Auerbach quoted in Francis Thomson, 'The Corpus of Slavonic Translations Available in Muscovy: The Cause of Old Russia's Intellectual Silence and a Contributory Factor to Muscovite Cultural Autarky', in Boris Gasparov and Olga Raevsky-Hughes (eds), *Slavic Cultures in the Middle Ages*, 3 vols (Berkeley, 1993), vol. 1, pp. 179–214 (p. 209); Serge Zenkovsky (ed.), *Medieval Russia's Epics, Chronicles, and Tales* (New York, 1974), p. 366; James Billington, *The Icon and the Axe: An Interpretive History of Russian Culture* (New York, 1966), p. 94 – or was not: Thomson, 'The Corpus of Slavonic Translations', p. 209 – a pupil of Maxim the Greek in a literal sense. What is beyond dispute, however, is that the younger Kurbsky both knew Maxim and was influenced by his late hesychast views. Billington argues that Kurbsky's first-documented usage of 'Holy Russia' 'the humiliated and suffering ... wife and mother ... a ideal opposed to the mechanical and unfeeling state' was an extrapolation from Maxim's writings (Billington, *The Icon and the Axe*, pp. 92–4, 664).

10. Zenkovsky (ed.), *Medieval Russia's Epics*, p. 260.

11. Theophanes' painting style is described by Epiphanius, apparently an eyewitness, in a letter of 1414 or 1415 to St Cyril of Tver. See Robin Milner-Gulland, 'Art and Architecture of Old Russia, 988–1700', in Robert Auty and Dimitri Obolensky (eds), *Companion to Russian Studies*, 3 vols (Cambridge, 1981), vol. 3, pp. 34–9; George Hamilton, *The Art and Architecture of Russia*, 3rd edn (New Haven, 1983), pp. 92–6, 128–9; Tamara Rice, *A Concise History of Russian Art* (New York, 1963), pp. 74–8, 116–20.

12. Billington, *The Icon and the Axe*, p. 51.

13. Fairy von Lilienfeld, 'The Spirituality of the Early Kievan Caves Monastery', in Gasparov and Raevsky-Hughes (eds), *Slavic Cultures in the Middle Ages*, vol. 1, pp. 63–76 (pp. 65–7).

14. Michael Cherniavsky, '"Holy Russia": A Study in the History of an Idea', *American Historical Review* 63, no. 3 (1958), pp. 617–37 (p. 635).

15. Despite the accepted scholarly view of a split as between Josephian possessors [*stiazhateli*] and Nil's non-possessors [*nestiazhateli*] of monastic lands, a younger generation of scholars (Donald Ostrowski, 'Church Polemics and Monastic Land Acquisition in Sixteenth-Century Moscow', *Slavonic and East European Review* 64 [July 1986], pp. 355–79; J. E. Kollmann, 'The Moscow *Stoglav* [Hundred Chapters] Church Council of 1551', Ph D dissertation, University of Michigan, 1978) now increasingly questions this assumption, doubting the existence of distinct Church parties with consistent positions on monastic land-owning. A clearer (i.e. better documented) split, both between these two men and within Russian spirituality, of this era concerned the issue of monastic rule.

16. Its full title by the time of its probable completion in 1514 or 1515, shortly before Joseph's death, was 'The Authentic and Detailed Last Will and Spiritual Charter of the Reverend Abbot Iosif – "To the Spiritual Superior Who Shall Succeed Me and to All My Brothers in Christ, from the First Down to the Last" – Concerning the Monasterial and Monastic Institution, According to the Witness of the Divine Scriptures, from the Cloister of the Venerable and Glorious Dormition of the All-Glorious Mother-of-God, in Whom We Dwell'. See David Goldfrank, 'New and Old Perspectives on Iosif Volotsky's Monastic Rules', *Slavic Review* 34 (1975), pp. 279–301 (p. 281).

17. Goldfrank, 'Perpectives on Iosif Volotsky's Monastic Rules', pp. 291, 293.

18. Ia. Lur'e and A. Zimin (eds), *Poslaniia Iosifa Volotskogo* (Moscow–Leningrad, 1959), pp. 239–40. Goldfrank, 'Perpectives on Iosif Volotsky's Monastic Rules', p. 294.

19. Scholars also differ in their assessment of Josephite dominance after their apparent victory in the Church Councils of 1503–4 and 1531. Lur'e and Likhachev are most strongly convinced of an intemperate and vituperative alliance between Josephite victors and the state (see D. S. Likhachev, *Razvitie russkoi literatury X–XVIII vekov: Epokhi i stil'* [Leningrad, 1973], pp. 124–37; Ia. Lur'e, *Ideologicheskaia bor'ba v russkoi publitsistike kontsa XV–nachala XVI veka* [Moscow–Leningrad, 1960]). Bushkovitch and Fedotov, on the other hand, see a more tempered, gradual compromise emerging from this period (Bushkovitch, *Religion and Society in Russia*, p. 17; G. Fedotov, *Sviatye drevnei Rusi*, 3rd edn [Paris, 1985], pp. 187–90). Meyendorff argues that all extremes, including ardent proponents of the Third Rome, were marginalised and what emerged was a moderate Josephite compromise, stressing national identity rather than Byzantine continuity (John Meyendorff, 'Universal Witness and Local Identity in Russian Orthodoxy', in Gasparov and Raevsky-Hughes [eds], *Slavic Cultures in the Middle Ages*, vol. 1, pp. 11–29 [p. 21]). Berdiaev's analysis implicitly allies itself with Likhachev and Lur'e.

20. Billington, *The Icon and the Axe*, pp. 93–4.

21. The principal difference I would stress here is functional and stylistic rather than semantic. 'Holy Russia' is a medieval term that differentiates, as Cherniavsky suggests, nation from ruler. 'Russian Idea' is a modern (and highly self-conscious) term that retroactively attempts to fuse with the nation through a similar cultural pattern disavowing power.

22. Cherniavsky, 'Holy Russia', p. 621.

23. Fedotov (ed.), *A Treasury of Russian Spirituality*, p. 281.

24. Aleksandr Ianov, *Russkaia ideia i 2000-yi god* (New York, 1988); Donald Lowrie, *Rebellious Prophet: A Life of Nicolai Berdyaev* (New York, 1960); Matthew Spinka, *Nicolas*

Notes to Chapter 3

Berdyaev, Captive of Freedom (Philadelphia, 1950). See also James P. Scanlon (ed.), *Russian Thought After Communism: The Recovery of a Philosophical Heritage* (Armonk, New York, 1994).

25. The first major publications were, not surprisingly, Berdiaev's *pre*-emigration writings *The Philosophy of Freedom* [Filosofiia svobody, 1911] and *The Meaning of Creation* [Smysl tvorchestva, 1916]. These began to appear in the second half of 1989 in the series 'From the History of National Philosophical Thought' [Iz istorii otechestvennoi filosofskoi mysli], as a supplement to the journal *Questions of Philosophy* [Voprosy filosofii]. The decision, initially made at the highest political level, to sanction the Berdiaev publication by the Pravda publishing house of the CPSU Central Committee, testifies to his anticipated problematic popularity within the intelligentsia. See Robin Aizlewood, 'The Return of the "Russian Idea" in Publications, 1988–91', *Slavonic and East European Review* 71, no. 3 (July 1993), pp. 490–9, (p. 490).

26. *Voprosy filosofii* 1 (1990), pp. 77–144; 2 (1990), pp. 87–154. It was also published by V. A. Kotel'nikov in *Russkaia literatura* 2 (1990), pp. 85–133; 3 (1990), pp. 67–102; 4 (1990), pp. 59–111. See Aizlewood, 'The Return of the "Russian Idea"'.

27. Igor' Chubais, *Ot Russkoi idei k idee novoi Rossii: kak nam preodolet' ideinyi krizis* (Moscow, 1996); Arsenii Gulyga, *Russkaia ideia i ee tvortsy* (Moscow, 1995); Z. A. Krakhmal'nikova (ed.), *Russkaia ideia i evrei: rokovoi spor: khristianstvo, antisemitizm, natsionalizm* (Moscow, 1994); M. A. Maslin (ed.), *Russkaia ideia* (Moscow, 1992); Mikhail Nazarov, *Russkaia ideia i sovremennost'* (Moscow, 1991); V. M. Piskunov (ed.), *Russkaia ideia*, 2 vols (Moscow, 1994); V. Sh. Sabirov, *Russkaia ideia spaseniia: zhizn' i smert' v russkoi filosofii* (St Petersburg, 1995); V. N. Sagatovskii, *Russkaia ideia: prodolzhim li prervannyi put'* (St Petersburg, 1994); Aleksandr Shchelkin, 'Russkaia ideia: iskushenie dukhovnost'iu', *Nevskoe vremia*, 30 December 1992; E. S. Troitskii (ed.), *Russkaia ideia i sovremennost'* (Moscow, 1992); A. Ia. Zis' (ed.), *Russkaia ideia v krugu pisatelei i myslitelei russkogo zarubezhiia* (Moscow, 1994); G. A. Ziuganov (ed.), *Sovremennaia Russkaia ideia i gosudarstvo* (Moscow, 1995). In addition to these publications, a number of major conferences and symposia have been organised on topics relevant to the discussion here. The most noteworthy are the December 1990 conference 'The Russian Idea and Contemporary Life' (part of the so-called December Events, since 1983 an annual meeting of Russian scholars and cultural figures); the round table 'The Russian Idea and the Rebirth of Russia' at the Congress of Compatriots, held in Moscow in August 1991, during (it turned out) the August coup; the Tenth Annual 'December Events' meeting, 'Congregationalism: Sources and Contemporary Thought' (December 1991); and the Transnational Institute Conference 'The Renewal of Russian Spiritual Life', held at Dartmouth College, New Hampshire, in July 1992. For an excellent commentary and extensive critical assessments of the post-Soviet religious thought, see Scanlon (ed.), *Russian Thought After Communism*, and Caryl Emerson, 'The Russian Intelligentsia and Post-Soviet Religious Thought', *Cross Currents* 43, no. 2 (Summer 1993), pp. 184–203.

28. Oleg Kovalov, Chapter 2, p. 12.

29. Tarkovsky's inheritance is a complex topic beyond the scope of this article. My position, briefly, accords with that of Liubov' Arkus, film scholar (her major work is on Sokurov) and editor of the St Petersburg film journal *Seans*, who argues convincingly that, despite evident formal similarities, no 'direct heir' would claim Tarkovsky's path of tortured personal and professional sacrifice. In strictly cinematic terms, however, Kaidanovsky is the closest to a continuation of Tarkovsky's cinematic style.

4. Now that the Party's Over

1. 1983 interview cited in B. Eisenschitz, 'A Fickle Man, or Portrait of Boris Barnet as a Soviet Director', in R. Taylor and I. Christie (eds), *Inside the Film Factory. New Approaches to Russian and Soviet Cinema* (London and New York, 1991), p. 163.

2. There is, of course, considerable controversy over the nature of Eisenstein's relationship to Stalin, but see L. Kozlov, 'The Artist and the Shadow of Ivan', in R. Taylor and D. Spring (eds), *Stalinism and Soviet Cinema* (London and New York, 1993), pp. 109–30; and O. Bulgakowa, *Sergej Eisenstein: eine Biographie* (Berlin, 1998).

3. This account owes a great deal to conversations over more years than either of us would care to remember with Ian Christie and to his introduction to R. Taylor and I. Christie (eds), *The Film Factory. Russian and Soviet Cinema in Documents, 1896–1939* (London and Cambridge, MA, 1988; paperback edn, London and New York, 1994,) pp. 1–17.

4. See the audience statistics under the relevant entries in S. Zemlianukhin and M. Segida, *Domashniaia sinemateka: otechestvennoe kino, 1918–1996* (Moscow, 1996).

5. M. Turovskaia, 'I. A. Pyr'ev i ego muzykal'nye komedii. K probleme zhanra', *Kinovedcheskie zapiski* 1 (1988), pp. 111–46; the quotation is from p. 116. Cf. also Turovskaia's remarks in Dana Ranga's film *East Side Story* [1997].

6. This film has been so thoroughly wiped from the collective memory that it is not even mentioned in the otherwise comprehensive F. Albera and R. Cosandey (eds), *Boris Barnet. Ecrits, Documents, Etudes, Filmographie* (Locarno, 1985).

7. E. Margolit and V. Shmyrov, *(iz'iatoe kino) 1924–1953* (Moscow, 1995).

8. A. Lawton, *Kinoglasnost: Soviet Cinema in Our Time* (Cambridge, 1992), pp. 111–25.

9. O. Kovalov, Chapter 2, p. 12.

10. See, for instance, I. Avdeev and L. Zaitseva (compilers), *Vse belorusskie fil'my. Katalog-spravochnik. Tom I: Igrovoe kino 1926–1970* (Minsk, 1996).

11. Ironically, Lawton (*Kinoglasnost*, p. 175) refers to this as a 'Latvian picture' but spells the director's name in the Russian fashion, which illustrates the pitfalls perfectly.

12. A decree of 4 January 1936 changed 'film factories' into 'studios': V. Vishnevskii and P. Fionov, *Sovetskoe kino v datakh i faktakh* (Moscow, 1973), p. 103. This was either part of the process of 'normalisation' associated with the adoption of the new constitution later that year, or part of Shumyatsky's plan to create a 'Soviet Hollywood' by imitating the original. The Russian word for 'film' changed from the feminine 'fil'ma' to the masculine 'fil'm' at the end of the 1920s; nobody has ever been able to explain this strange phenomenon to me but it may have been part of the general militarisation of cultural terminology during the cultural revolution of 1928–32.

13. G. Mar'iamov, *Kremlevskii tsenzor. Stalin smotrit kino* (Moscow, 1992); V. Mikhailov, 'Stalinskaia model' upravleniia kinematografom', in L. Mamatova, *Kino: politika i liudi (30-e gody)*, Moscow, 1995; V. Fomin, *Kino i vlast'. Sovetskoe kino: 1965–1985 gody. Dokumenty, svidetel'stva, razmyshleniia* (Moscow, 1996); E. Gromov, *Stalin: vlast' i iskusstvo* (Moscow, 1998).

14. *Piatyi s'ezd kinematografistov SSSR. 13–15 maia 1986 goda. Stenograficheskii otchet* (Moscow, 1987).

15. Document dated February 1933: A. V. Lunacharskii, *Sobranie sochinenii v 8 tomakh* (Moscow, 1967), vol. 8, pp. 615–16; translated in Taylor and Christie, *The Film Factory*, p. 327.

16. '*Chapaeva* smotrit vsia strana', *Pravda*, 21 November 1934, translated in Taylor and Christie, *The Film Factory*, pp. 334–5.

17. The work done by a team of Moscow scholars under the leadership of Maya Turovskaya and shortly to be published under the title *The Film Process* will clarify many of these questions.

18. Yu. Vorontsov and I. Rachuk, *The Phenomenon of Soviet Cinema* (Moscow, 1980).

19. *Time*, 14 September 1981.

5. Russian Cinema – National Cinema?

Translated and annotated by Birgit Beumers. Dondurei's speech is published here with kind permission of the author. Mikhalkov's speech is published with kind permission of the Gorky Studio and adapted from the Gorky Studio's Information Bulletin, no. 21 (37), 3 June 1998, pp. 6–7.

1. *Samogon* is home-distilled vodka; distilling alcohol was an illegal activity.

2. Selianov here paraphrases Pushkin's 'Deep in Siberia's mines ... ' (1827) dedicated to the Decembrists.

3. Three of the most well-known directors of 'Soviet' times: Andrei Tarkovsky (1932–86); the Georgian director Otar Ioseliani (b. 1934); and Armenian film-maker Sergo Paradzhanov (1924–94).

4. Films which show a bleak reality and focus on pornographic scenes.

5. Ivan-the-Fool is a fairytale character; he performs heroic deeds, in between which he fails to cope with everyday reality.

6. Sergei Soloviev addressed the Congress in his function of Chairman on 22 December 1997. Dondurei's speech was given on the same day.

7. The Federal Law on Cinema was authorised by the President on 22 August 1996.

8. A film by Alexei Sakharov based on Pushkin's stories, in which he dwells on the 'eternal values of love and the family'.

9. The films with their original title, director(s) and production date are: *The Year of the Dog* [God sobaki], Semen Aranovich, 1994 (Russia/France); *Limits* [Limita], Denis Evstigneev, 1993; *Peshawar Waltz* [Peshavarskii val's], Timur Bekmambetov, Gennadi Kaiumov, 1994; *Life with an Idiot* [Zhizn' s idiotom], Alexander Rogozhkin, 1993 (based on V. Erofeev); *Riaba la poule* [Kurochka Riaba], Andrei Konchalovsky, 1994 (Russia/France); *The Muslim* [Musul'manin], Vladimir Khotinenko, 1995; *Schizophrenia* [Shizofreniia], Viktor Sergeev, 1997; *Brother* [Brat], Alexei Balabanov, 1997.

10. Nautilus Pompilius: St Petersburg rock band, headed by Viacheslav (Slava) Butusov.

11. *The Vampire* [Upyr'], Sergei Vinokurov, 1997; *The Cutter* [Mytar'], Oleg Fomin, 1997; *Good Trash – Bad Trash* [Drian' khoroshaia, drian' plokhaia], Alexander Khvan, 1998.

12. Gilles Jacob, director of the Cannes Film Festival; Moritz de Hadeln, Berlin Film Festival; Marco Müller, Locarno Film Festival.

13. For comparison: 'All those who interested themselves even a little in the national situation saw the difficult situation in agriculture, but Stalin had never even noted it. Did we tell Stalin about this? Yes, we told him, but he did not support us. Why? Because Stalin never travelled anywhere, did not meet city or kolkhoz workers; he did not know the actual situation in the provinces. He knew the country and agriculture only from films. And those films had dressed up and beautified the existing situation in agriculture. Many films so pictured kolkhoz life that the tables were bending from the weight of turkeys and geese. Evidently, Stalin thought it was actually so.' N. S. Khrushchev, 'The Secret Speech', 1956. Quoted from the edition by Zhores and Roy Medvedev, 1976 (p. 72).

14. Chapayev, hero of the civil war, portrayed in the 1934 film by the Vasiliev Brothers. Stirlitz was a hero-spy in the Great Patriotic War (World War II) as portrayed in *Seventeen Moments of Spring* [17 mgnovenii vesny], a 1970s television serial based on Yulian Semenov's novel of the same title.

6. Tinkling Symbols

1. Viktor Tsoi, leader of the rock band Kino, died in 1990.
2. Sergei Livnev in the Russian TV talk show 'National Interest', October 1997.
3. Valeri Chkalov (1904–38), pilot who pioneered non-stop flights from Moscow to the Far East and to Vancouver.
4. The author here lists a number of figures from the artistic scene: the film-maker Petr Lutsik (b. 1960), the actors Alexander Negreba (b. 1961) and Oleg Boretsky, the actress and scriptwriter Renata Litvinova (b. 1967), the actor, playwright and film-maker Ivan Okhlobystin (b. 1966), and the film-maker Andrei I. [B.B.]
5. 'Ivan Okhlobystin – ditia solntsa', interview with A. Titov, *Iskusstvo kino* 4 (1991), p. 14.
6. Sergei Livnev, 'Ekonomika v kino opredeliaet estetiku ... ' *Iskusstvo kino* 12 (1997), pp. 6–9.
7. See Gorky Studio Information Bulletin no. 4, 8 October 1997, p. 1.
8. N. A. Berdiaev, *Istoki i smysl' russkogo kommunizma* (Moscow, 1990), p. 109.
9. See M. Allenov, 'Ochevidnosti sistemnogo absurdizma skvoz' emblematiku moskovskogo metro', *Iskusstvo kino* 6 (1990), pp. 81–2.
10. Viktor Borisov-Musatov (1870–1905), painter, expressing in his decorative painting the dream of man's harmony with nature.
11. Aleksandr Khvan, 'Kino – kollektivnoe snovidenie chelovechestva', *Kinovedcheskie zapiski* 16 (1992), p. 166.
12. Slavoi Zhizhek, 'Kiberprostranto, ili Nevynosimaia zamknutost' bytiia' (Cyberspace, or the Unbearable Closeness of Being), *Iskusstvo kino* 2 (1998), p. 124.
13. Vladimir Soloviev, 'O narodnosti i narodnykh delakh Rossii', in *Literaturnaia kritika* (Moscow, 1990), p. 295.

7. Viewed from Below

1. Nikolai Berdiaev, *Sud'ba Rossii* (Moscow, 1990), p. 65. Written in 1915, first published 1919.
2. While recognising the historical problems in this definition, I will refer to the Soviet Union as a 'nation' for these purposes, as the question of the 'national' space is central to my argument.
3. For an examination of these themes, see my article, 'An Unmappable System: The Collapse of Public Space in Late Soviet Cinema', *Film Criticism* XXI, 2 (Winter 1996), pp. 8–24.
4. See Il'ia Alekseev, 'Den' voskreseniia: fil'my Sergeiia Sel'ianova na fone russkoi kul'turnoi traditsii', *Iskusstvo kino* 7 (1993), pp. 10–19, for discussion of Selianov's first films in the context of Russian identity.
5. Andrei Platonov, 'Gosudarstvennyi zhitel'', in Platonov, *Gosudarstvennyi zhitel': proza, rannie sochineniia, pis'ma* (Minsk, 1990), pp. 370–80 (p. 371).
6. Vladimir Erofeev was a key figure in the development of the Soviet travelogue during the late 1920s. See for example *Far Away in Asia* [Daleko v Azii, 1931] and *The Roof of the World: An Expedition to Pamir* [Krysha mira: ekspeditsiia na Pamir, 1927].

7. The Turksib railway, linking Turkestan and Siberia, opened in 1930, provoking a storm of documentary films, press eulogies and literature in celebration. The most famous and successful of the films was Viktor Turin's 1930 film *Turksib*.

8. For Russian criticism of *Hammer and Sickle*, see *Seans* 10 (1994), pp. 10–11.

9. Henri Bergson, *L'évolution créatrice* (Paris, 1909), pp. 330–1. First published Paris, 1907. Bergson's conception of movement as heterogeneous and indivisible was set out in *Matter and Memory* in 1896.

8. To Moscow! To Moscow?

The author wishes to thank the Arts Faculty Research Fund of the University of Bristol for supporting research for this article.

1. See Sergei Dobrotvorsky, 'Cinema Myths and the Future of Culture', in E. Berry and A. Miller-Pogacar (eds), *Re-Entering the Sign* (Ann Arbor, 1995), pp. 311–23 (p. 312).

2. See Evgenii Margolit, 'Signal o nalichii zhizni', *Iskusstvo kino* 2 (1996), p. 6.

3. See *Seans* 16 (1997) for a dossier on the hero-figure of the killer in Russian cinema.

4. Nina Tsyrkun, 'Zhizn' kak siuzhet', *Iskusstvo kino* 4 (1993), p. 57.

5. Karina Dobrotvorskaia, 'Uvidet' Parizh i vyzhit'', *Seans* 9 (1994), p. 85.

6. Zara Abdullaeva, 'Popular Culture,' in D. Shalin (ed.), *Russian Culture at the Crossroads* (Boulder, CO and Oxford, 1996), p. 212.

7. Tatiana Moskvina, 'Istochniki zhizni eshche ne issiakli', *Seans* 12 (1996), p. 26.

8. See Valerii Todorovskii, 'Rossiia perezhivaet burnyi roman s den'gami', Interview with Roman Khrishch, *Seans* 16 (1997), p. 102.

9. Evgenii Margolit, 'Plach po pioneru, ili Nemetskoe slovo "Iablokitai"', *Iskusstvo kino* 2 (1998), p. 58.

10. Mikhail Brashinskii, 'Ubiitsy sredi nas', *Seans* 16, pp. 104–9 (p. 109).

11. Viktor Matizen in his review 'Skromnoe ocharovanie ubiitsy', *Seans* 16 (1997), p. 41, disputes the verisimilitude of his actions.

12. Margolit, 'Plach po pioneru', p. 59.

13. See Alla Bossart, 'Son na porazhenie', *Seans* 16 (1997), p. 40.

14. Brashinskii, 'Ubiitsy sredi nas', p. 109.

15. Katerina Clark, *The Soviet Novel: History as Ritual*, 2nd edn (Chicago, 1985).

16. See Vladimir Papernyi, *Kul'tura dva* (Moscow, 1996).

9. La Grande Illusion

This article was first published in *Iskusstvo kino* 6 (1997) and is reprinted here with kind permission.

1. 'Nikita Mikhalkov: dela semeinye' (dossier of interviews and articles), *Domovoi* 10 (1995), pp. 45–60 (p. 60).

2. Mikhalkov's debut as an actor was made in this film by Daneliya. [B.B.]

3. Vladislav Khodasevich, 'Pered zerkalom', in *Sobranie sochinenii* vol. 1 (Ardis, 1983), p. 161. [B.B.]

4. Moskvina here alludes to the title of Leonid Lukov's film *A Great Life* [Bol'shaia zhizn'], the first part released in 1940, while the second was shelved in 1946. [B.B.]

5. *Novoe vremia* 31 (1996), p. 36.

6. Moskvina here refers to 'The time is out of joint' as rendered by Pasternak in his translation of 1940. [B.B.]

7. Konstantin Rudnitskii, in 'O chem? Vo imia chego?' (Critics' views, ed. Alla Gerber), *Sovetskii ekran* 1 (1975), p. 2 (on Mikhalkov's debut as a director).

8. 'Stop, moment, you are beautiful' is a paraphrase of Goethe's *Faust*, 'Zum Augenblicke dürft ich sagen: Verweile doch, du bist so schön!' [B.B.]

9. Vera Shitova, 'Segodnia, 20 let spustia,' *Iskusstvo kino* 2 (1984), p. 66.

10. Kamchatka is a peninsula in the Pacific Ocean; Chukotka is a region on the Bering Sea in the far north-east, the closest point of Soviet/Russian territory to the USA. [B.B.]

11. Shitova, 'Segodnia'.

12. Sergei Nikolaevich in *Domovoi* 10 (1995), p. 59.

13. Elena Stishova, 'Neokonchennaia p'esa dlia mechanicheskogo pianino,' *Iskusstvo kino* 7 (1989), p. 87.

14. Nikolaevich, *Domovoi*.

15. Iurii Bogomolov, 'Rol' i sud'ba: Sluchai N. Mikhalkova,' *Stolitsa* 25 (1992), p. 51.

16. Urga: a pole thrust into the steppe to mark a territory for making love. [B.B.]

17. *The Government Inspector*, directed by Sergei Gazarov with a cast including the stars of contemporary Russian cinema: Evgeni Mironov, Marina Neelova, Oleg Yankovsky, Armen Dzhigarkhanian, Vladimir Ilyin, Avangard Leontev. [B.B.]

18. *Nezavisimaia gazeta*, 20 July 1996, p. 3.

19. Moskvina here refers to two moments in history when the people (rather than the professional military) defended the country: in 1612 a second national army was formed under Minin and Pozharsky; and in 1812 the people's resistance to the invasion of Napoleon's army led to his defeat. [B.B.]

20. Nina Zarkhi in 'O chem? Vo imia chego?' (Critics' views, ed. Alla Gerber), *Sovetskii ekran* 1 (1975), p. 3.

21. Aleksandr Kaliagin, b. 1942, played in *A Stranger* ... , *Unfinished Piece* ... , and *A Slave of Love*; since 1971 actor at the Moscow Arts Theatre; now runs his own theatre ('Et Cetera'). Svetlana Kriuchkova, b. 1950, played in *Kinfolk* and is an actress in the Bolshoi Drama Theatre in St Petersburg. [B.B.]

22. Oleg Menshikov, b. 1960, winner of the Russian State Prize and numerous other awards; roles in the theatre include Esenin in London (1991) and Nijinsky (1993); roles in cinema include: Sergei Sinitsyn in *My Favourite Clown* [Moi liubimyi kloun, 1986]; Arteniev in *Moonsund* [Moonzund, 1987]; Andrei Pletnev in *Diuba-Diuba* [1992]; Mitia in *Burnt by the Sun*; Sasha in *The Prisoner of the Mountains* [Kavkazskii plennik, 1996]. [B.B.]

23. Menshikov performed in English in a production of *The Gamblers* in London in 1992. [B.B.]

24. Maia Turovskaia, 'P'esa bez nazvaniia', in A. Sandler (ed.), *Nikita Mikhalkov* (Moscow, 1989), p. 58.

25. Klara Shul'zhenko (1906–84). Her songs were very popular in the 1930s and 1940s. [B.B.]

26. Aleksandr Adabashian, b. 1945, wrote the following scenarios with Mikhalkov: *Unfinished Piece* ... , *Five Evenings, Oblomov, A Stranger* ... , *A Slave of Love, Kinfolk*. [B.B.]

27. Rustam Ibragimbekov, b. 1939, has collaborated with Mikhalkov since the mid-1980s. He also wrote the screenplay for *The White Sun of the Desert* (1970). [B.B.]

28. 'Cranberry juice in a fairbooth' – the use of red liquid for scenes of bloodshed in street theatre. [B.B.]

29. Mikhalkov, *Domovoi* 10 (1995), p. 60.

30. T. Moskvina, 'Nikita Mikhalkov: V shutku i vser'ez,' *Iskusstvo kino* 4 (1987). pp. 77–85.

31. These lines are taken from the Tsarist anthem.

Notes to Chapters 10 and 11

10. Fathers for the Fatherland

1. For a survey of recent Russian films on Stalinism, see Julian Graffy, 'Unshelving Stalin: After the Period of Stagnation', in Richard Taylor and Derek Spring (eds), *Stalinism and Soviet Cinema* (London and New York), 1993, pp. 212–27.

2. Both *To Kill the Dragon* and *The Servant* are discussed in Anna Lawton, 'The Ghost that Does Return: Exorcising Stalin', in Taylor and Spring (eds), *Stalinism and Soviet Cinema*, pp. 186-200.

3. The Moika is one of the main canals through St Petersburg.

4. For further discussion of Mamin's films see Andrew Horton and Michael Brashinsky, *The Zero Hour: Glasnost and Soviet Cinema in Transition* (Princeton, 1991), especially, pp. 201–7.

5. For discussion of the nationalistic themes in Russian cinema of recent years, see David Gillespie, 'Identity and the Past in Recent Russian Cinema', in Wendy Everett (ed.), *European Identity in Cinema* (Exeter, 1996), pp. 53–60.

6. Elena Stishova, 'Razryv', *Iskusstvo kino* 1 (1995), p. 47.

7. Alexandra Heidi Karriker, *Turmoil on the Screen: Shifting Perspectives in Soviet and Post-Communist Cinema* (Morgantown, 1993), p. 18.

11. New Versions of Old Classics

1. Boris Eikhenbaum, 'Literature and Cinema' (trans. by T. L. Aman), in Stephen Bann and John E. Bowlt (eds), *Russian Formalism: A Collection of Articles and Texts in Translation* (Edinburgh, 1973), pp. 122–7 (pp. 122–3).

2. Morris Beja, *Film and Literature: An Introduction* (New York and London, 1979), p. 82. See also the seminal study on this theme, Robert Richardson, *Literature and Film* (Bloomington and London, 1969).

3. Brian McFarlane, *Novel to Film: An Introduction to the Theory of Adaptation* (Oxford, 1996), p. 26.

4. I do not intend here to examine the cinematic treatment of post-1917 Russian literature, although some of the greatest Soviet films belong to this category. These include Mark Donskoi's Maxim Gorki Trilogy (1938–40) and Alexander Askoldov's *The Commissar* [Komissar, 1967, rel. 1987]. Donskoi's trilogy is a superb example of realism, with an explicit ideological content. *The Commissar*, based on the story 'In the Town of Berdichev' ('V gorode Berdicheve') by Vasili Grossman, blends themes of anti-Semitism, feminism and motherhood with startling images of death and violence to evoke the loss and futility of revolution and civil war. This film, along with Evgeni Tsymbal's film *Tale of the Unextinguished Moon* [Povest' nepogashennoi luny, 1987], based on the 1926 novella by Boris Pilniak, was released within the context of Gorbachev's policy of *glasnost* in the arts. Both films therefore became part of a political agenda, very much, though obviously for vastly differing purposes, like Donskoi's epic trilogy fifty years earlier.

5. Classical Russian literature has always been part of the staple diet of Russian cinema, since its early, silent beginnings. During the Stalin years, the otherwise severe strictures of Socialist Realism gave directors such as Vladimir Petrov the opportunity to produce faithful renditions of the classics, remaining as faithful as possible to the original text, while portraying the life of nineteenth-century Russia in stark and bleak terms; Petrov made a number of films based on the plays by Alexander Ostrovsky. In the 1960s and 1970s the 'giants' of the nineteenth century, such as the works of Dostoevsky and Tolstoi, were given lavish screen treatment. Nevertheless, it is possible to see in these films, despite their fidelity, at times word-for-word, to the original text, the attempt, as

with *The Lady with the Lapdog,* to put a Socialist Realist gloss on the classics. Pyriev's version of *The Brothers Karamazov* makes no mention of the uplifting theme of children and the future with which Dostoevsky ends his novel, thereby adding to the feeling of gloom and hopelessness in pre-revolutionary Russia.

6. There were only forty-six films made in Russia in 1995, compared to 300 in 1990. See Julian Graffy, 'Everything Will Be OK', *Sight and Sound*, October 1996, pp. 24–5.

7. In a recent survey of the cinema, V. Pritulenko characterised the recent trend of screening the literary classics as the 'new escapism', which sees directors in 'flight from actuality and into another reality, the saving bosom of literature'. See V. Pritulenko, 'Svoimi slovami', *Iskusstvo kino* 9 (1996), pp. 65–71 (p. 71).

8. Boris Eikhenbaum's comments in 1926 are again illuminating: 'my general thesis [is] that the word is not completely excluded from film. From this assertion follows another: that the word has a special role in film, and that film opposes the culture of reading, and hence of literature. The competition of cinema with literature is an undeniable fact of our present culture. The development of film undoubtedly threatens the culture of reading so long as its success is connected with the rejection of books by the masses. By the same token, the gravitation of cinema toward literature should be examined, not only as a pull of syncretic tendencies but also as a strugle for dominance. If this is a marriage, then film plays the role of the husband' ('Literature and Cinema', p. 126). See also Julian Graffy's review of 'Katia Izmailova', *Sight and Sound*, February 1996, p. 46.

9. Bodrov affirms that work on the screenplay actually began before the outbreak of the Chechen war. See his interview 'Ne tol'ko o chechenskoi voine', *Literaturnaia gazeta*, 7 August 1996, p. 8. For further discussion of this film, see David Gillespie and Natasha Zhuravkina, 'Sergei Bodrov's "A Prisoner in the Caucasus"', *Rusistika* 14 (December 1996), pp. 56–9, and Julian Graffy, 'Soldier, Soldier', *Sight and Sound*, March 1998, pp. 34–5.

10. The theme of the 'noble savage' of the mountains, notably absent in Tolstoi's story but not in Pushkin's poem, is also present in the 1978 Soviet TV production of *A Prisoner of the Caucasus,* directed by Georgi Kalatozishvili and starring Yuri Nazarov and Vladimir Solodnikov as the captured Russian officers. The ending, when Zhilin's life is spared, is similar to that of Bodrov's film. It was shown on BBC TV in 1980 and repeated in 1982.

11. Bodrov himself said that he initially wanted to make the film in Bosnia (Bodrov, 'Ne tol'ko o chechenskoi voine'); in another interview, he does not hide the fact that the film criticises Russian imperial attitudes. See Sergei Bodrov, 'Govoriat, my sdelali anti-russkuiu kartinu', *Obshchaia gazeta*, 3 July 1996, p. 8.

12. As a political film, *The Prisoner of the Mountains* can stand comparison with recent British films about Northern Ireland, such as Neil Jordan's *Michael Collins* [1996] and *The Crying Game* [1994], and Thaddeus O'Sullivan's *Nothing Personal* [1995], all of which have courted controversy in the British media for their handling of a topical and fiercely debated issue.

13. Susan Layton, *Russian Literature and Empire: Conquest of the Caucasus from Pushkin to Tolstoy* (Cambridge, 1994), p. 288.

12. Representation – Mimicry – Death

Translated by Birgit Beumers.

1. Hubert Robert (1733–1808), landscape painter, also known as 'Robert des Ruines'. [B.B.]

2. Giovanni Paolo Panini (1691–1765), painter of Roman topography, especially views of ruins. [B.B.]

3. Giovanni-Niccolo Servandoni (1695–1766), theatre designer and architect; in 1732 created the façade of Saint-Sulpice. [B.B.]

4. Giambattista Piranesi (1720–78), draughtsman and etcher, especially famous for his prints of Roman ruins. His 'Carceri d'invenzione' ('Imaginary Prisons') date from c. 1745. [B.B.]

5. Philippe Hamon, *Expositions* (Berkeley, 1992), p. 62. 'Objective riddle' is an expression borrowed from Hegel.

6. Rainer-Maria Rilke, *Selected Letters 1902–1926* (London, 1988), p. 240.

7. Alois Riegl, 'The Modern Cult of Monuments: Its Character and its Origin', *Oppositions* 25 (Fall 1982), pp. 38–9.

8. Georg Simmel, 'The Ruin', *Selected Works [Izbrannoe]*, vol. 2 (Moscow, 1996), p. 230.

9. Barbara Stafford has explored in detail the analogy between anatomic figurativeness and the depiction of ruins. The destruction, the shedding of skin, play an important role in her analysis: Barbara Maria Stafford, *Body Criticism* (Cambridge, MA, 1991), pp. 58–66.

10. Michael Fried, *Art and Objecthood* (Chicago, 1998), p. 153. The most uncompromising and protracted critique of Fried's aesthetics belongs to Rosalind Krauss. See Rosalind Krauss, 'Using Language to Do Business as Usual', in Norman Bryson (ed.), *Visual Theory. Painting and Interpretation* (New York, 1991), pp. 79–94.

11. Fried, *Art and Objecthood*, p. 197.

12. Theodor Adorno, *In Search of Wagner* (London and New York, 1981), p. 34.

13. Roger Caillois, 'Mimicry and Legendary Psychasthenia', in Annette Michelson (ed.), *October. The First Decade* (Cambridge, MA), 1987, p. 70.

14. Rosalind Krauss, *The Optical Unconscious* (Cambridge, MA, 1993), p. 183.

15. Martin Kemp (ed.), *Leonardo on Painting* (New Haven, 1989), p. 88.

16. Daniel Arasse, *Vermeer. Faith in Painting* (Princeton, 1994), p. 73.

17. Ibid., p. 75.

18. Jean-Luc Nancy, *The Birth to Presence* (Stanford, CA, 1993), p. 86.

19. Jean-Luc Nancy, 'De l'évidence', *Cinémathèque* 8 (Autumn 1995), p. 55.

20. On this theme in *The Stone* see Mikhail Iampolski, *Demon i labirint* (Moscow, 1996), pp. 117–70.

21. See Georges Didi-Huberman, *La Ressemblance informe* (Paris, 1995), pp. 98–100.

22. The classical analysis of the colossus belongs to Jean-Pierre Vernant, *Mythe et pensée chez les Grecs, II* (Paris, 1965), p. 65–78.

23. Giorgio Agamben, *Homo Sacer. Sovereign Power and Bare Life* (Stanford, CA, 1998), p. 98.

24. Aleksandr Sokurov, 'Tvorcheskii alfavit', *Kinograf* 3 (1997), p. 88.

25. See Carl Schmitt, *Political Romanticism* (Cambridge, MA, 1986), pp. 11–15.

13. The Meaning of Death

1. For an overview of Muratova's film career before the break-up of the Soviet Union, see Jane A. Taubman, 'The Cinema of Kira Muratova', *Russian Review* 52 (1993), pp. 367–81.

2. See for example V. Bozhovich, 'Rentgenoskopiia dushi', *Iskusstvo kino* 9 (1987), pp. 51–70; and V. Fomin, 'Ot cheloveka k "chelovecheskomu faktoru"', *Iskusstvo kino* 4 (1989), pp. 78–87. Taubman (p. 368) talks of Muratova's 'Tolstoyan moral absolutism'. Taubman's comment notwithstanding, Muratova's image in the West is largely that of

a non-conformist feminist film-maker interested in the 'woman question'. See for example Lynne Attwood (ed.), *Red Women on the Silver Screen* (London, 1993), pp. 84–7. A press release at the 47th Berlin International Film Festival where *Three Stories* was screened in January 1997 described the film as a 'feminist thriller'.

3. Taubman, 'The Cinema of Kira Muratova', p. 369.

4. For an interview with the director see L. Gersova (comp.), 'Kira Muratova otvechaet zriteliam', *Kinovedcheskie zapiski* 13 (1992), pp. 157–68.

5. A full study of Muratova's output is beyond the scope of the present chapter. For a discussion of the continuity between her early work and *Asthenic Syndrome*, see Graham Roberts, 'Look Who's Talking: The Politics of Representation and the Representation of Politics in Two Films by Kira Muratova', *Elementa* 3 (1997), pp. 309–23.

6. Like most aesthetic/philosophical categories, the Absurd has been defined in a number of different ways. Amazingly, the definitive survey of the Absurd as a literary genre remains Martin Esslin, *The Theatre of the Absurd*, 3rd edn (Harmondsworth, 1987). For a short bibliography on the Absurd, see Péter Müller, *Central European Playwrights Within and Without the Absurd: Václav Havel, Slawomir Mrozek, and István Erkény* (Pécs, 1996); he draws a useful distinction (p. 18) between *writers* of the Absurd (Ionesco, Beckett, Genet), and *philosophers* of the Absurd (the existentialists Camus and Sartre): 'The existentialist thinkers tried to create *tragic* forms using the structures of realism to examine and demonstrate the metaphysics of their philosophy. The Theatre of the Absurd, on the other hand, produced a new genre, a new dramatic form and a unique theatrical language.' As we shall see, Muratova is far closer to the latter group than to the former.

7. Viktor Gul'chenko, 'Mezhdu "ottepeliami"', *Iskusstvo kino* 6 (1991), pp. 57–69. Barbara Heldt went so far as to describe *Asthenic Syndrome* as 'the best *glasnost* film to date': 'Gynoglasnost: Writing the Feminine', in Mary Buckley (ed.), *Perestroika and Soviet Women* (Cambridge, 1991), pp. 160–75 (p. 168).

8. In a recent interview, Muratova has insisted that in her films she tries merely to *reflect* reality, rather than to articulate a moral message which might help to *change* that reality ('Kira Muratova otvechaet zriteliam').

9. A detailed summary of *Asthenic Syndrome* can be found in Frank Beardow, 'Women's Films', Part 3, *Rusistika* 11 (June 1995), pp. 35–42 (pp. 38–41). On this film, see also Andrew Horton and Michael Brashinsky, *The Zero Hour: Glasnost and Soviet Cinema in Transition* (Princeton, 1991), pp. 105–8.

10. Such use of cinematic *mise en abyme* links *Asthenic Syndrome* to films as diverse as Dziga Vertov's *Man with a Movie Camera* [Chelovek s kinoapparatom, 1928] and Peter Greenaway's *The Baby of Macon* [UK, 1992].

11. Muratova has in fact suggested that Natasha and Nikolai suffer from different forms of an identical 'asthenic syndrome' ('Kira Muratova otvechaet zriteliam', p. 160).

12. This sends us back to one of the first stories we hear, in the 'Natasha' film.

13. See Samuel Beckett, *The Unnamable* (New York, 1970).

14. One critic has suggested that the 'death of Man' in this film amounts to the same thing as the 'death of God': see Andrei Plakhov, 'Legkaia muza, ili Esteticheskii sindrom', *Iskusstvo kino* 8 (1994), pp. 3–7.

15. Quoted in Esslin, *The Theatre of the Absurd*, p. 23.

16. Taubman ('The Cinema of Kira Muratova', p. 380) sees, in the strange way Tolia dances around the cabbage patch in the opening sequence, echoes of filming and acting techniques first elaborated in Russia in the 1920s by the collective known as 'The Factory of the Eccentric Actor' (FEKS). This combination of incongruity and theatricality will be a feature of *Three Stories* (see below).

17. Despite the fact that *The Sentimental Policeman* has much in common thematically with its predecessor, Muratova has claimed that this film was 'the polar opposite of *Asthenic Syndrome* in all respects' (quoted in Taubman, op. cit., p. 380).

18. Russian cinema may be said to have come full circle with this courtroom scene, since in many respects it is the mirror image of the trial scene in Pudovkin's *Mother* [Mat', 1926], which satirised the pre-Soviet, tsarist legal system.

19. Chance and fate are the central theme of Muratova's film *A Change of Fate* [Peremena uchasti, 1987], in which a woman, accused of murdering her lover, is unexpectedly saved by her husband.

20. According to Taubman ('The Cinema of Kira Muratova', p. 381), 'the film continues [Muratova's] investigation into the dynamics of intimate human relationships and the relation of speech to reality'.

21. The idea that Natasha might in fact be the physical realisation of Tolia's belief system looks forward to the way in which the boundary between the imaginary and the real is blurred in Muratova's subsequent film, *Enthusiasms*.

22. According to our reading, however, this film is less optimistic than is suggested by Jane Taubman, for whom, 'Muratova clearly intends *The Sentimental Cop* [sic] as a companion-piece to the apocalyptic *Asthenic Syndrome*, an assertion that life and love will and must go on even after the death of Russia' ('The Cinema of Kira Muratova', p. 381).

23. Quoted in Plakhov, 'Legkaia muza', p. 4.

24. Quoted in Sergei Zemlianukhin and Miroslava Segida, *Domashniaia sinematika: otechestvennoe kino, 1918–1996* (Moscow, 1996), p. 465.

25. This is not to imply that 'surreal' is in any way synonymous with 'absurd'.

26. The monologues in this film were written by the actress Renata Litvinova, who plays the role of the nurse. A slightly different version of this monologue can be found in Renata Litvinova, 'Boites' svoikh zhelanii – oni sbyvaiutsia', *Iskusstvo kino* 8 (1994), pp. 10–14 (p. 13). An interview with Litvinova, which contains the monologues featured in *Enthusiasms*, can also be found in *Kinostsenarii* 5 (1994), pp. 112–33. For a discussion of the metaphysical implications of language in this film, see I. Mantsov, 'Kollektivnoe telo kak romanticheskii geroi-liubovnik', *Iskusstvo kino* 8 (1994), pp. 7–9.

27. A version of this text can be found in Litvinova, 'Boites' svoikh zhelanii', p. 12.

28. Compare this with the way Ionesco's and Beckett's characters keep on talking in order to fill the void, in plays such as *Endgame, Happy Days, The Chairs* or *The Bald Prima Donna*.

29. Compare this with the closing lines of Beckett's *Waiting for Godot* (1952): '[*Vladimir*]: Well? Shall we go? [*Estragon*]: Yes, let's go. [They do not move]' (Samuel Beckett, *Waiting for Godot* [London, 1965], p. 94). The issue of identity is just as significant in *The Sentimental Policeman*, where Natasha's 'identity' is the subject of the dispute between the couple and the doctor.

30. See Plakhov, 'Legkaia muza', and Litvinova, 'Boites' svoikh zhelanii'.

31. On *Three Stories*, see Iuliia Tarantul, 'Poznavaia kriminal'nyi mir', *Novoe vremia* 12 (1997), p. 43.

32. The figure of Zhenia, who seems everywhere out of place, has its roots in the nineteenth-century Russian literary tradition of the 'superfluous man'. Indeed, Zhenia tells Gennadi at one moment that he feels like the 'superfluous men' Pechorin and Onegin.

33. This detail is reminiscent of the senseless, exaggerated violence in the prose of one of Russia's proto-absurdists, namely Daniil Kharms (1905–42). On Kharms and the Absurd, see Neil Cornwell (ed.), *Daniil Kharms and the Poetics of the Absurd: Essays and Materials* (Basingstoke and London, 1991).

34. The very fact that male homosexual characters are featured in a Russian film – one of Veniamin's clients propositions the man and kisses him on the lips – is one of the most striking incongruities of *Three Stories*.

35. On the 'surrealist' features of Muratova's *Among the Grey Stones* [Sredi serykh kamnei, 1987], see Taubman, 'The Cinema of Kira Muratova', p. 378.

36. In a visual allusion to Muratova's own film *Asthenic Syndrome*, the woman who plays Ofa's mother here also played the role of the deputy director of Nikolai's school.

37. Taubman ('The Cinema of Kira Muratova', p. 377) talks of 'the tendency to ornamentalism in Muratova's work'.

38. As this last example highlights, Muratova's camera frequently lingers on an image or a scene much longer than we might expect, thereby suggesting that significance is not where it seems. This is a feature of a number of proto-absurdist Russian prose writers. See Cathy Popkin, *The Pragmatics of Insignificance: Chekhov, Zoshchenko, Gogol* (Stanford, CA, 1993).

39. Interestingly, this echoes an otherwise isolated comment by one of the residents (an old woman) who complain about the dog fight in *The Sentimental Policeman* to the effect that 'everything is forbidden' [*vse zapreshchaetsia*].

14. Dmitri Astrakhan

I wish to express my gratitude to Birgit Beumers for supplying me with copies of several of the films discussed in this article.

1. Dmitrii Savel'ev has described him as a worthy successor of El'dar Riazanov whose comedies had for several decades made him the ruler of this kingdom. See D. Savel'ev, 'Chetvertaia popytka', *Iskusstvo kino* 2 (1996), pp. 20–1 (p. 20).

2. On the return to Jewish themes, see, for example, Lev Anninskii, 'Evreiskoe kinoschast'e', *Vestnik Evreiskogo universiteta v Moskve* 3 (1993), pp. 78–107.

3. The dual vision of the film, adapting the pre-revolutionary past in order to speak of the late Soviet present, was noted upon the film's release in articles by Mikhail Gorelik, 'Popytka ekzortsizma', *Iskusstvo kino* 5 (1992), pp. 53–6, and Andrei Shemiakin, 'Most nad bezdnoi', ibid., pp. 57–9. Gorelik also notes that the idealisation of the Jewish hero follows a model set by Babel in his Odessan Stories.

4. Ironically the St Petersburg that is so bereft in *You are My Only One* was the dream destination of the protagonists of *Get Thee Hence!*

5. The emigration of Kolyvanov was the result of an overtly exaggerated version of this paradigm – he met his future wife, the daughter of an American senator, on a *Bulgarian* beach. This and other details of *You are My Only One* mark an increasing tendency in Astrakhan's work to express his argument in brazenly programmatic terms.

6. The hold that this dream has over the post-Soviet imagination is apparent in its recurrence in other films. See, for example, the variant in Gennadi Baisak's *Agape* [Agape, 1996], in which the hero inherits a villa in Australia from a long-lost brother, though the machinations of the underworld ensure that he is not destined to see it.

7. See, in particular, his 1922 article 'Amerikanshchina', translated as 'Americanism' in R. Taylor and I. Christie (eds), *The Film Factory. Russian and Soviet Cinema in Documents 1896–1939* (London, 1988), pp. 72–3.

8. On this see J. Graffy, 'Emigré Experience of the West as Related to Soviet Journals', in Arnold B. McMillin (ed.), *Under Eastern Eyes. The West as Reflected in Recent Russian Emigré Writing* (London, 1991), pp. 115–57.

9. See, for example, Bushmelev's *Our American Boria* [Nash amerikanskii Boria, 1992];

Notes to Chapter 14

Eiramdzhan's *The Fiancé from Miami* [Zhenikh iz Maiami, 1993]; Shchegolev's *The American Grandfather* [Amerikanskii dedushka, 1993]; Shengelaia's *The Restless Archer* [Strelets neprikaiannyi, 1993]; Ursuliak's *Russian Ragtime* [Russkii regtaim, 1993]; Dykhovichnyi's *Music for December* [Muzyka dlia dekabria, 1994]; Surikova's *Moscow Holidays* [Moskovskie kanikuly, 1995] and Sukhorebryi's *The Raving* [Besnovatye, 1994–96].

10. For a comparison of this song with the Beatles' 'Back in the USSR' and an analysis of the mutual misreading of each other's culture, see Svetlana Boym, 'From Russia with a Song: from "Back in the USSR" to "Bye-Bye Amerika"', *New Formations* 22 (1994), pp. 33–47.

11. On this compare Sergei Dobrotvorsky's words about the fact that post-Soviet cinema has only recently discovered that Russians must live in their own country, and his further contention that the sooner Russians stop sighing about 'abroad' the sooner they will also stop sighing about the past, in his 'Zagranitsa, kotoruiu my poteriali', *Seans* 9 (1994), pp. 136–43 (pp. 142, 143).

12. Interviewed about the film by Dmitrii Saveliev, Astrakhan speaks of the constant audience demand for melodrama and of his readiness to work through sentimentality to move audiences. See Dmitrii Astrakhan, 'Vopros tol'ko v tom, kogo vybirat'. Ia vybiraiu zritelei', *Iskusstvo kino* 4 (1994), pp. 105–7 (p. 105).

13. On the conscious crudity and exaggeration of this scene, and the concomitant use of melodramatic archetypes, see Elena Stishova, 'Dym otechestva', *Iskusstvo kino* 4 (1994), pp. 88–93 (p. 89). On the gender analysis of the film, see also Lynne Attwood, 'Gender Angst in Russian Society and Cinema in the Post-Stalin Era', in Catriona Kelly and David Shepherd (eds), *Russian Cultural Studies. An Introduction* (Oxford, 1998), pp. 352–67 (pp. 364–5).

14. The performance and the star personality of the actor Alexander Zbruev are central to the effect of this role. See Stishova, 'Dym otechestva', p. 90.

15. Both Dobrotvorskii and Stishova point out that the words 'You are My Only One' could be applied both to Timoshin's wife and to his country. See Stishova, 'Dym otechestva', p. 89; Dobrotvorskii, 'Zagranitsa, kotoruiu my poteriali', p. 143.

16. An indulgent attitude towards displays of gargantuan Russian drinking has marked a number of recent popular Russian cinematic hits, notably Alexander Rogozhkin's *Peculiarities of the National Hunt* [Osobennosti natsional'noi okhoty, 1995] and Valeri Chikov's *Stop Playing the Fool* [Ne valiai duraka, 1997].

17. Natal'ia Sirivlia, 'Pole chudes … ', *Seans*, 12 (1996), pp. 164–6 (p. 165).

18. This scene precisely echoes a famous scene near the end of Elem Klimov's 1964 satire of Soviet conformism *Welcome, or No Unauthorised Admission* [Dobro pozhalovat', ili postoronnim vkhod vospreshchen] in which the prize of 'queen of the fields' at a carnival at a pioneer camp has been fixed in advance by the camp commandant for the niece of a Party official but is seditiously given instead to the camp's boy rebel. The change in *dramatis personae* between the two films is an eloquent expression of the changes Russia has undergone.

19. This connection of the past and the present is emphasised by the parallels in the experiences of Smirnov and his son, played by Aleksandr Zbruev and Mark Goronok, and, for Astrakhan veterans, by the fact that the actors who in this film play father and son played the same character, Timoshin, as a young man and as a middle-aged man in *You are My Only One*. Astrakhan's use of a 'repertory company' of actors from film to film will be discussed later in this chapter.

20. The motif of boxing, and fighting generally, as a conventional measure of male worth recurs in *You are My Only One*, *Everything will be OK* and *The Fourth Planet*.

21. Elena Stishova notes the speed with which Olia sizes up the situation and concludes sardonically that the concerns of Pushkin's Tatiana in *Evgenii Onegin*, 'But I am given to another and will be faithful to him for ever', are not for her: Elena Stishova, 'Ot kakogo geroia', *Iskusstvo kino* 2 (1996), pp. 12–15 (p. 14).

22. Natalia Sirivlia invokes the world of the Latin American soap operas popular on post-Soviet television, but also the story of Odysseus and Penelope, in her discussion of the film's recurrent motif of waiting for a true love to return (Sirivlia, 'Pole chudes ...', p. 165). Evidence that the characters themselves inhabit a world of popular belief is provided in a female guest's noting the 'bad omen' when Olia drops the ring at her wedding.

23. 'Moia militsiia menia berezhet' is a sentence from the final section of Maiakovskii's 1927 epic poem 'Khorosho'. See Vladimir Maiakovskii, *Polnoe sobranie sochinenii*, 13 vols (Moscow, 1955–61), vol. 8, p. 324. Recently the figure of the policeman has been brought under ironic scrutiny in Russian art, notably in the poetry of Dmitrii Prigov and in Kira Muratova's 1992 film *The Sentimental Policeman* [Chuvstvitel'nyi militsioner].

24. Elena Stishova calls this the 'intentional banalising' of Astrakhan's poetics (Stishova, 'Ot kakogo geroia', p. 14).

25. When the journal *Iskusstvo kino* devoted eighteen pages to Astrakhan in its February 1996 issue, it prefaced them with an apology for doing so, insisting that this was not a sign that it was 'renouncing [its] aesthetic principles', *Iskusstvo kino* 2 (1996), p. 4. The materials on *Everything will be OK* in *Seans* 12 (1996) included brief assessments by nineteen Russian critics who accused him of everything from Socialist Realism to cynicism, from the 'heights of disgracefulness' to 'having no world view' to being a cinematic Zhirinovsky. See *Seans* 12, pp. 34–7, 64–5, 164–6. Margolit's views are articulated in his 'Signal o nalichii zhizni', *Iskusstvo kino* 2 (1996), pp. 5–8 (p. 5).

26. That she has no need for the bra asked for by Natasha in *You are My Only One* is evident from the cameo role hers plays in this scene.

27. This speech by a sympathetic middle-aged woman renouncing the unexpected chance of love and happiness with a New Russian businessman in the name of duty to family is almost exactly echoed by the heroine played by Elena Safonova in a big popular hit of 1997, Vilen Novak's *Princess on Beans* [Printsessa na bobakh, 1997].

28. This 'search for a good man' recalls another hugely successful conservative fairytale in Soviet cinema, Vladimir Menshov's *Moscow Does Not Believe in Tears* [Moskva slezam ne verit, 1980], most specifically the comic machinations of the character Liudmila, whose trawl for a wealthy but manipulable husband takes her to the Lenin Library in Moscow.

29. The sentimental relationship of the child and surrogate grandfather, played by the veteran star Mikhail Ulianov, is savagely reversed by Kira Muratova in the 'Death and the Maiden' ['Devochka i smert''] episode of her 1997 film, *Three Stories* [Tri istorii], in which another wheelchair-bound surrogate grandfather is played by another veteran star actor, Oleg Tabakov, but in which the child, this time a young girl, wearying of his sententious glozings, poisons him. See Graham Roberts's contribution to this volume.

30. The song recurs, in an ostentatiously unhappy context, at the start of another 1995 film, Alexander Sukhochev's *A Principled and Compassionate Look* [Printsipial'nyi i zhalostlivyi vzgliad].

31. When the film premièred on Russian Public Television (ORT) on 30 June 1996 it was preceded by interviews with eight of the people involved in making it, most of whom told tales of how it had brought them happiness, but Anatoli Zhuravlev, the actor playing Kolia, was conspicuously not among them.

Notes to Chapter 14

32. Both these words, and the disgust at being 'dressed' by a New Russian American, have already characterised Evgeni Timoshin in *You are My Only One*, see above.

33. That these rural excursions will not be without their alcoholic lubrication is suggested by the scene of three Russian 'fishermen' seeing granddad Volodia's triumphant progression in his wheelchair, complete with helicopter retinue, and taking it for the effect of delirium tremens.

34. Though both films were made in 1995, *The Fourth Planet* was released slightly after *Everything will be OK*. See D. Savel'ev, 'Chetvertaia popytka', p. 20.

35. Two films made in the late 1980s, Vladimir Khotinenko's *Mirror for a Hero* [Zerkalo dlia geroia, 1987] and Valeri Ogorodnikov's *Prishvin's Paper Eyes* [Bumazhnye glaza Prishvina, 1989], had transported their contemporary heroes into 1949, but in both films the point of the exercise was to shed light upon the uncertain present, to which the heroes were duly returned. This is not Astrakhan's intention

36. The popularity of this song in the Soviet Union is attested by its use as a marker in a number of Soviet and post-Soviet films, including Rostotski's *It Happened in Pen'kovo* [Delo bylo v Pen'kove, 1957], Menshov's *Moscow Doesn't Believe in Tears*, Shugarev's *The Scent of Desires* [Ham Hyyal, Turkmenistan, 1995], and Chikov's *Don't Play the Fool* [Ne valiai duraka, 1997].

37. 'I na Marse budut iabloni tsvesti', words by Evgeni Dolmatovsky, music by Vano Muradeli, see *Pesnia ostaetsia s chelovekom. Populiarnye pesni shestidesiatykh godov*, compiled by V. K. Solonenko (Moscow, 1994), pp. 69–70. The song begins: 'Zhit' i verit' – eto zamechatel'no! / Pered nami nebyvalye puti. / Utverzhdaiut kosmonavty i mechtateli, / Chto na Marse budut iabloni tsvesti!', and ends: 'Pokidaia nashu Zemliu, obeshchali my, / Chto na Marse budut iabloni tsvesti!'

38. Sergei Anashkin reports Astrakhan's remark – little short of sacrilege in the post-Soviet period – that 'Tarkovsky is a very boring director', and accuses him of making '*Solaris* for slobs – *The Fourth Planet*': Sergei Anashkin, '"Sovok-lubok", ili ostorozhno – Astrakhan!', *Iskusstvo kino* 2 (1996), pp. 9–11 (p. 10). In fact there are conscious echoes of Tarkovsky in this film, both in Sam Styron's freeway drive, which recalls the one made at the start of *Solaris*, and in the fact that three symbolically differentiated travellers make a journey through a symbolic landscape, as in *Stalker*.

39. *The Fourth Planet* makes a nod in the direction of Klimov's film when one of the banners displayed at the start reads *Welcome* ('Dobro pozhalovat''). A subversive attitude to space flight is also present in the films of Georgii Daneliia, *33* [1965] and *Kin-dza-dza!* [1986].

40. On the use of the motif of space flight in Eldar Riazanov's film *Promised Heavens* [Nebesa obetovannye, 1991], See Savel'ev, 'Chetvertaia popytka', p. 21.

41. The working title of *Everything will be OK* was *The Right to Happiness* [Pravo na schast'e]. See Savel'ev, op. cit., p. 21.

42. When, in *Everything will be OK*, Katia realises that Smirnov the millionaire is the Smirnov of her youth, she says, 'Oh, Konstantin Smirnov, from the company "Astron". Is that you?' When Tania realises that Sergei Beliaev is the boy she went to school with, she says, 'Serezha, is that really you?'

43. Evgeni Margolit stresses the importance of this factor in his sensitive analysis of the acting in Astrakhan's films, Margolit, 'Signal o nalichii zhizni', pp. 7–8.

44. Olga Beliaeva, Astrakhan's wife, graduates from the subsidiary role of Natasha Samsonova in *Everything will be OK* to that of Tania, the heroine, in *The Fourth Planet*. See Natal'ia Rtishcheva, 'Dmitrii Astrakhan. Marsianin na krepkikh nogakh', *Ekran* 2 (1995), pp. 9–11. But the hero of *The Fourth Planet* is given her surname, Beliaev, making him, in this sense, a double of Astrakhan. Thus the journey of *The Fourth Planet*

can be seen to stand for the investigations into the contemporary Russian sensibility and its sources in Astrakhan's first four films. Rtishcheva also suggests that his fellow film-makers treat Astrakhan as an extra-terrestrial, and that 'the heroes of his films are all to some degree Martians'.

45. This term is used by Petr Cherniaev as the title of his review of *Everything will be OK*; see P. Cherniaev, 'Astrakhan-lend', *Kinoglaz*, 1 (1996), p. 38.

46. For a reaction to this work by the scriptwriter Natal'ia Riazantseva see Riazan-tseva, 'Razmyshleniia v "zale ozhidaniia",' *Iskusstvo kino* 7 (1998), pp. 79–81.

47. *Otkrytyi rossiiskii kinofestival'. Open Russian Film Festival* (Sochi, 1998), p. 23.

48. *Sobach'e serdtse* [The Heart of a Dog] was filmed by Vladimir Bortko in 1988.

49. Astrakhan, 'Vopros tol'ko v tom, kogo vybirat'', p. 105.

Filmography

Listed here are only films released in the 1990s. Films which have been released or televised in the UK are asterisked. The English title is followed by the original Russian, the director's surname and the year of release.

Adam's Rib (Rebro Adama; Krishtofovich, 1990)

Afghan Breakdown (Afganskii izlom; Bortko, 1991)

Agape (Baisak, 1996)

All Souls' Day (Dukhov den'; Selianov, 1990)

American Bet (Amerikanka; Meskhiev, 1998)

American Daughter (Amerikanskaia doch'; Shakhnazarov, 1995)

Anna from 6 to 18 (Anna ot 6 do 18; Mikhalkov, 1993)

Anna Karamazoff (Khamdamov, 1991)

Arrival of a Train (Pribytie poezda, 1995). Almanac of four short films: Exercise No. 5 (Ekzersis No. 5, Meskhiev); Trofim (Balabanov); Road (Doroga, Khotinenko); Wedding March (Svadebnyi marsh, Khvan).

Assassin of the Tsar (Tsareubiitsa; Shakhnazarov, 1991)

Asthenic Syndrome (Asteicheskii sindrom; Muratova, 1991)*

Barber of Siberia (Sibirskii tsiriul'nik; Mikhalkov, 1998)

Black Veil (Chernaia vual'; Proshkin, 1995)

Body will be Committed to the Earth and the Senior Warrant Officer will Sing, The (Telo budet predano zemle, a starshii michman budet pet'; Makarov, 1998)

Bomb (Bomba; Meskhiev, 1997)

Brother (Brat; Balabanov, 1997)

Burnt by the Sun (Utomlennye solntsem; Mikhalkov, 1994)*

Casanova's Cloak (Plashch Kazanovy; Galin, 1993)

Castle (Zamok; Balabanov, 1994)

Chekist (Rogozhkin, 1991)

Children of a Bitch (Sukiny deti; Filatov, 1990)

Children of Iron Gods (Deti chugunnykh bogov; Tot, 1993)

Circus Burnt Down, and the Clowns Ran Away ... , The (Tsirk sgorel, i klouny razbezhalis'; Bortko, 1998)

Composition for Victory Day (Sochinenie ko dniu pobedy; Ursuliak, 1998)

Comrade Chkalov's Crossing of the North Pole (Perekhod tovarishcha Chkalova cherez severnyi polius; Pezhemsky, 1990)

Concert for a Rat (Kontsert dlia krysy; Kovalov, 1995)

Contract with Death (Kontrakt so smert'iu; Astrakhan, 1998)

Cops and Thieves (Politseiskie i vory; Dostal, 1997)

Cutter (Mytar'; Fomin, 1997)

Cynics (Tsiniki; Meskhiev, 1991)

Day of the Full Moon (Den' polnoluniia; Shakhnazarov, 1997)

Dead Man's Friend (Priiatel' pokoinika; Krishtofovich, 1997)

Diuba-Diuba (Khvan, 1992)

Dog's Feast (Sobachii pir; Menaker, 1990)

Dreams (Sny; Shakhnazarov, 1993)

Drum Roll (Barabaniada; Ovcharov, 1993)

Eastern Elegy (Vostochnaia elegiia; Sokurov, 1996)

Encore, Another Encore! (Ankor, eshche ankor!; P. Todorovsky, 1992)

Enthusiasms (Uvlechen'ia; Muratova, 1993)

Ermak (Krasnopolsky and Uskov, 1996)

Everything will be OK (Vse budet khorosho; Astrakhan, 1995)

Exercise No. 5 (Ekzersis No. 5; Meskhiev, 1995), see Arrival of a Train (Pribytie poezda)

Fatal Eggs, The (Rokovye iaitsa; Lomkin, 1995]

First Love (Pervaia liubov'; Balayan, 1995)

Fourth Planet (Chetvertaia planeta; Astrakhan, 1995)

From Hell to Hell (Iz ada v ad; Astrakhan, 1996)

Gambrinus (Meskhiev, 1990)

Gardens of Scorpio (Sady skorpiona; Kovalov, 1991)

Get Thee Hence! (Izydi!; Astrakhan, 1991)

Giselle's Mania (Mania Zhizeli; Uchitel, 1995)

Good Trash, Bad Trash (Drian' khroroshaia, drian' plokhaia; Khvan, 1998)

Good Weather on Deribasov Street (Na Deribasovskoi khoroshaia pogoda ... ; Gaidai, 1992)

Government Inspector (Revizor; Gazarov, 1996)

Hammer and Sickle (Serp i molot; Livnev, 1994)

Happy Days (Schastlivye dni; Balabanov, 1991)

Happy New Year, Moscow (S novym godom, Moskva; Piankova, 1993)

Heads or Tails (Orel i reshka; Daneliya, 1995)

Hello, Fools! (Privet, duralei!; Riazanov, 1996)

Horses are Carrying Me Away (Nesut menia koni; Motyl, 1996)

I Wanted to See Angels (Ia khotela uvidet' angelov; Bodrov, 1992)*

In That Land (V toi strane; Bobrova, 1997)

Russia on Reels

Inner Circle (Blizhnii krug; Konchalovsky, 1992)

Iron Heel of Oligarchy (Zheleznaia piata oligarkhii; Bashirov, 1998)

Island of the Dead (Ostrov mertvykh; Kovalov, 1992)

Katia Izmailova (Podmoskovnye vechera; V. Todorovsky, 1994)*

Katka and Schizo (Kat'ka i shiz; Keosayan, 1992)

Khrustalev, the Car! (Khrustalev, mashinu!; German, 1998)

Kiks (Livnev, 1991)

Kiss the Bride (Gor'ko!; Mamin, 1998)

Ladies' Tailor (Damskii portnoi; Gorovets, 1990)

Lady-Peasant (Baryshnia-krestianka; Sakharov, 1995)

Land of the Deaf (Strana glukhikh; V. Todorovsky, 1997)

Life with an Idiot (Zhizn' s idiotom; Rogozhkin, 1993)

Limits – Outsiders on a Contract (Limita; Evstigneev, 1993)

Line of Life (Liniia zhizni; Lungin, 1996)

Little Demon (Melkii bes; Dostal, 1995)

Little Giant of Great Sex (Malen'kii gigant bol'shogo seksa; Dostal 1992)

Little Princess (Malen'kaia printsessa; Grammatikov, 1997)

Love (Liubov'; V. Todorovsky, 1991)

Luna Park (Lungin, 1992)

Makarov (Khotinenko, 1993)

Man for a Young Woman (Muzhchina dlia molodoi zhenshchiny; M. Ibragimbekov, 1996)

Menage à trois (Retro v troem; P. Todorovsky, 1998)

Middle-Age Crisis (Krizis srednego vozrasta; Sukachev, 1997)

Monday Children (Deti ponedel'nika; Surikova, 1998)

Moscow Holidays (Moskovskie kanikuly; Surikova, 1995)

Moscow Parade (Prorva; Dykhovichny, 1992)

Mother and Son (Mat' i syn; Sokurov, 1997)*

MuMu (Grymov, 1998)

Music for December (Muzyka dlia dekabria; Dykhovichny, 1994)

Muslim, The (Musul'manin; Khotinenko, 1995)

Of Freaks and Men (Pro urodov i liudei; Balabanov, 1998)

Operation 'New Year' (Operatsiia 'S novym godom'; Rogozhkin, 1996)

Out of this World (Mama ne goriui; Pezhemsky, 1997)

Over Dark Waters (Nad temnoi vodoi; Meskhiev, 1993)

Papa, Santa Claus is Dead (Papa, Ded Moroz umer; Yufit, 1991)

Paradise-Cloud (Oblako-rai; Dostal, 1991)

Passport (Pasport; Daneliya, 1990)

Patriotic Comedy (Patrioticheskaia komediia; Khotinenko, 1992)

Peculiarities of the National Hunt (Osobennosti natsional'noi okhoty; Rogozhkin, 1995)

Filmography

Peshawar Waltz (Peshavarskii val's; Bekmambetov, Kaiumov, 1994)

Play for a Passenger (P'esa dlia passazhira; Abdrashitov, 1995)

Poor Sasha (Bednaia Sasha; Keosayan, 1997)

President and his Woman (President i ego zhenshchina; Raiskaya, 1996)

Princess on Beans (Printsessa na bobakh; Novak, 1997)

Principled and Compassionate Look (Printsipial'nyi i zhalostlivy vzgliad; Sukhochev, 1995)

Prisoner of the Mountains (Kavkazskii plennik; Bodrov, 1996)*

Prisoners of Fortune (Plenniki udachi; Pezhemsky, 1993)

Promised Heavens (Nebesa obetovannye; Riazanov, 1991)

Raving (Besnovatye; Sukhorebry, 1994–96)

Riaba la Poule (Kurochka Riaba; Konchalovsky, 1994)

Road (Doroga; Khotinenko, 1995), *see* Arrival of a Train (Pribytie poezda)

Russian Ragtime (Russkii regtaim; Ursuliak, 1993)

Russian Symphony (Russkaia simfoniia; Lopushansky, 1994)

Schizophrenia (Shizofreniia; Sergeev, 1997)

Scientific Section of Pilots (Nauchnaia sektsiia pilotov; I., 1996)

Second Circle (Krug vtoroi; Sokurov, 1990)

See Paris and Die (Uvidet' Parizh i umeret'; Proshkin, 1992)

Sentimental Policeman (Chuvstvitel'nyi militsioner; Muratova, 1992)

Shell (Pantsir'; Alimpiev, 1990)

Shirly Myrli (Menshov, 1996)

Sideburns (Bakenbardy; Mamin, 1990)

Silver Heads (Serebriannye golovy; Yufit, 1998)

Snake Spring (Zmeinyi istochnik; Lebedev, 1997)

Stone (Kamen'; Sokurov, 1992)

Stop Playing the Fool (Ne valiai duraka; Chikov, 1997)

Strange Time (Strannoe vremia; Piankova, 1997)

Summer Folk (Letnie liudi; Ursuliak, 1995)

Sympathy Seeker (Sirota kazanskaia; Mashkov, 1997)

Taxi Blues (Lungin, 1990)

Ten Years without Correspondence (Desiat' let bez prava perepiski; Naumov, 1990)

Thief (Vor; Pavel Chukhrai, 1997)*

Three Stories (Tri istorii; Muratova, 1997)

Time for Sadness Has Not Yet Come, The (Vremia pechali eshche ne prishlo; Selianov, 1995)

Time of the Dancer (Vremia tantsora; Abdrashitov, 1997)

Trofim (Balabanov, 1995), *see* Arrival of a Train (Pribytie poezda)

Tsar Aleksei (Melnikov, 1997)

Tsar's Murderer (Tsareubiitsa; Shakhnazarov, 1991)

Two Moons, Three Suns (Dve luny, tri solntsa; Balayan, 1998)

Urga. Close to Eden (Urga, territoriia liubvi; Mikhalkov, 1991)*

Vampire (Upyr'; Vinokurov, 1997)

Wedding March (Svadebnyi marsh; Khvan, 1995), *see* Arrival of a Train (Pribytie poezda)

What a Wonderful Game (Kakaia chudnaia igra; P. Todorovsky, 1995)

Whispering Pages (Tikhie stranitsy; Sokurov, 1993)

Window on Paris (Okno v Parizh; Mamin, 1993)

Wooden Room (Dereviannaia komnata, Yufit, 1995)

Year of the Dog, The (God sobaki; Aranovich, 1996)

You are My Only One (Ty u menia odna; Astrakhan, 1993)

Select Bibliography

Contemporary Russian films are regularly reviewed in *Iskusstvo kino*, *Kinostsenarii* and *Seans*.

The Russian Idea

Aizlewood, Robin, 'The Return of the "Russian Idea" in Publications, 1988–91', *Slavonic and East European Review* 71, no. 3 (July 1993), pp. 490–9.

Berdyaev, Nicolas, *The Russian Idea* (transl. by R. M. French), (Boston, 1962).

Kovalov, Oleg, 'Russkaia Ideia: sinopsis stsenariia', *Seans* 12 (1996), pp. 75–82.

McDaniel, Tim, *The Agony of the Russian Idea* (Princeton, 1996).

Scanlon, James P. (ed.), *Russian Thought After Communism: The Recovery of a Philosophical Heritage* (Armonk, NY, 1994).

Solov'ev, Vladimir S., 'Russkaia ideia' (transl. from French by G. A. Rachinskii), in *Sobranie sochinenii*, 14 vols (Brussels, 1969), vol. 11, pp. 91–117.

Contemporary Russian Film

Arkus, Liubov' (ed.), *Sokurov* (St Petersburg, 1994).

Attwood, Lynne (ed.), *Red Women on the Silver Screen: Soviet Women and Cinema from the Beginning to the End of the Communist Era* (London, 1993).

Berry, E. and A. Miller-Pogacar (eds), *Re-Entering the Sign* (Ann Arbor, 1995).

Buckley, Mary (ed.), *Perestroika and Soviet Women* (Cambridge, 1991).

Condee, Nancy (ed.), *Soviet Hieroglyphics: Visual Culture in Late Twentieth-century Russia* (Bloomington and London, 1995).

Freidin, Gregory (ed.), *Russian Culture in Transition* (Stanford, 1993).

Horton, Andrew and Michael Brashinsky, *The Zero-Hour: Glasnost and Soviet Cinema in Transition* (Princeton, 1991).

Kelly, C. and D. Shepherd (eds), *Russian Cultural Studies: An Introduction* (Oxford, 1998).

Lawton, Anna, *Kinoglasnost: Soviet Cinema in Our Time* (Cambridge, 1992).

Roberts, Graham, 'Look Who's Talking: The Politics of Representation and the Representation of Politics in Two Films by Kira Muratova', *Elementa* 3 (1997), pp. 309–23.

Sandler, A. (ed.), *Nikita Mikhalkov* (Moscow, 1989).

Shalin, D. (ed.), *Russian Culture at the Crossroads* (Boulder CO, and Oxford, 1996).

Russia on reels

Suminova, T., *Nikita Mikhalkov: Fil'mograficheskii i bibliograficheskii ukazatal'* (Moscow, 1995).

Taubman, Jane A., 'The Cinema of Kira Muratova', *Russian Review* 52 (1993), pp. 367–81.

Zemlianukhin, Sergei and Miroslava Segida, *Domashniaia sinematika: otechestvennoe kino, 1918–1996* (Moscow, 1996).

Websites

Russian Database of Films 1917–present @ http://russia.agama.com/r_club/cinema

Internet Movie Database @ http://us.imdb.com/Sections/Languages/Russian/

Index